NEW

중등교원 임용고시 시험대비

최시원 전공영어
영어교육학

Conceptual

📖 영어교육학 최고의 선택
명/쾌/한 설명으로 영어교육학이 쉬워진다!

최시원 전공영어 영어교육학
English Education Conceptual

PREFACE

영어교육학에서 고득점을 얻는 비결

중등 영어 임용 1차 시험에서 영어 교육의 이론과 실제를 동시에 다루는 영어 교육학의 중요성은 더 이상 강조할 필요가 없어진 것이 주지의 사실입니다. 게다가 영어 교육학에서 다루는 실제적인 수업 상황의 해석과 지침은 2차 수업 실연에서도 밑바탕이 되기 때문에 그 중요성은 더욱 크다고 할 수 있습니다.

영어 교육론에서 고득점을 얻는 비결은 역시 기출 문제의 분석에서 시작됩니다. 현재 제시되는 문제의 유형은 기입형과 서술형 문항입니다. 우선 기입형 문제의 해결을 위해서는 영어 교육론과 관련된 원서의 내용을 읽고 내용을 파악한 뒤 체계적인 정리를 통해 수험장에서 키워드를 도출해내는 능력을 기르는 것이 최우선입니다. 그러기 위해서는 출제 빈도가 높은 관련 교재의 원문 내용을 가지고 공부하는 것이 가장 효율적인 방법입니다. 그래서 이 교재는 이미 출제되었거나 출제 가능성이 높은 원서 교재에서 핵심 내용을 발췌하여 체계적으로 정리했습니다. 한글로 된 교재로 이해를 하고 원서를 따로 보는 것은 비효율적일 뿐만 아니라 영어로 사고하고 문제를 해결해야 할 중등 임용 시험 응시자에게 적합하지 않은 방법입니다. 게다가 다음의 서술형 문항을 대비하는 데에 도움이 되지 않습니다.

기입형 문제와 달리 서술형 문제는 수험생에게 기본적으로 읽기 능력 이외에 쓰기 능력을 요구합니다. 쓰기 능력 또한 구와 절을 완성하고 문장과 문단을 완성하는 식으로 기초를 다듬는 것은 영어 전공자에게는 비효율적이며 시간이 많이 소모되는 부적합한 방법입니다. 오히려 문항에서 요구하는 수준의 영어 교육과 관련된 내용의 글을 읽고 나름대로 자신의 언어로 요약하고 정리(summarizing & paraphrasing)해 보는 것이 수험장이라는 극도의 긴장된 상황에서 실수를 줄이는 최선의 방법입니다. 즉, 우리가 알고 있는 말뭉치(chunk)를 통해 어색한 한국어식 표현을 줄이고 영어로 이해하고 영어로 표현해야만 평가자가 수긍할 수 있는 깔끔한 답안을 작성할 수 있습니다.

이 수험서의 특징은 기입형 문항의 풀이를 위해 관련 내용의 설명 첫 부분에 중요 키워드를 기출 표시와 함께 마인드맵과 표로 처리하여 가독성을 높인 것입니다. 줄글을 읽기 전에 중요한 키워드를 선행조직자로 형성한다면 한 번을 읽더라도 의미 있는 이해와 인지적 정착 비율을 높일 수 있습니다. 줄글로 된 부분은 실제 시험 문항에 제시될 수 있는 원서의 내용으로써 의미가 있을 뿐만 아니라 서술형 문항에서 어떤 식으로 답안을 작성하는 것이 적절한가에 대한 지침을 마련해 줄 것입니다. 따라서 이 책의 내용을 여러 번 정독하고 나름대로 정리한다면 1차 시험에서 고득점을 할 수 있고, 이 영어 교육론의 내용은 2차 시험에서도 좋은 바탕을 마련해줄 것입니다.

여러 해 동안의 기출 문제를 살펴보면 우리가 읽어야 할 영어 교육론의 지문은 저자와 출처를 달리하지만 거의 비슷한 수준으로 이전 시험 문항에서 출제되었던 키워드가 반복해서 나타나는 것을 알 수 있습니다. 따라서 이 교재로 기초를 다지고, 모의고사에서 출제되는 여러 원서의 새로운 표현 방식에 대해 실전적인 감각을 익힌다면 무리 없이 시험에서 좋은 성적을 거둘 수 있을 것입니다. 이 책이 임용 시험을 준비하는 학우들에게 효율적으로 공부하는 데 조그만 보탬이 되기를 바랍니다. 감사합니다.

2020년 12월
편저자 최시원

CONTENTS

Chapter 01 — Approaches to Language Acquisition

A	Three Approaches: Behaviorist / Nativist / Interactionist	12
B	Recent Cognitive Perspectives	18

Chapter 02 — Models of Second Language Acquisition

A	An Innatist Model: Krashen's Five Hypotheses	22
B	Cognitivist Models: Attention-Processing Model, Implicit & Explicit Processing, Noticing Hypothesis, and others	23
C	Social Constructivist Models: Swain's & Long's Hypotheses	31

Chapter 03 — Language Analyses

A	Contrastive Analysis	38
B	Interlanguage	38
C	Stages of Learner Language Development	39
D	Error Analysis	42
E	Communicative Competence	47
F	Discourse Analysis	50
G	Conversation Analysis	53
H	Types of Nonverbal Communication	62

Chapter 04 — Learner Variables

A	Age & the Critical Period Hypothesis	66
B	Cognitive factors & Learning Styles	66
C	Affective factors	70
D	Socio-cultural factors	74
E	Techniques in Teaching Culture	75
F	World Englishes	76
G	Autonomy	79
H	Strategies	79

Chapter 05 — Teaching Methodologies

A	Traditional Approaches	86
B	Innovative Approaches	90
C	Communicative Approaches	93
D	Roles of the Interactive Teacher	108

Chapter 06 — Syllabus Design and Material Development

A	Curriculum components	112
B	Classification of Syllabus	114
C	Types of Syllabus	116
D	Material Development	119
E	Lesson Objectives	124

CONTENTS

Chapter 07 — Teaching Listening

A	Types of Spoken Language (L/S)	128
B	Bottom-up vs. Top-down Processing (L/R)	129
C	Features of authentic materials in Listening	132
D	Types of Listening Performance	135
E	Process Listening (PWP)	137
F	Listening Exercises	138
G	Listening Techniques and Tasks	139

Chapter 08 — Teaching Speaking

A	Fluency vs. Accuracy issues	144
B	Types of Speaking Performance	145
C	Speaking Techniques and Tasks	147

Chapter 09 — Teaching Reading

A	Bottom-up vs. Top-down Process	150
B	Schema Theory	153
C	Comprehension Level	153
D	Authenticity vs. Readability issues in Choosing Text	154
E	Process Reading (PWP)	155
F	Reading Techniques and Tasks	157

Chapter 10 — Teaching Writing

A	Product- vs. Process-oriented Writing	162
B	Process Writing (PWP; Writing Techniques and Tasks)	163
C	Types of Writing Performance	167

Chapter 11 — Teaching Grammar

A	Approaches to Teaching Grammar & FFI	172
B	Deductive vs. Inductive teaching	175
C	Techniques and Tasks in teaching grammar	175

Chapter 12 — Teaching Vocabulary

A	Incidental vs. Intentional learning	184
B	Corpus	186
C	Lexis	186
D	Techniques and Tasks in teaching vocabulary	189

Chapter 13 — Teaching Pronunciation

A	Segments vs. Suprasegmentals	194
B	Teachability issues in teaching pronunciation	195
C	Intelligibility issues in teaching pronunciation	196
D	Techniques and tasks in teaching pronunciation	196

CONTENTS

Chapter 14 — Technology in Language Learning and Teaching

A	CALL & MALL	200
B	CMC	202
C	Types of CALL Activities	204
D	Corpora and Concordancers	207
E	Computer Adaptive Testing	208

Chapter 15 — Language Assessment

A	Principles of Language Assessment	210
B	Types of Testing: in terms of Purposes	215
C	Types of Test Items	216
D	Multiple-choice Tests	220
E	Integrative Testing	232
F	Alternative Assessments	235
G	Holistic vs. Analytic Scoring	238

★ APPENDIX

★	Glossary on English Education	244

최시원 전공영어 영어교육학

Chapter 01 Approaches to Language Acquisition

Chapter 02 Models of Second Language Acquisition

Chapter 03 Language Analyses

Chapter 04 Learner Variables

Chapter 05 Teaching Methodologies

Chapter 06 Syllabus Design and Material Development

Chapter 07 Teaching Listening

Chapter 08 Teaching Speaking

Chapter 09 Teaching Reading

Chapter 10 Teaching Writing

Chapter 11 Teaching Grammar

Chapter 12 Teaching Vocabulary

Chapter 13 Teaching Pronunciation

Chapter 14 Technology in Language Learning and Teaching

Chapter 15 Language Assessment

최시원 전공영어 영어교육학
English Education Conceptual

Chapter 01~02 MindMap

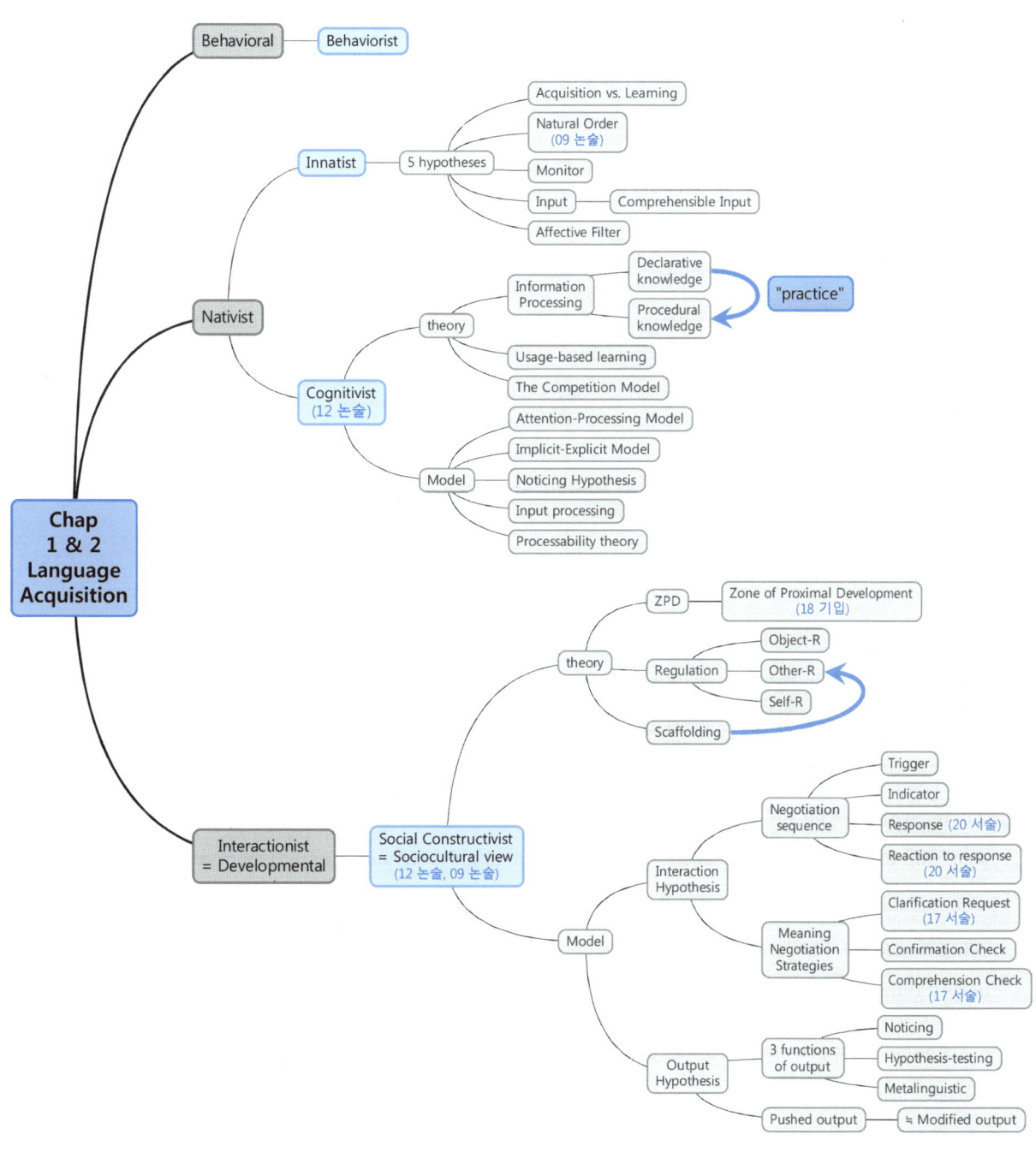

Chapter 01 Approaches to Language Acquisition

A Three Approaches: Behaviorist / Nativist / Interactionist

L1 Approach	Behaviorist	Nativist		Interactionist
Psychology	Behaviorism	Cognitivism		Constructivism
Linguistics	Structural	Transformational-generative		
SLA Model	Behaviorist	Innatist	Cognitivist	Social Constructivist
Language Analysis	Contrastive Analysis	Error Analysis		Discourse Analysis, Conversation Analysis
Methodology	ALM	NA / TPR		CLT / TBLT

A1 Structural Linguistics and Behavioral Psychology

In the 1940s and 1950s, the structural, or descriptive, school of linguistics prided itself in a rigorous application of scientific observations of human languages. Only 'publicly observable responses' could be subject to investigation. The linguist's task, according to the structuralist, was to ***describe*** human languages and to identify the structural characteristics. An important axiom of structural linguistics was that languages can differ from each other without limit, and that no preconceptions should apply across languages. Freeman Twaddell (1935), among others, underscored the mandate for the structural linguist to examine only ***overtly observable*** data, and to ignore any mentalistic theorizing that might entertain unobservable guesses, hunches, and intuition about language. Of further importance to the structural or descriptive linguist was the notion that language could be dismantled into small pieces or units and that these units could be described scientifically, contrasted, and added up again to form the whole.

Similar perspectives were shared by psychologists of this era. In the behavioral paradigm, the only legitimate 'responses' were those that could be objectively perceived, recorded, and measured. The unreliability of observation of states of consciousness, thinking, concept formation, or the acquisition of knowledge made such topics impossible to examine in a behavioral framework.

A2 (Transformational-) Generative Linguistics and Cognitive Psychology

In the decade of the 1960s, generative-transformational linguistics emerged through the influence of Noam Chomsky and a number of his colleagues. Chomsky was trying to show that human language cannot be scrutinized simply in terms of *observable* stimuli and responses or the volumes of raw data gathered by field linguists. The generative linguist was interested not only in describing language (achieving the level of descriptive adequacy) but also in arriving at an explanatory level of adequacy in the study of language that is, a 'principled basis, independent of any particular language, for the selection of the descriptively adequate grammar of each language'.

Similarly, cognitive psychologists asserted that meaning, understanding, and knowing were significant data for psychological study. Cognitive psychologists, like generative linguists, sought to discover underlying motivations and deeper structures of human behavior by using a **rational** approach. For cognitive psychologists, going beyond merely descriptive adequacy to explanatory power took on the utmost importance.

Both the structural linguist and the behavioral psychologist were interested in description, in answering *what* questions about human behavior by means of objective measurement in controlled circumstances. The generative linguist and cognitive psychologist were, to be sure, interested in the *what* question. But they were far more interested in a more ultimate question, *why?* What underlying factors — innate, psychological, social, or environmental circumstances — caused a particular behavior in a human being?

A3 Constructivist Psychology

Developmental psychologists argue that the innatists place too much emphasis on the 'final state' (the competence of adult native speakers) and not enough on the developmental aspect of language acquisition. They see no need to assume that there are specific brain structures devoted to language acquisition. They focused on the interplay between the innate learning ability of children and the environment in which they develop. These researchers attribute considerable more importance to the environment than the innatists do even though they also recognize a powerful learning mechanism in the human brain.

In order to understand constructivism, it will be helpful to think of two branches of constructivism: cognitive and social. In the cognitive version of constructivism, emphasis is placed on the importance of learners constructing their own representation of reality. For Jean Piaget, 'learning is a developmental process that involves change, self-generation, and construction, each building on prior learning experiences'.

Social constructivism emphasizes the importance of social interaction and cooperative learning in ultimate attainment. The champion of social constructivism is Lev Vygotsky, who advocated the view that 'children's thinking and meaning-making is socially constructed and emerges out of their social interactions with their environment'.

One of the most popular concepts advanced by Vygotsky was the notion of a **zone of proximal development** (**ZPD**): the distance between learners' existing developmental state and their potential development. The ZPD is an important facet of social constructivism because it involves tasks 'that a child cannot yet do alone but could do with the assistance of more competent peers or adults'.

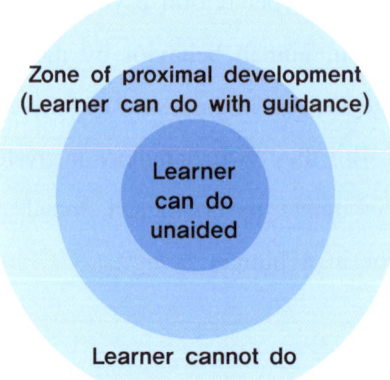

Vygotsky's concept of the ZPD contrasted rather sharply with Piaget's theory of learning in that the former saw a unity of learning and development while the latter saw stages of development setting a precondition, or readiness, for learning. Piaget stressed the importance of individual cognitive development as a relative solitary act. Biological timetables and stages of development were basic; social interaction was claimed only to trigger development at the right moment in time. On the other hand, Vygotsky maintained that social interaction was foundational in cognitive development and rejected the notion of predetermined stages.

All three of the historical perspectives described in this section — structural/behavioral, generative/cognitive, and constructivist — must be seen as important in creating balanced description of second language acquisition.

(A3a) Scaffolding

Scaffolding refers to the supportive environment created through the guidance and feedback learners receive during collaboration. When learners collaborate with others, they master what they have not been able to master independently. This happens particularly when learners interact with a more capable person.

(A3b) Regulation

According to Vygotsky, children learn to engage in activity as an individual in social interactions between themselves and peers or more experienced members of the same culture. Gradually, children acquire conscious control and individuality through three levels of **regulation** in interaction known as object-regulation, other-regulation, and self-regulation.

The first stage, **object-regulation**, refers to the process in which a person is controlled directly by environment and his/her attention is focused on objects that dominate cognition at that moment. At this stage, people are not able to exert control over the environment that instead influences them at the early stage of mental development. Furthermore, as some research shows, even if children are able to carry out tasks by themselves, they are not able to pursue independent action whenever a particular goal is not 'directly suggested by the environment'.

The second stage is **other-regulation,** a process in which a person is regulated by another more knowledgeable or experienced person (e.g. adult, peer, and teacher) in the shared social activity. At this stage, people are able to carry out some tasks with linguistically mediated assistance from a parent, teacher, or more capable peer. This linguistically mediated assistance normally refers to dialogic speech that is regarded as the primary means of carrying out other-regulation.

The third stage is **self-regulation**, the final stage, which refers to the ability to accomplish activities with minimal or no external support. Self-regulation is made possible through internalization — the process of making what was once external assistance a resource that is internally available to the individual.

Some researchers apply Vygotsky's framework of self-regulation in first language acquisition to EFL/ESL language classrooms. For example, Foley (1991) claims that the traditional type of EFL/ESL teaching is actually dominated by object-regulation or/and other-regulation, that is, students are regulated by texts, exercises, or other-regulated by teachers. Upon analysis of Foley, it is agreeable that in traditional language classrooms, teachers tend to force learners to speak or write while self-regulation is not permitted when they are using the target language. Long and Crookes (1987) pointed out that traditional language teachers allow for little two-way interaction, while in the natural settings, speakers self-regulate through the complete interaction.

A4 Child First Language Acquisition

Primarily coming from research on child language acquisition, during the 1950s and 1960s there were challenges to the behaviorist theory of language and language learning. Language came to be seen not as a set of automatic habits, but as a set of structured rules. These rules were claimed to be learned not by imitation, but by actively formulating them on the basis of innate principles as well as on the basis of exposure to the language being learned. Three examples from the child language literature are often cited as evidence against the imitation view of language acquisition.

(1) From Cazden (1972; no age given)

Child: My teacher holded the baby rabbits and we patted them.

Adult: Did you say your teacher held the baby rabbits?

Child: Yes.

Adult: What did you say she did?

Child: She holded the baby rabbits and we patted them.

Adult: Did you say she held them tightly?

Child: No, she holded them loosely.

Despite the adult's modeling of the correct past tense form, the child continues to regularize the past tense by adding *-ed* rather than by changing the vowel. Imitation clearly played no role at this point in this child's talk.

> (2) From McNeill (1966; no age given)
>
> Child: Nobody don't like me.
>
> Mother: No, say "nobody likes me."
>
> Child: Nobody don't like me.
>
> (eight repetitions of this dialogue)
>
> Mother: No, now listen carefully; say "nobody likes me."
>
> Child: Oh! Nobody don't likes me.
>
> ---
>
> (3) Original data, Age 3
>
> Child: I don't see no trees.
>
> Mother: I don't see any trees. Not no trees, any trees.
>
> Child: No any trees. No any trees.
>
> Mother: I don't see any trees.

In examples (2) and (3), the mother attempts unsuccessfully to model the correct form or even to overtly instruct the child. This type of example is often mocked in cartoons. One such cartoon shows a small child saying, "Mommy, Dolly hitted me." The mother responds "Dolly HIT me." The little boy's response was "You too?! Boy, she's in trouble!" (Time Magazine, November 1, 1999).

Bloomfield clearly stated that when the child produces an incorrect form, the child receives a disappointing response with the admonition, "No, say it like this." The assumption is that the correct modeling (coupled with negative reinforcement) is sufficient to perfect the child's speech. However, as we have seen in the preceding examples, neither imitation nor reinforcement is a sufficient explanation of a child's linguistic behavior.

It became commonplace in the 1960s to see children as actively involved in creating grammars of their language, as opposed to being passive recipients imitating their surroundings. Children do not just soak in what goes on around them but actively try to make sense of the language they are exposed to. They construct grammars. In so doing they make generalizations, they test those generalizations or hypotheses, and they alter or reformulate them when necessary — or abandon them in favor of some other generalization.

During the 1950s and 1960s it became clear that the utterances of children displayed systematicity. Their language could be studied as a system, not just as deviations from the language they were exposed to. Thus, early utterances by children such as **no shoe** and **no book** are not best described as faulty imitation but rather as representing the child's attempt to systematically express negation. It is these assumptions that have come to guide work in second language acquisition as well.

B   Recent Cognitive Perspectives

Since the 1990s, psychological theories have become increasingly central to research in SLA. Some of these theories use the computer as a metaphor for the mind, comparing language acquisition to the capacities of computers for storing, integrating, and retrieving information.

B1   Information Processing

| Declarative knowledge | 'knowing that' | Declarative → Procedural |
| Procedural knowledge | 'know how' | through 'practice' (to fluency) |

Cognitive psychologists working in an information-processing model see SLA as the building up of knowledge that can eventually be called on automatically for speaking and understanding. Norman Segalowits (2003) and others have suggested that learners have to pay attention at first to any aspect of the language that they are trying to understand or produce. However, the information processing model suggests that there is a limit to the amount of focused mental activity we can engage in at one time. Thus, learners at the earliest stages will use most of their resources to understand the main words in a message. In that situation, they may not notice the grammatical morphemes attached to some of the words, especially those that do not substantially affect meaning. Gradually, through experience and practice, information that was new becomes easier to process, and learners become able to access it quickly and even automatically. This frees them to pay attention to other aspects of the language that, in turn, gradually become automatic.

Similar 'information processing' approaches to SLA have been explored by other researchers. Robert Dekeyser (1998, 2001) and others have investigated SLA as 'skill learning', starts with '**declarative knowledge**', also referred to as knowledge that. The hypothesis is that, through practice, declarative knowledge may become '**procedural knowledge**', or knowledge how, in the same way that someone learns other skills like driving a car or skating. Indeed, once skills become proceduralized and automatized, thinking about the declarative knowledge while trying to perform the skill actually disrupts the smooth performance of it. In SLA, the path from declarative to procedural knowledge is sometimes associated with the kind of learning that takes place in a classroom, where rule learning is followed by practice. With enough practice, procedural knowledge eclipses the declarative knowledge, which, in time, may be forgotten. For this reason, fluent speakers may not even realize that they once possessed the declarative knowledge that set the process in motion.

Sometimes changes in language behaviour do not seem to be explainable in terms of a gradual build-up of fluency through practice. These changes have been described in terms of '**restructuring**' (Lightbown 1985; McLaughlin 1990). They seem to be based on some qualitative change in the learner's knowledge. Restructuring may account for what appear to be sudden bursts of progress, when learners suddenly seem to 'put it together', even though they have not had any new instruction or apparently relevant exposure to the language. It may also explain apparent **backsliding**, when a systematic aspect of a learner's language incorporates too much or incorporates the wrong things. For example, when a learner finally masters the use of the regular *-ed* ending to show past tense, irregular verbs that had previously been 'practised' correctly may be affected. Thus after months of saying 'I saw a film', the learner may say 'I seed' or even 'I sawed'. Such errors are not based on practice of those specific items but rather on their integration into a general pattern.

B2 Usage-based learning (Connectionism)

Usage-based learning proponents, unlike innatists, see no need to hypothesize the existence of a neurological module dedicated exclusively to language acquisition. They argue that what is innate is simply the ability to learn, rather than any specific 'linguistic' principles. Some usage-based theories also attribute less importance to the kind of declarative knowledge that characterizes skill learning and traditional structure-based approaches to second language instruction. As Nick Ellis (2002) explains, the emphasis is on the frequency with which learners encounter specific linguistic features in the input and the frequency with which language features occur together. According to this view, learners develop a stronger and stronger network of associations or connections between these features as well as between language features and the contexts in which they occur. Eventually, the presence of one situational or linguistic feature will activate the other(s) in the learner's mind. For example, learners might get subject-verb agreement correct, not because they know a rule but because they have heard examples such as 'I say' and 'he says' so often that each subject pronoun activates the correct verb form.

Connections may be strong because the language features have occurred together frequently or they may be relatively weaker because there have been fewer opportunities to experience them together. Some of the evidence for usage-based views comes from the observation mentioned above that much of the language we use in ordinary conversation or in particular genres is predictable, and to considerable extent based on formulaic units or chunks. As suggested by Nick Ellis (2003, 2005) and others, language is at least partly learned in units larger than single words, and sentences or phrases are not usually put together one word at a time. Usage-based research has shown that a learning mechanism, simulated by a computer program, can not only 'learn' from input but can also generalize, even making overgeneralization errors.

B3 The Competition Model

The competition model is closely related to the connectionist perspective. It is also based on the hypothesis that language acquisition occurs without the necessity of a learner's focused attention or the need for any innate brain module that is specifically for language. Through exposure to thousands of examples of language associated with particular meanings, learners come to understand how to use the 'cue' with which a language signals specific functions.

For example, the relationship between words in a sentence may be signaled by word order, grammatical markers, and the animacy of the nouns in the sentence. Most languages make use of multiple cues, but they differ in the primacy of each. This becomes clear in a situation where the meaning of a sentence is not immediately obvious. What helps you figure out the meaning? English uses word order as the most common indicator of the relationships between sentence components. Most English sentences have the order SVO. Two- and three-year old English speaking children use cues of animacy and their knowledge of the way things work in the world to interpret odd sentences. Thus, if they hear a string of words such as 'Box push boy', they will act it out by making a boy doll push a tiny box, focusing on the fact that the 'boy' is the natural agent of action in this situation. However, the SVO pattern is so strong in English that, before they are four years old, children will give an SVO interpretation to such strings of words. They will ignore the fact that boxes don't normally move on their own, and carefully demonstrate how the box pushes the boy. Word order patterns are stronger than animacy cues at this point. According to the competition model SLA requires that learners learn the relative importance of the different cues appropriate in the language they are learning.

Chapter 02 — Models of Second Language Acquisition

A An Innatist Model: Krashen's Five Hypotheses

One of the most talked-about models within this tradition was Stephen Krashen's *acquisition-learning hypothesis*, also known as the *input hypothesis* as well as the *monitor model*. Five claims were made by Krashen:

A1 Acquisition vs. Learning Hypothesis

Adult learners' 'fluency in L2 performance is due to what we have acquired, not what we have learned'. Subconscious acquisition is separate from conscious learning and is superior in the long run.

A2 Input Hypothesis

Comprehensible input — input that is 'a bit beyond' one's level of competence — is 'the only *true cause* of second language acquisition' (Krashen 1984). That input may be represented as $i+1$, that is, neither too far beyond one's reach nor so close that it poses no challenge ($i+0$). Further, speech will naturally 'emerge' with sufficient comprehensible input.

A3 Monitor Hypothesis

Monitoring, 'watchdogging' one's output, and other explicit, intentional learning, ought to be largely avoided, as it presumed to hinder acquisition.

A4 Natural Order Hypothesis

Extrapolating from morpheme order studies (Dulay & Burt 1976), later confirmed by Goldschneider and Dekeyser (2001), we acquire language rules in a predictable or 'natural' order.

A5 Affective Filter Hypothesis

The best acquisition will occur in environments of low anxiety, that is, in contexts where the affective filter is low.

B Cognitivist Models: Attention-Processing Model, Implicit & Explicit Processing, Noticing Hypothesis, and others

B1 An Attention-Processing Model

Focal ⇔ Peripheral	Attention	Processing	Controlled ⇔ Automatic
controlled·focal → controlled·peripheral / automatic·focal → automatic·peripheral			

One domain within cognitivism that 'remains one of the key puzzles confronting the scientific worldview' (Koch 2004) is defining and understanding consciousness. Recognizing this conundrum, Barry McLaughlin directed the attention of SLA researchers away from quibbling over consciousness and toward two features of human cognition: controlled and automatic processing. **Controlled processing** was described as typical of anyone learning a brand new skill (e.g., L2 beginners) in which only a very few elements of the skill can be retained, while **automatic processing** is used in more accomplished skills (advanced L2 learners), in which the 'hard drive' of one's brain manages multiple of bits of information simultaneously.

Both ends of this continuum of processing can occur with either **focal** (intentional, explicit) or **peripheral** (incidental, implicit) **attention** to the task at hand, that is, focusing attention either centrally or on the periphery. Both focal and peripheral attention to some tasks may be quite conscious (Hulstijn 1990). When you are driving a car, for example, your focal attention may center on cars directly in front of you as you move forward; but your peripheral attention to cars beside you and behind you, to potential hazards, and of course to the other thoughts running through your mind is all very much within your conscious awareness. In SLA your focal attention could be on form at times and on meaning at others, but an important stage to reach in SLA is to be able to focus on meaning while attending peripherally to form. Such a perspective on SLA entirely obviates the need to distinguish conscious and subconscious processing.

Let's look at some specific examples in the following table.

Processes	Examples
1. Controlled / Focal	Explaining a specific grammar point / Giving an example of a word usage / Learning prefabricated routines / Repeating after the teacher
2. Controlled / Peripheral	Giving simple greetings / Playing a simple language game / Using memorized routines in new situations / Completing very limited conversations
3. Automatic / Focal	Monitoring output / Giving brief attention to form during conversation / Scanning for specific keywords / Editing writing, including peer editing
4. Automatic / Peripheral	Participating in open-ended group work / Skimming and rapid reading / Freewriting / Engaging in natural unrehearsed conversation

A plausible interpretation of the four processes, with some overlap among them, would place most classroom learners roughly on a line of progression from #1 (controlled/focal) to #4 (automatic/peripheral). The latter might also be known as **fluency**, an ultimate communicative goal for language learners (Wood 2001). In FFI, for example, the ultimate goal is not to leave the learner focused on form, but rather to incorporate a correct form peripherally into the learner's automatic processing mechanisms.

B2 Implicit and Explicit Processing

Explicit knowledge	facts that a learner knows *about* language
Implicit knowledge	information that is automatically and spontaneously used in language tasks

The constructs of explicit/implicit knowledge have drawn the attention of numerous researchers over the years. Arguments were raised about the definition of implicit and explicit and about how to apply both processing types in the classroom.

In linguistic terms, **implicit knowledge** is information that is automatically and spontaneously used in language tasks, while **explicit knowledge** includes facts that a learner knows ***about*** language (Williams 2009). Children implicitly learn phonological, syntactic, semantic, and pragmatic rules for language, but do not have access to an explicit description of those rules. Implicit processes enable a learner to perform language but not necessarily to cite rules governing the performance. Ellen Bialystok (1990), Rod Ellis (1997), and Nick Ellis (1994) argued the importance of distinguishing implicit and explicit processing.

Another way of looking at the implicit/explicit dichotomy (or is it a dichotomy?) is to think of language processing as analyzed and unanalyzed knowledge (Bialystok 1982). The former includes the verbalization of linguistic rules and facts, as in a grammar-focus exercise, while the latter is synonymous with implicit learning. Other terminology has been used to describe virtually the same dichotomy: intentional vs. incidental learning (Gass & Selinker 2001), as well as declarative vs. procedural knowledge. These terminological contrasts underscore the interplay, in all classroom learning of an L2, of directing learner's attention to form while at the same time encouraging those forms to move to the periphery. On the periphery, learners are aware of forms, but are not focused on (or overwhelmed by) those forms.

B3   Schmidt's Noticing Hypothesis

Noticing	the essential starting point to acquisition, noticing-the-gap

Richard Schmidt (2001) proposed the '**noticing hypothesis**', suggesting that nothing is learned unless it has been noticed. Noticing does not itself result in acquisition, but it is the essential starting point. From this perspective, comprehensible input does not lead to growth in language knowledge unless the learner becomes aware of a particular language feature.

The question of whether learners must be 'aware' that they are 'noticing' something in the input is the object of debate. According to information processing theories, anything that uses up our mental 'processing space', even if we are not aware of it or attending to it intentionally, can contribute to learning. From a usage-based perspective, the likelihood of acquisition is best predicted by the frequency with which something is available for processing, not by the learner's awareness of something in the input.

The extent to which learner's noticing of language features affects their second language development comes up in our discussion of research on the following example. This example is taken from a classroom where a group of 12-year-old French speakers are learning English. In this example, they are engaged in an activity where the words in sentences are reordered to form new sentences. The following sentence has been placed on the board: 'Sometimes my mother makes good cakes'.

T:	Another place to put our adverb?
S1:	After makes?
T:	After makes.
S2:	Before good?
T:	My mother makes sometimes good cakes.
S3:	No.
T:	No, we can't do that. It sounds yucky.
S3:	Yucky!
T:	Disgusting. Horrible. Right?
S4:	Horrible!

This is hardly a typical grammar lesson! And yet the students' attention is being drawn to an error that virtually all of them make in English.

Researchers suggest that the focused instruction will allow learners to notice the target features in subsequent input and interaction. Form-focused instruction as it is understood in this position does not always involve metalinguistic explanations, nor are learners expected to be able to explain why something is right or wrong. They claim simply that the learners need to notice how their language use differs from that of a more proficient speaker. They assume that much of language acquisition will develop naturally out of meaningful language use, without formal instruction that focuses on the language itself.

B4 Input processing

processing instruction	comprehension practice > production practice

In his research with American university students learning foreign languages, Bill VanPatten (2004) observed many cases of students misinterpreting sentences. For example, as predicted by the competition model, when these English speakers heard sentences such as '*La sigue el señor*', they interpreted it as 'She (subject pronoun) follows the man'. The correct interpretation is 'Her (object pronoun) follows the man (subject of the sentence).' In other words, the correct English translation would be 'The man follows her.' In order to understand that, students need to learn that in Spanish, a pronoun object precedes the verb and that it is essential to pay attention to whether the pronoun is a subject or an object rather than to the word order alone.

VanPatten argued that the problem arose in part from the fact that learners have limited processing capacity and cannot pay attention to form and meaning at the same time. Not surprisingly, they tend to give priority to meaning. When the context in which they hear a sentence helps them make sense of it, that is a good strategy for understanding the general idea, but it may interfere with learners' progress in acquiring the language. VanPatten developed instructional procedures that require learners to focus on the specific language features in order to interpret the meaning, thus pushing them to acquire those features.

Two groups were compared in the study, one receiving processing instruction, the other following a more traditional approach. The processing instruction group received explicit explanations about object pronouns and did some activities that drew their attention to the importance of noticing that object pronouns could occur before the verb. Then, through a variety of focused listening and reading exercises, learners had to pay attention to how the target forms were used in order to understand the meaning. For example, they heard or read '*La sigue el señor*' and had to choose which picture — a man following a woman or a woman following a man — corresponded to the sentence. A second group of learners also received explicit information about the target forms but instead of focusing on comprehension practice through **processing instruction**, they engaged in production practice, doing exercises to practice the forms being taught. After the instruction, learners who had received the comprehension-based processing instruction not only did better on the comprehension tasks than learners in the production group, they also performed as well on production tasks.

Comprehension of meaningful language is the foundation of language acquisition. Active listening and reading for meaning are valuable components of classroom teachers' pedagogical practices. Nevertheless, considerable research and experience challenge the hypothesis that comprehensible input is enough. VanPatten's research showed that forcing students to rely on specific linguistic features in order to interpret meaning increased the chances that they would be able to use these features in their own second language production.

B5 Processability theory

developmental features	learned along a predictable developmental path
variational features	learned at different developmental stages

Manfred Pienemann (1999, 2003) developed the **processability theory** on the basis of his research with learners of different languages in a variety of settings, both instructional and informal. One important aspect of his theory is the integration of developmental sequences with first language influence. He argues that his theory explains why learners do not simply transfer features from their L1 at early stages of acquisition. Instead, they have to develop a certain level of processing capacity in the second language before they can use their knowledge of the features that already exist in their L1.

Manfred Pienemann have tried to explain why it often seems that some things can be taught successfully whereas other things, even after extensive or intensive teaching, seem to remain unacquired. Their research provides evidence that some linguistic structures, for example, basic word order in sentences (both simple and complex) develop along a predictable developmental path. These were labeled 'developmental features'. (Some language features which could be learned and used by learners who were at different developmental stages were referred to as 'variational features'.) They also described a sequence in the acquisition by learners of English from a variety of first language backgrounds. The developmental stages of questions are based on the following research. According to Pienemann, any attempt to teach a Stage 4 word-order pattern to learners at Stage 1 will not work because learners have to pass through Stage 2 and get to Stage 3 before they are ready to acquire what is at Stage 4.

[The developmental stages of question]

Stage 1

Single words, formulae, or sentence fragments.
- Dog? / Four children?

Stage 2

Declarative word order, no inversion, no fronting.
- It's a monster in the right corner?
- The boys throw the shoes?

Stage 3

Fronting: *do*-fronting; *wh*-fronting without inversion; other fronting.
- Do you have a shoes on your picture?
- Where the children are playing?
- Does in this picture there is four astronauts?
- Is the picture has two planets on top?

Stage 4

Inversion in *wh*- + copula; 'yes/no' questions with other auxiliaries.
- Where is the sun?
- Is there a fish in the water?

Stage 5

Inversion in *wh*- questions with both an auxiliary and a main verb.
- How do you say *proche*?
- What's the boy doing?

Stage 6

Complex questions.
- question tag: It's better, isn't it?
- negative question: Why can't you go?
- embedded question: Can you tell me what the date is today?

In Example 1 below, we see a teacher trying to help students with the word order of questions. The students seem to know what the teacher means, but the level of language the teacher is offering them is beyond their current stage of development. Students are asking Stage 3 questions, which the teacher recasts as Stage 5 questions. The students react by simply answering the question or accepting the teacher's formulation.

> **Example 1**
>
> Students in intensive ESL (11-12 year old French speakers) interviewing a student who had been in the same class in a previous year.
> S1: Mylène, where you put your 'Kid of the Week' poster?
> T: Where did you put your poster when you got it?
> S2: In my room.
>
> (two minutes later)
>
> S3: Beatrice, where you put your 'Kid of the Week' poster?
> T: Where did you put your poster?
> S4: My poster was on my wall and it fell down.

In Example 2, the student is using the 'fronting' strategy that is typical of Stage 3 questions. The teacher's corrective feedback leads the student to imitate a Stage 4 question.

> **Example 2**
>
> (The same group of students engaged in 'Famous person' interviews.)
> S1: Is your mother play piano?
> T: 'Is your mother play piano?' OK. Well, can you say 'Is your mother play piano?' or 'Is your mother a piano player?'
> S1: 'Is your mother a piano player?'
> S2: No.

The result of this study suggests that while 'variational features' of the language can be taught successfully at various points in the learners' development, 'developmental features' are best taught according to the learner's internal schedule. Furthermore, although learners may be able to produce more advanced forms on tests or in very restricted pedagogical exercises, instruction cannot change the 'natural' developmental course. The recommendation is to assess the learners' developmental level and teach what would naturally come next.

One component of language learning that has seen a renewal of interest within the cognitive perspective is practice. As we saw in discussions of the behaviourist perspective, an approach to learning that is based on drill and that separates practice from meaningful language use does not usually lead to communicative competence. This does not mean, however, that practice is not an essential component of language learning. Researchers are now looking more closely at how practice converts declarative knowledge to procedural knowledge and then to automatic performance. Note that from the cognitive perspective, the practice needed for language development is not mechanical, and it is not limited to the production of language. Listening and reading are also affected by opportunities for practice. Elizabeth Gatbonton and Norman Segalowitz have developed an approach to language teaching which is based on classroom activities which, by their nature, require learners to use meaningful units of language repetitively in contexts where there are genuine exchanges of meaning. The goal is to provide opportunities for using these units with sufficient frequency that they will become automatic. Segalowitz (2010) has emphasized the importance of increasing the amount of language that can be used automatically, thus freeing more cognitive resources for learning new things.

C Social Constructivist Models: Swain's & Long's Hypotheses

C1 Swain's Output Hypothesis

Noticing function	be aware of the gap
Hypothesis-testing function	modify by feedback
Metalinguistic function	learn by internalization

Theoretical interest in output as a source of language acquisition was stimulated by Swain's (1985) proposal that **comprehensible output** as well as comprehensible input may be required in order for learners to achieve high levels of grammatical and sociolinguistic competence in an L2. Swain argued that what she called 'pushed output' obligated learners to engage in syntactic processing, as opposed to the kind of semantic processing involved in comprehension. That is, pushed output allowed them to move from what they want to say (e.g., the vocabulary they need) to how they say it (e.g., the grammar and syntax to make their meanings clear and appropriate to the context), and this fostered acquisition. Swain (1995) discusses three functions of output where accuracy is concerned.

① **Noticing function**: Producing language helps learners to notice their problems.

② **Hypothesis-testing function**: Producing language enables learners to test out hypotheses about the L2. This occurs through the **modified output** that learners produce following negative feedback.

③ **Metalinguistic function**: Output allows learners to reflect consciously about L2 forms. This can occur in the context of communicative tasks where the content is grammar (i.e. when learners negotiate for meaning as they grapple with a grammar problem).

Input-intake-output

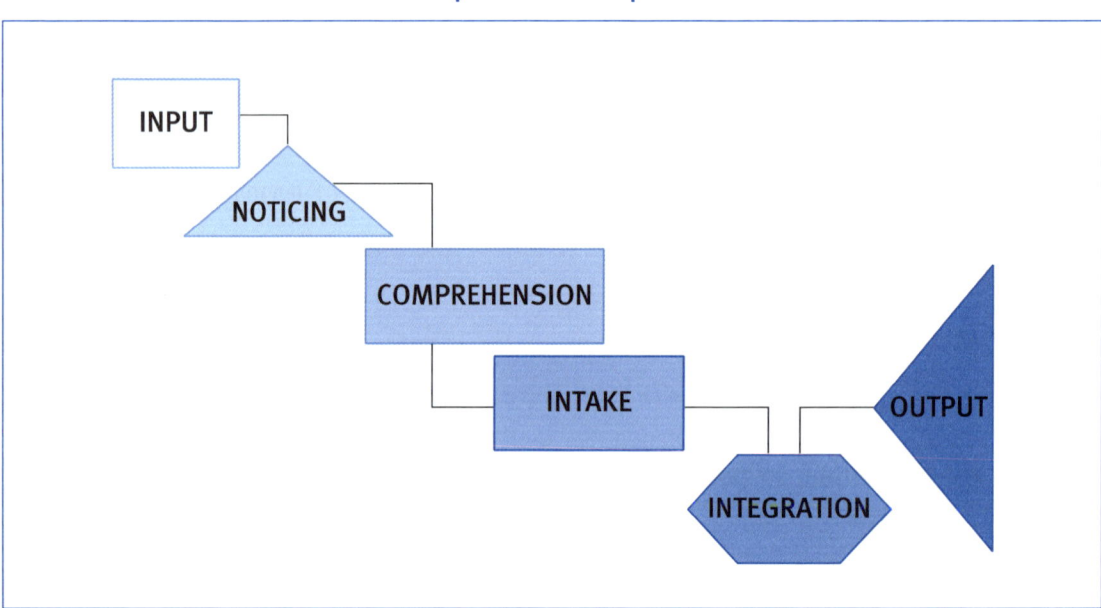

(C1a) Input vs. Output

The most crucial difficulty in Krashen's Input Hypothesis is found in his explicit claim that 'comprehensible input is the only causative variable in SLA'. In other words, success in a foreign language must be attributed to input alone. Such a theory ascribes little credit to learners and their own active engagement in the process. Moreover, it is important to distinguish between **input** and **intake**. The latter is the subset of all input that actually gets assigned to our long-term memory store. For example, reading a book is a kind of your input. But your intake is what you take with you over a period of time and can later remember. Krashen did suggest that input gets converted to intake through a learner's process of linking forms to meaning and noticing 'gaps' between the learner's current internalized rules system and the new input. However, others have been against his proposal. They suggest that Krashen's comprehensible input must at the very least be complemented by a significant amount of output that gives credit to the role of the learner's production. Swain offered convincing evidence that output was at least as significant as input, if not more so, in explaining learner success in her Output Hypothesis.

(C1b) Modified Output (vs. Pushed Output)

The term **pushed output** has been defined as 'output that reflects what learners can produce when they are pushed to use the target language accurately and concisely' (Ellis 2003), and Ellis pointed out the necessity of distinguishing between modified output and pushed output. Pushed output does not necessarily include modification of the initial non-targetlike utterance because it could be a simple repetition, which is illustrated in the example below.

> Non-native speaker (NNS): I go cinema.
> Native speaker (NS): Uh?
> NNS: I go cinema last night.
> NS: Oh, last night.

Here the NNS is pushed into clarifying her initial utterance, which is not marked for time. She responds by adding a lexical marker of past time reference ('last night') and the conversation proceeds. Thus, successful communication takes place without the learner needing to modify her output by incorporating the past tense marker. This example demonstrates the need to distinguish between pushed and modified output, showing that not all pushed output is in fact modified.

C2 Long's Interaction Hypothesis

According to Long (1983), input comes to the individual from a variety of sources, including others. Individuals make their input 'comprehensible' in three ways: 1) by simplifying the input, i.e., using familiar structures and vocabulary; 2) by using linguistic and extralinguistic features, i.e., familiar structures, background knowledge, gestures; and 3) by modifying the interactional structure of the conversation.

This third element is the basis of Long's (1981) **Interaction Hypothesis**, which accounts for ways in which input is modified and contributes to comprehension and acquisition. Long (1983, 1996) maintains that speakers make changes in their language as they interact or 'negotiate meaning' with each other. **Negotiation of meaning** has been characterized as 'exchanges between learners and their interlocutors as they attempt to resolve communication breakdown and to work toward mutual comprehension' (Pica et al. 1989). Speakers negotiate meaning to avoid conversational trouble or to revise language when trouble occurs. Through negotiation of meaning, interactions (i.e., between native and nonnative speakers or between nonnative speakers) are changed and redirected, leading to greater comprehensibility. Further, these negotiations can lead to language development by the learner (Long 1996). That is, by working toward comprehension, language input is made available for intake, cognitive inspection, and thus acquisition.

(C2a) Negotiation of Meaning

Clarification Request	by Listener	Pardon?
Confirmation Check	by Listener	[repetition] ↗
Comprehension Check	by Speaker	[tag question] ~ right?

Negotiation of meaning occurred most often to overcome communication problems during chat exchange rather than in direct relation to errors. Long (1980) defined a number of negotiation devices that interlocutors might employ as they negotiate for meaning during social interaction, such as **clarification requests**, **confirmation checks**, and **comprehension checks**.

1) Clarification requests

They refer to moves by which one speaker seeks assistance in understanding the other speaker's preceding utterance through questions, statements such as "I don't understand.", or imperatives such as "Please repeat." and "Try again.".

> I: So you came here by yourself or did you come with friends?
> L: No no I – what? what you say? (clarification request)
> I: Did you come to the states with friends or did you come alone?
> L: No, alone – from Toronto.
>
> **Learner (NNS English) & Interlocutor (NS English)**

2) Confirmation checks

They refer to moves by which one speaker seeks confirmation of the other's preceding utterance through repetition, with rising intonation, of what was perceived to be all or part of the preceding utterance.

> I: Did you get high marks? Good grades?
> L: High marks? (confirmation check)
> I: Good grades A's and B's. Did you get A in English?
> L: Oh no in English yes em B.
>
> **Learner (NNS English) & Interlocutor (NS English)**

3) Comprehension checks

They refer to moves by which one speaker attempts to determine whether the other speaker has understood a preceding message often formed with a tag question.

> I: OK, he's dancing with the woman doctor.
> L: Excuse me? (clarification request)
> I: The young man doctor is dancing with the woman doctor, right? (comprehension check)
> L: Mmhm.
>
> **Learner (NNS English) & Interlocutor (NS English)**

(C2b) Structure of 'non-understanding routines'

Trigger	the utterance that creates a problem of understanding
Indicator	the utterance indicating that something was not understood
Response	the utterance of response to the indicator
Reaction to Response	(optional)

The study of interactional modifications involves examining the speech of both participants in a conversation. As Long (1983) has pointed out, acts such as requests for clarification and confirmation take place within a discourse context — they have life across utterances and speakers. However, the study of individual discourse acts does not show how sequences of discourse are constructed. For this it is necessary to examine the structure of discourse.

Gass and Varonis (1985) have developed a model to describe the structure of 'non-understanding routines' where meaning negotiation takes place. It consists of a 'trigger' (i.e. the utterance or part of an utterance that creates a problem of understanding), an 'indicator' which indicates that something in a previous utterance was not understood, a 'response' to the indicator, and finally a 'reaction to the response', which is optional. The model is recursive in that it allows for the 'response' element itself to act as a 'trigger' for a further non-understanding routine. The following table provides a simple illustration of the model.

Utterance	Function
NNS1: My father now is retire.	Trigger
NNS2: Retire?	Indicator
NNS1: Yes.	Response
NNS2: Oh yeah.	Reaction to Response

<Table: A simple discourse model of the negotiation of meaning>

Chapter 03 MindMap

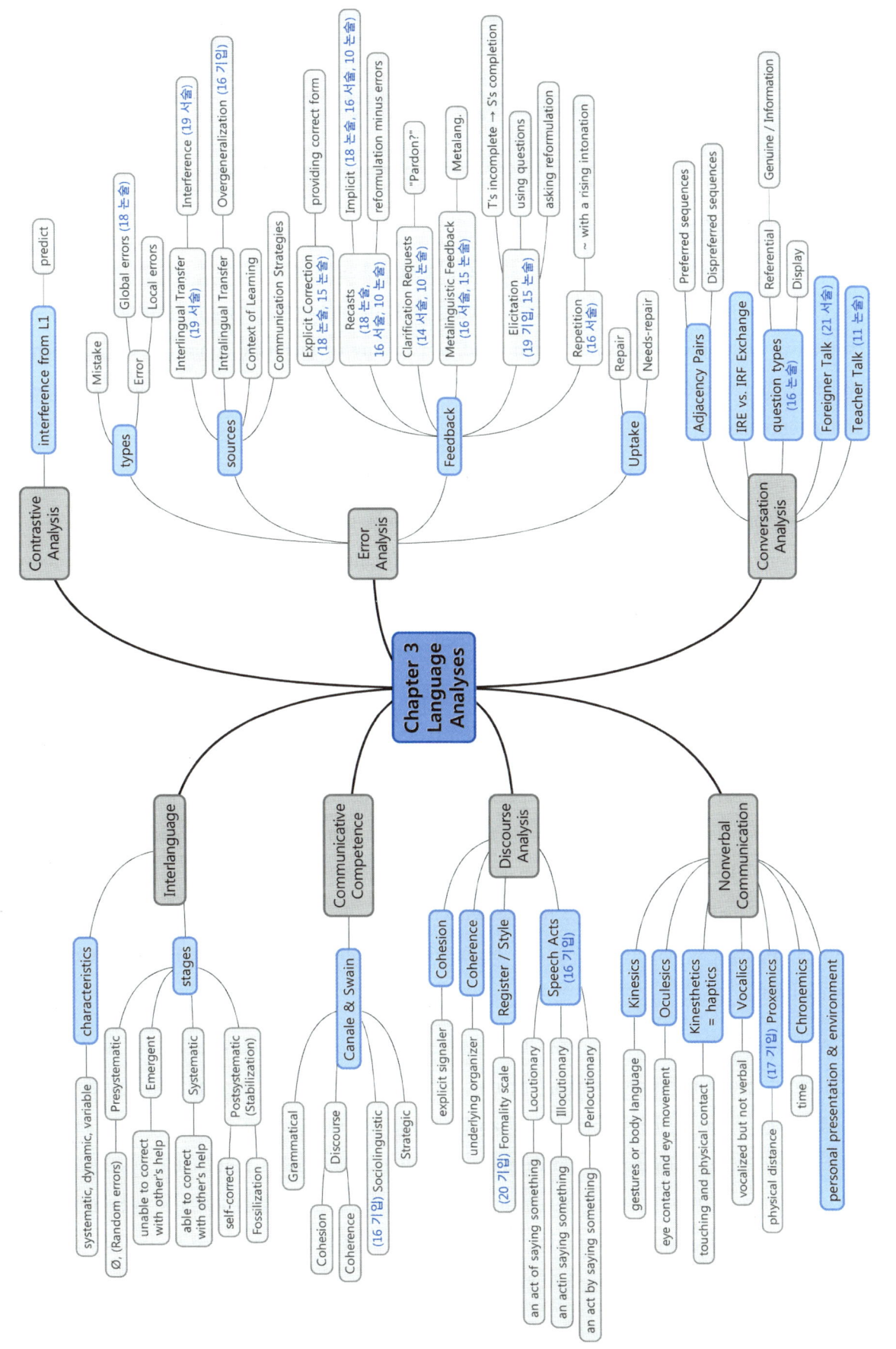

Chapter 03　Language Analyses

A　Contrastive Analysis

The **Contrastive Analysis** claimed that the principal barrier to SLA is the interference of the first language system with the second language system, and that a scientific structural analysis of the two languages in question would yield a taxonomy of linguistic contrasts between them which in turn would enable linguists and language teachers to predict the difficulties a learner would encounter.

According to the Contrastive Analysis Hypothesis (CAH), where the first language and the target language are similar, learners should acquire target language structures with ease; where there are differences, learners should have difficulty. However, researchers have found that learners do not make all the errors predicted by the CAH. Instead, many of their actual errors are not predictable on the basis of their first language.

B　Interlanguage

Until the 1960s, L2 learners had been viewed for perhaps centuries as incomplete users of their foreign language, slow and imperfectly approximating nativelike proficiency. However, this view of the L2 learners' journey markedly changed. Learners were looked on not as producers of malformed language replete with mistakes, but as intelligent beings proceeding through logical, systematic stages of acquisition, creatively acting upon their linguistic environment.

A number of terms were coined to describe the perspective that stresses the legitimacy of learners' second language systems. The best known of these is interlanguage by Larry Selinker. **Interlanguage** refers to the separateness of an L2 learner's system, a system that has a structurally intermediate status between the native and target languages. This is neither the system of L1 nor the system of the L2, but a system based upon the best attempt of learners to bring order and structure to the linguistic stimuli surrounding them. The interlanguage hypothesis led to a new era of second language research and teaching and represented a significant breakthrough for the study of SLA. The most obvious approach to analyzing interlanguage is to study the speech and writing of learners, or what is also called **learner language** (James, 1990).

C Stages of Learner Language Development

Students progress through various stages of development when it comes to the errors they make. This, of course, parallels their language level.

Presystematic	∅
Emergent	unable to correct errors when pointed out
Systematic	able to correct errors when pointed out
Postsystematic (Stabilization)	self-correct (but Fossilization)

① **stage 1** - '**presystematic**' stage

L2 learners may make a number of random errors, since they are only marginally aware of a given subset of the L2 system. Consider these actual written utterances by ESL students, in which the intended meaning is quite a mystery.

> The different city is another one in the another two.
> Society has it's hard-living's bitterness way into the decaded-dragging life.

② **stage 2** - '**emergent**' stage

The learner's linguistic production becomes more consistent as certain rules, words, and phrases (possibly correct in the learner's mind) are induced and applied. A hearer or reader should at this stage be able to discern what the intended meaning is. While meaning may be interpretable, this stage may also be characterized by some **backsliding** (Selinker 1972), in which the learner seems to have grasped a rule or principle and then regresses to a previous stage. This phenomenon of moving from a correct form to an incorrect form and then back to correctness is referred to as **U-shaped learning** (Gass & Selinker 2001). In general the learner is still unable to correct errors when they are pointed out by someone else. Consider the following conversation between a learner (L) and a native speaker (NS) of English:

L:	I go New York.	NS:	When?
NS:	You're going to New York?	L:	Uh, 1992.
L:	[*doesn't understand*] What?	NS:	Oh, you went to New York in 1992.
NS:	You will go to New York?	L:	Yes, uh, ... I go 1992.
L:	Yes.		

③ **stage 3** - '**systematic**' stage

The learner is now able to manifest more consistency in producing the second language. The most salient difference between the second and third stages is the ability of learners to repair their errors when they are pointed out — even very subtly — to them. Consider the English learner who described a popular fishing-resort area:

L: Many fish are in the lake. These fish are serving in the restaurants near the lake.
NS: [*smiling*] The *fish* are serving?
L: Oh, no, [*laughing*] uh, fish are *being served* in restaurants!

④ **stage 4** - '**postsystematic**' stage

In the final stage, which some researchers (Long 2003) call **stabilization**, the learner has relatively few errors and has mastered the system to the point that fluency and intended meanings are not problematic. This fourth stage is characterized by the learner's ability to self-correct.

He passed out with very high score — sorry, I mean, he *passed* test — with high score.
I like Abraham Lincoln because he has known many people in Japan — um, ah, no, no, he ... many, many Japan people know *him*!

In the fourth stage, learners can stabilize too fast, allowing minor errors to slip by undetected, and thus manifest **fossilization** (Selinker & Lamendella 1979) of their language, which refers to the relatively permanent incorporation of incorrect linguistic forms into a person's second language competence.

C1 Sequences of Acquisition

When learners acquire a grammatical structure they do so gradually, moving through a series of stages *en route* to acquiring the native-speaker rule. The acquisition of a particular grammatical structure, therefore, must be seen as a *process* involving **transitional constructions**. As an example of this process, let us consider how L2 learners acquire irregular past tense forms (for example, 'ate'). Learners are likely to pass through the different stages shown in the following table.

Table. Stages in the acquisition of the past tense of 'eat'

Stage	Description	Example
1	Learners fail to mark the verb for past time.	'eat'
2	Learners begin to produce irregular past tense forms.	'ate'
3	Learners overgeneralize the regular past tense form.	'eated'
4	Sometimes learners produce hybrid forms.	'ated'
5	Learners produce correct irregular past tense forms.	'ate'

Such sequences are instructive because they reveal that the use of a correct structural form (for example, 'ate') does not necessarily mean that this form has been 'acquired'. Indeed, in this sequence, learners producing 'eated' and 'ated' are, in fact, more advanced than learners at stage 2 who produce 'ate'. Acquisition follows a **U-shaped course of development**; that is, initially learners may display a high level of accuracy only to apparently regress later before finally once again performing in accordance with target-language norms. It is clear that this occurs because learners reorganize their existing knowledge in order to accommodate new knowledge. Thus, stages 3 and 4 only arise when learners have begun to acquire regular *–ed* (as in 'jump*ed*'). Forms like 'eated' and 'ated' represent an overgeneralization of the regular *–ed* past tense. This kind of reorganization, which is believed to be prevalent in L2 acquisition, is referred to as **restructuring**. As learners restructure their grammatical systems, they may appear to regress whereas in fact they are advancing. Sequences such as that for irregular past reveal how restructuring occurs and how it can lead to U-shaped development.

It is clear that the acquisition of what looks like a simple grammatical feature such as past tense is, in fact, a highly complex affair. Not only are there general stages in the acquisition of grammatical features like past tense, as illustrated in the above table, but there may also be stages within stages. Thus, when learners begin to use past tense markers (either irregular markers as in 'ate' or regular markers as in 'painted'), they do not do so on all verbs at the same time. Learners find it easier to mark verbs for past tense if the verb refers to events (for example, 'arrive'), somewhat more difficult to mark verbs that refer to activities (for example, 'sleep'), and most difficult to mark verbs that refer to states (for example, 'want')

The kind of verb also influences the kind of errors learners make. For example, with activity verbs learners are more likely to substitute a progressive form for the past tense form:

> After that the weather was nice so we swimming in the ocean.

In contrast, with state verbs they substitute the simple form of the verb:

> Last night everything seem very quiet and peaceful.

Learners, then, pass through highly complex stages of development. These stages are not sharply defined, however. Rather they are blurred as learners oscillate between stages. Thus, in the case of past tense, at any one time a learner may mark some verbs correctly for past tense, fail to mark others at all, and overgeneralize the regular *-ed* and the progressive *-ing* forms with yet other verbs. Despite the complexity of learners' behaviour, however, it is clear that it is far from random.

D Error Analysis

The fact that learners do make errors, and that these errors can be observed, analyzed, and classified to reveal something of the system operating within the learner, led to a surge of study of learners' errors, called **error analysis** (**EA**). Error analysis became distinguished from contrastive analysis hypothesis (CAH) by its examination of errors attributable to all possible sources, not just those resulting from negative transfer of the native language. Error analysis differed from contrastive analysis hypothesis in that it did not set out to predict errors. Rather, it sought to discover and describe different kinds of errors in an effort to understand how learners process second language data.

D1 Sources of error

Interlingual Transfer	L1 → L2, = interference
Intralingual Transfer	L2 → L2, = overgeneralization
Context of Learning	environment (classroom / social situation)
Communication Strategies	production strategies

① **Interlingual Transfer** (generalization between L1 and L2): The beginners of learning a second language are especially vulnerable to interlingual transfer from the native language, or **interference**. e.g. 'sheep' for 'ship'

② **Intralingual Transfer** (generalization within L2): Once learners have begun to acquire parts of the target language, intralingual transfer is manifested. Negative intralingual transfer, or **overgeneralization** is typical in this category.
   e.g. "Does John can sing?", "He goed."

③ **Context of Learning**: '**Context**' refers, for example, to the classroom with its teacher and its materials in the case of school learning or the social situation in the case of untutored second language learning. In a classroom context the teacher or the textbook can lead the learner to make faulty hypotheses about the language. The sociolinguistic context of natural, untutored language acquisition can give rise to certain dialect acquisition that may itself be a source of error.

④ **Communication Strategies**: Learners obviously use production strategies in order to enhance getting their messages across, but at times these techniques can themselves become a source of error. Word coinage, circumlocution, false cognates and prefabricated patterns can all be sources of error.

D2 Categories of error treatment

Explicit Correction	explicit provision of the correct form
Recasts	reformulation minus the error
Clarification Requests	requiring a repetition / reformulation
Metalinguistic Feedback	using metalanguage w/o E. C.
Elicitation	eliciting S's completion
Repetition	repeating with a rising intonation

① **Explicit correction**: It refers to the explicit provision of the correct form. As the teacher provides the correct form, he clearly indicates that what the student had said was incorrect.

> S: The dog runs fastly.
> T: 'Fastly' doesn't exist. 'Fast' does not take '-ly'. That's why I picked 'quickly'.
>
> ---
>
> S1: Is your favourite house is a split-level?
> S2: Yes.
> T: You're saying 'is' two times, dear. 'Is your favourite house a split-level?'
> S1: A split-level.

② **Recasts**: They involve the teacher's reformulation of all or part of a student's utterance, minus the error. Recasts are generally **implicit** in that they are not introduced by 'You mean', 'Use this word', or 'You should say'.

> T: Would you close the door please, Bernard? Claude, what is he doing?
> S1: Close the door.
> T: He is closing the door. What are you doing, Mario?
> S2: I listen to you.
> T: You're listening to me.
> S2: Yes.
>
> ---
>
> S: Mylène, where you put your 'Kid of the Week' poster?
> T: Where did you put your poster when you got it?

③ **Clarification requests**: They indicate to students either that their utterance has been misunderstood by the teacher or that the utterance is ill-formed in some way and that a repetition or a reformulation is required. A clarification request includes phrases such as 'Pardon me?' or 'I'm sorry?'. It may also include a repetition of the error as in 'What do you mean by ~?'

> T: How often do you wash the dishes?
> S: Fourteen.
> T: Excuse me? (Clarification request)
> S: Fourteen.

> T: Fourteen what? (Clarification request)
> S: Fourteen for a week.
> T: Fourteen times a week? (Recast)
> S: Yes. Lunch and dinner.

④ **Metalinguistic feedback**: It contains information, or questions, related to the well-formedness of the student's utterance, without explicitly providing the correct form. Metalinguistic comments generally indicate that there is an error somewhere. Metalinguistic information provides either some grammatical metalanguage that refers to the nature of error or a word definition in the case of lexical errors. Metalinguistic questions also point to the nature of the error but attempt to elicit the information from the student.

> S: We look at the people yesterday.
> T: What's the ending we put on verbs when we talk about the past?

⑤ **Elicitation**: It refers to at least three techniques that teachers use to directly elicit the correct form from students. First, teachers elicit completion of their own utterance. Second, teachers use questions to elicit correct forms. Third, teachers occasionally ask students to reformulate their utterance.

> S: My father cleans the plate.
> T: Excuse me, he cleans the …….
> S: Plates?

⑥ **Repetition**: It refers to the teacher's repetition, in isolation, of the student's erroneous utterance. In most cases, teachers adjust their intonation so as to highlight the error.

> S: We is ….
> T: We is? (Repetition) But it's two people, right? You see your mistake? You see the error? (Metalinguistic feedback) When it's plural it's 'we are'. (Explicit correction)
>
> ----
>
> S: He's in the bathroom.
> T: Bathroom? (Repetition) Bedroom. He's in the bedroom. (Recast)

D3 Uptake: Responses to Feedback

We (Lyster & Lanta 1997) have drawn on speech act theory to introduce the notion of uptake into the error treatment sequence. **Uptake** in our model refers to a student's utterance that immediately follows the teacher's feedback and that constitutes a reaction in some way to the teacher's intention to draw attention to some aspect of the student's initial utterance (this overall intention is clear to the student although the teacher's specific linguistic focus may not be). A description of uptake, then, reveals what the student attempts to do with the teacher's feedback. If there is no uptake, then there is topic continuation, which is initiated by either the same or another student (in both cases, the teacher's intention goes unheeded) or by the teacher (in which case the teacher has not provided an opportunity for uptake).

> L: (to another student) What means this word?
> T: Uh, Luis, how do we say that in English, What does?
> L: Ah, what does this word mean?

Uptakes are categorized as follows:

1) (other-initiated) Repair

① **Repetition**: refers to a student's repetition of the teacher's feedback when the latter includes the correct form.

② **Incorporation**: refers to a student's repetition of the correct form provided by the teacher, which is then incorporated into a longer utterance produced by the student.

③ **Self-repair**: refers to a self-correction, produced by the student who made the initial error, in response to the teacher's feedback when the latter does not already provide the correct form.

④ **Peer-repair**: refers to peer-correction provided by a student, other than the one who made the initial error, in response to the teacher's feedback.

2) Needs-repair

① **Acknowledgment**: generally refers to a simple 'yes' on the part of the student in response to the teacher's feedback, as if to say, "Yes, that is indeed what I meant to say (but you've just said it much better!)." Acknowledgment may also include a "yes" or "no" on the part of the student in response to the teacher's metalinguistic feedback.

② **Same error**: refers to uptake that includes a repetition of the student's initial error.

③ **Different error**: refers to a student's uptake that is in response to the teacher's feedback but that neither corrects nor repeats the initial error; instead, a different error is made.

④ **Off target**: refers to uptake that is clearly in response to the teacher's feedback turn but that circumvents the teacher's linguistic focus altogether, without including any further errors.

⑤ **Hesitation**: refers to a student's hesitation in response to the teacher's feedback.

⑥ **Partial repair**: refers to uptake that includes a correction of only part of the initial error.

The needs-repair category is one that can lead to additional feedback from the teacher and thus allows for error treatment sequences to go beyond the third turn.

E Communicative Competence

grammatical competence	linguistic knowledge, 'formally possible'
discourse competence	inter-sentential relationship [cohesion, coherence]
sociolinguistic competence	following sociocultural rules, understanding the social context
strategic competence	using verbal/nonverbal tech. to compensate for com. breakdown

The term, **communicative competence** (CC) was coined by Dell Hymes (1972), who asserted that Chomsky's (1965) notion of competence was too limited. This opposition has been adopted by those who seek new directions toward a communicative era by taking for granted the basic motives and the appropriateness of this opposition behind the development of communicative competence.

E1 Canale & Swain's Model

In Canale and Swain's definition, four different components, or subcategories, made up the construct of CC. The first two subcategories reflected the use of the *linguistic system* itself; the last two defined the functional aspect of *communication*.

① **Grammatical competence**: "Knowledge of lexical items and of rules of morphology, syntax, sentence-grammar semantics, and phonology" (Canale & Swain 1980). It is the competence that we associate with mastering the linguistic code of a language, the linguistic competence referred to by Hymes (1972).

② **Discourse competence**: The ability to connect sentences in stretches of discourse and to form a meaningful whole out of a series of utterances. With its inter-sentential relationships, discourse encompasses everything from simple spoken conversations to lengthy written texts.

③ **Sociolinguistic competence**: The ability to follow sociocultural rules of language. This type of competence "requires an understanding of the social context in which language is used: the roles of the participants, the information they share, and the function of the interaction." (Savignon 1983)

④ **Strategic competence**: The ability to use verbal and nonverbal communicative techniques to compensate for breakdowns in communication of insufficient competence. It includes the ability to make repairs, and to sustain communication through paraphrase, circumlocution, repetition, hesitation, avoidance, and guessing.

E2 Later Modification of CC Models

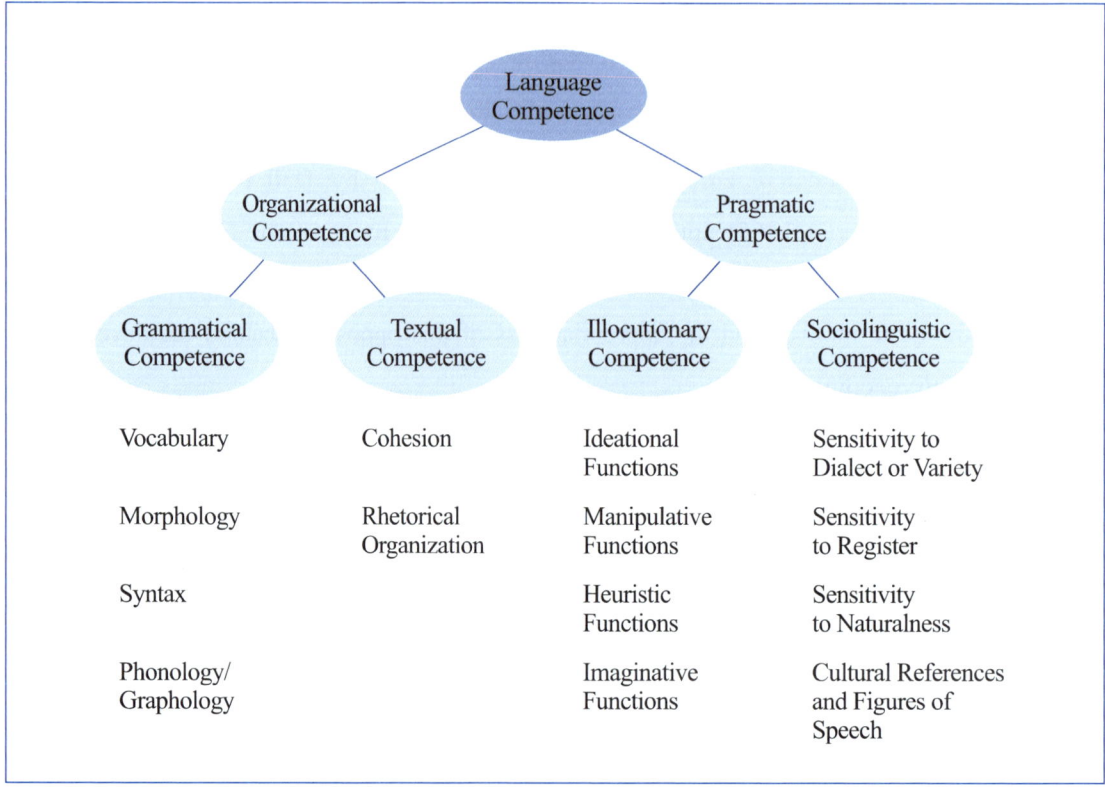

The conceptualization of CC through the years saw a number of different interpretations. One promising version of CC was offered by Bachman (1990), who proposed a reclassification of Canale and Swain's model under an overarching mode, language competence, or language ability.

Bachman placed grammatical and discourse (renamed 'textual') competence under organizational competence: the rules and systems that govern what we can do with the forms of language, whether they be sentence-level (grammar) or rules that specify how we 'string' sentences together (discourse). Canale and Swain's sociolinguistic competence was divided into two separate pragmatic categories: functional aspects of language (illocutionary competence, pertaining to sending and receiving intended meanings) and sociolinguistic aspects (which deal with such considerations as politeness, formality, metaphor, register, and culturally related aspects of language).

Bachman considered strategic competence to be an entirely separate element of communicative language ability, serving an 'executive' function of making the final 'decision', among many possible options, on wording, phrasing, and other productive and receptive means for negotiating meaning. In such a model, a user of a language utilizes both organizational and pragmatic knowledge in the moment-by-moment (strategic) decisions about how exactly to word an utterance or written communication, and how to interpret linguistic strings perceived through listening or reading competencies.

In more recent years, William Littlewood (2011) provided yet another conceptualization of CC using five separate dimensions, mostly a rearrangement of Canale and Swain's and Bachman's definitions. Three competencies are borrowed from the previous concepts, linguistic, discourse, and sociolinguistic, with virtually no redefinition. However, Littlewood added pragmatic competence as a separate node: the ability to 'use linguistic resources to convey and interpret meanings in real situation, including those where they encounter problems due to gaps in their knowledge'. In other words, he prefers the concept of 'pragmatic' to 'strategic'. And a fifth dimension, sociocultural, is added to include 'cultural knowledge and assumptions that affect the exchange of meanings'.

What we have with these three conceptions is comprehensive picture of what is meant, in broad strokes, by communicative competence. The classifications and redefinitions should not be a cause for confusion if one understands that there are no major theoretical disagreements among the three. The following table summarizes the three positions.

Canale and Swain (1980)	Bachman (1990)	Littlewood (2011)

1. Grammatical
2. Discourse
3. Sociolinguistic
4. Strategic
	A. Organizational
	   1. Grammatical
	   2. Textual
	B. Pragmatic
	   3. Illocutionary
	   4. Sociolinguistic
		1. Linguistic (= Grammatical)
		2. Discourse (= Textual)
		3. Pragmatic (= Strategic)
		4. Sociolinguistic
		5. Sociocultural

F Discourse Analysis

The analysis of the relationship between forms and functions of language is commonly called **discourse analysis**, which encompasses the notion that language is more than a sentence-level phenomenon.

cohesion	explicit signaler	grammatical ~ / lexical ~
coherence	underlying organizer	

F1 Cohesion

Cohesion is linguistically explicit and signals underlying semantic relationships between text elements. (Halliday 1976) In *Cohesion in English*, Halliday and Hasan identify five general categories of cohesive devices that create coherence in texts: reference, ellipsis, substitution, lexical cohesion and conjunction. They can be grouped into two main types: **grammatical cohesion** which is based on structural content, and **lexical cohesion** which is based on lexical content and background knowledge.

1) Grammatical Cohesion

Categories		Examples
Reference	Personal	I just met your brother. <u>He</u> is a nice guy.
	Demonstrative	You failed the test. <u>This</u> is bad news.
	Comparative	It is the <u>same</u> town we visited last year.

Substitution	Nominal	Can you give me a few nails? I need <u>one</u>.
	Verbal	Did you meet Kate last Sunday? Yes, I <u>did</u>.
	Clause	Will Tom win the match? I hope <u>so</u>.
Ellipsis	Nominal	Jane's paintings are better than Tom's Ø.
	Verbal	Mark will go to the cinema, but I don't think Kate will Ø.
	Clause	Somebody has stolen my car, but who Ø?
Conjunction	Adversative	I didn't study. <u>However</u>, I still passed.
	Additive	He didn't study. <u>And</u> he failed.
	Temporal	She studied hard. <u>Then</u> she sat the test.
	Causal	They studied hard. <u>Therefore</u>, they deserve to pass.

2) Lexical Cohesion

Categories		Examples
Reiteration	Repetition	She had a <u>flower</u>. The beauty of the <u>flower</u> is overwhelming.
	Synonym	I turned to the <u>ascent</u> of the peak. <u>The climb</u> is easy.
	Superordinate	Tom bought a new <u>Mercedes</u>. A color of that <u>car</u> is black.
	General Item	<u>Rebecca</u> is scared of spiders. You should give support to this <u>girl</u>.
Collocation		<u>Once upon a time</u>, there lived a king named Midas.

F2 Coherence

Coherence is an underlying organizer which makes the words and sentences into a unified discourse that conforms to a consistent world picture. (Halliday 1976) A coherent text is meaningful, unified, and gives the impression of 'hanging together'. But it is perfectly possible to construct a text which, although it is rich in cohesive devices, makes little sense because it is not coherent. The following example is fairly cohesive but it is not terribly coherent:

> This made her afraid. It was open at the letters page. His eyes were shut and she noticed the *Daily Mail* at his side. She knew then that he had read her contribution …

(F2a) Coherence without cohesion

Cohesion is not to be confused with coherence: A text may be ostensibly cohesive but make no sense (lacking coherence), and a text might lack overt cohesive devices yet be perfectly coherent if the ideas or information presented make logical connections with reality. In the following text we have a superficially cohesive text that makes no sense and is therefore not coherent:

> A cat is sitting on a fence. A fence is often made of wood. Carpenters work with wood. Wood planks can be bought from a lumber store.

In this text 'the overt, linguistically signaled relationships between propositions' are made evident, yet the propositions are not logically connected in terms of how we perceive the world. Carrell, on the other hand, provides a good example of short text that seemingly has no overt cohesion yet it makes perfect sense and enables the reader to perceive it as fully coherent:

> The picnic was ruined. No one remembered to bring a corkscrew.

Coherence in this text is created due to the fact that both the writer and the reader share knowledge and schemata that relates corkscrews to wine bottles and wine to picnics. The extratextual knowledge in this case is imperative for the perception of coherence in text. In fact nonnative speakers of English who do not drink wine often find Carrell's short text to be incoherent.

F3 Register

Register refers to a variety of a language used for a particular purpose or in a particular social setting. For example, when speaking in a formal setting contrary to an informal setting, an English speaker may be more likely to use features of prescribed grammar — such as pronouncing words ending in -ing with a velar nasal instead of an alveolar nasal (e.g. 'walking', not 'walkin'), choosing more formal words (e.g. father vs. dad), and refraining from using words considered nonstandard, such as 'ain't'.

As with other types of language variation, there tends to be a spectrum of registers rather than a discrete set of obviously distinct varieties — numerous registers could be identified, with no clear boundaries between them. Discourse categorization is a complex problem, and even in the general definition of 'register' given above (language variation defined by use not user), there are cases where other kinds of language variation, such as regional or age dialect, overlap.

F4 Speech acts

According to an American language philosopher J. R. Searle speaking a language is performing **speech acts**, acts such as making statements, giving commands, asking questions or making promises. J. R. Searle states that all linguistic communication involves linguistic (speech) acts. In other words, speech acts are the basic or minimal units of linguistic communication. They are not mere artificial linguistic constructs as it may seem, but their understanding together with the acquaintance of context in which they are performed is often essential for decoding the whole utterance and its proper meaning.

The locutionary, illocutionary and perlocutionary acts are, in fact, three basic components with the help of which a speech act is formed. Leech (1983) briefly defines them like this:

locutionary act	performing an act **of** saying something	language itself
illocutionary act	performing an act **in** saying something	purpose of the addresser
perlocutionary act	performing an act **by** saying something	effect on the addressee

The locutionary act can be viewed as a mere uttering of some words in certain language, while the illocutionary and perlocutionary acts convey a more complicated message for the hearer. An illocutionary act communicates the speaker's intentions behind the locution and a perlocutionary act reveals the effect the speaker wants to exercise over the hearer. This can be demonstrated on a simple example:

> *Would you close the door, please?*

The surface form, and also the locutionary act, of this utterance is a question with a clear content (Close the door.) The illocutionary act conveys a request from the part of the speaker and the perlocutionary act expresses the speaker's desire that the hearer should go and close the door. Every realization of a speech act has therefore three dimensions: locutionary meaning, illocutionary force, and perlocutionary effect.

G Conversation Analysis

Conversation analysis (**CA**) is a way of looking at the detailed, local aspects of interaction and the way participants in a conversation work hard to make it successful. CA is concerned with **turn-taking**, i.e., how speakers manage to take turns without interrupting one another, how they select who shall speak next, and how they show they are listening (e.g., by using backchannels, small noises and words such as 'uhum', 'yeah', 'right', 'mm'). It is also concerned with adjacency pairs, how two bits of language fit or do not fit appropriately with each other. For example, a greeting normally prompts a greeting in return, congratulations normally prompt thank-yous, etc. When the two pair-parts do not fit (what CA analysts call a **dispreferred sequence**), speakers have to work hard to repair potential problems. For instance, if I invite you to dinner and you have to decline, do you just say "No!" or do you say something like "I'd love to come, but I'm busy Friday. I'm so sorry."? CA is also concerned with openings and closings of conversations and with topic management (i.e., how speakers launch new topics, change the subject, decide what to talk about, etc.)

G1   Components of conversational competence

① Attention getting: Techniques include verbal gambits like "Excuse me," "Say," "By the way," "Got a minute?" and nonverbal signals such as eye contact, gestures, and proxemics. Without knowledge and use of such conventions, L2 learners may be reluctant to participate in a conversation because of their own inhibitions, or they may become obnoxious in securing attention in ways that 'turn off' their hearer.

② Topic nomination (initiating conversation): Once speakers have secured the hearer's attention, their task becomes one of initiating an exchange. If the topic is as simple as the weather, then a speaker may employ such gambits as, "Sure is hot today, isn't it?" Or sports: "How 'bout those Giants?" Or more seriously, "Did you see that program on global warming?"

③ Topic development (and 'holding the floor'): After a topic is nominated, participants in a conversation then use strategies for continuing the conversation, which sometimes involves discourse that holds the floor (as opposed to yielding the floor to another speaker). Techniques include using hesitation signals ("uh," "um," "and, well, like, I mean ...") when otherwise pauses might suffice.

④ Turn-taking: The counterpart of the conversational ability to hold the floor is to yield it to another speaker. Turn-taking is another culturally oriented set of rules that require finely tuned perceptions in order to communicate effectively.

⑤ Topic clarification: A list of components of interactional and conversational competence includes the ability to ask questions for clarification, which may arise from inaudibility ("What did you just say?"), lack of understanding ("What does 'eco-justice' mean?"), or disagreement ("I see your point, but have you considered ...")

⑥ Repair: In the case of conversations between second language learners and native speakers, topic clarification often involves seeking or giving repair of linguistic forms that contain error. These techniques range along a continuum of possibilities from indirect signals to outright correction. It is part of Canale and Swain's (1980) strategic competence.

⑦ Shifting, avoiding, and interrupting: These are among numerous conversational abilities that may be effected through both verbal and nonverbal signals. Changing a topic ("Well, speaking of music ..."), dancing around certain topics, and interrupting politely are especially difficult for an L2 learner to acquire, the rules for which vary widely across cultures and languages. Moreover, as Silberstein (2011) noted, L2 learners may be reluctant to display their confusion or misunderstanding in a conversation, relying instead on feigning comprehension.

⑧ Topic termination: The art of closing a conversation with a glance at a watch, a polite smile, or a "Well, I have to be going now," is not an easy one for an L2 learners to master.

G2 Adjacency Pairs

An adjacency pair is an example of conversational turn-taking. An **adjacency pair** is composed of two utterances by two speakers, one after the other. The speaking of the first utterance (the first-pair part, or the first turn) provokes a responding utterance (the second-pair part, or the second turn). Many actions in conversation are accomplished through established adjacency pairs, examples of which include:

① **greeting - greeting**
   "Heya!" - "Oh, hi!"

② **offer - acceptance/rejection**
   "Would you like to visit the museum with me this evening?" - "I'd love to!"

③ **request - acceptance/rejection**
   "Is it OK if I borrow this book?"
   "I'd rather you didn't, it's due back at the library tomorrow."

④ **question - answer**

"What does this big red button do?"

"It causes two-thirds of the universe to implode."

⑤ **complaint - excuse/remedy**

"It's awfully cold in here." "Oh, sorry, I'll close the window."

⑥ **degreeting - degreeting**

"See you!" - "Yeah, see you later!"

Some adjacency pairs will be easy to learn (e.g., the ritualized ones like greeting-greeting, offer-accept), but **dispreferred sequences** will require skill and practice.

G3   IRE vs. IRF exchange (Exchange Structure)

According to Lightbown and Spada (2006), the most common discourse sequence in the classroom is **initiation-response-evaluation** (**IRE**), a teacher-led discourse sequence. This consists of a three-part exchange:

1. The teacher asks a student a display question (one to which there is one correct answer) to find out whether the student can respond.

2. A student responds (with correct or incorrect information).

3. The student answer is evaluated by the teacher, who makes a brief reply such as "Good," or "No, that's not right."

T: Sentence number 5. Is it raining outside? Juan?	Initiation
S: Yes, it is.	Response
T: Right. Next, number 6. Are you tired? Ali?	Evaluation / Re-invitation

The interaction typically ends with Step 3. According to Hall and Walsh (2002), in this pattern the teacher assumes the role of expert, eliciting information from students and evaluating their responses as either right or wrong.

Closely related to IRE, but allowing for slightly more communicative classroom exchanges, is the **initiation-response-feedback** (**IRF**) sequence. This discourse sequence consists of this three-part exchange:

1. The teacher (or student) initiates the interaction by asking a referential question (one to which there are multiple possible answers) or introducing a topic.

2. A response is given.

3. The initiator uses the response to move the conversation forward.

T: How many brothers and sisters do you have? Juan?	Initiation
S: Seven.	Response
T: Wow, that's a big family.	Feedback
Who else has a big family?	Re-invitation

The interaction can continue for multiple turns and may include contributions from multiple class members.

The IRF sequence, though at first glance closely resembling the IRE sequence, represents an important reconceptualization of the teacher-student interaction pattern, allowing for more naturalistic interaction between teacher and student, a loosening of teacher control, and the chaining of student responses and contributions. As Hall and Walsh (2002) note, instead of closing down the interaction in the third move by providing an evaluation, the teacher's substitution of the feedback move invites students to expand on their response, justify or clarify their opinion, or share their personal experience.

Both IRE and IRF sequences are typical of teacher-student exchanges in the L2 classroom (both are sometimes conflated and considered one and the same). However, IRF/IRE sequence is not without its criticism. It is thought to limit meaningful student participation because teachers have the rights to initiate speech, to distribute turns and evaluate students' utterances, whereas students have much more restricted participation rights, opportunities to ask questions and negotiate meaning. But most studies in general claim that IRF/IRE sequences need not to have a restrictive function and can be used to create communicative, more life-like, teacher-student interaction.

More recently proposed alternatives to the IRE and IRF sequences are the 'instructional conversation' (Hall 2001) and the 'collaborative dialogue' (Richard & Farrell 2011), both of which entail scaffolded (or assisted) learning. In this process, the teacher or other more advanced peers provide supports, or scaffolds, to assist learners in acquiring and producing new aspects of the language, often modeling for them the desired outcome. The teacher also builds in opportunities for the learners to notice new language features and encourages them to practice using these features.

G4 Classroom interaction

(G4a) Referential vs. Display questions

Referential questions	not knowing the answer in advance (= Genuine Q / Information Q)
Display questions	knowing the answer in advance

There are many ways to classify what kinds of questions are effective in the classroom. Perhaps the simplest way to conceptualize the possibilities is to think of a range of questions, beginning with **display questions** that attempt to elicit information already known by the teacher, all the way to highly **referential questions** that request information not known by the teacher.

Working within sociocultural theory, the researchers chose the concept of scaffolding to investigate teacher questions. In the example below, they argue that the teacher's use of display question 'Who usually lives in palaces?' serves an important pedagogic function because it draws the learners' attention to the word 'palace' through the display question and facilitates the learners' comprehension of the word.

T: Palace?
S1: Like castle?
S2: Special place, very good.
S3: Very nice.
T: Castle, special place, very nice. Who usually lives in palaces?
Ss: Kings.
T: Kings, and queens, princes and princesses.
Ss: Yeah.
S4: Maybe beautiful house?
T: Big, beautiful house, yeah, really big.

(G4b) Open vs. Closed questions

Open questions	→ longer and more complex answers w/ explanation & reasoning
Closed questions	→ simple one-word responses, quick and easy to respond

Another distinction similar to the one between display and genuine questions is that between open and closed questions. **Closed questions** typically have only one possible answer and they usually lead to simple one-word responses, making them quick and easy to respond to. **Open questions** have more than one possible answer and invite elaboration, typically leading to longer and more complex answers, including, for example, explanation and reasoning.

G5 Foreigner Talk

What is the nature of the input to a language learner? Ferguson (1971), in a study designed to look at issues of linguistic simplicity, noted that in language directed toward linguistically deficient individuals (young children, NNSs of a language), NSs make adjustments to their speech in the areas of pronunciation, grammar, and lexicon. Speech directed toward young children he called ***baby talk*** (now known variably as ***motherese***, ***caretaker speech***, or ***child-directed speech***); speech directed toward linguistically deficient NNSs he called **foreigner talk**. His goal was to explore the similarities between these two speech varieties.

Table 1 presents examples from English, and Table 2, adapted from Hatch (1983), presents a partial listing of characteristics of foreigner talk speech. In general, foreigner talk adjustments reveal speech patterns that would not ordinarily be used in conversations with NSs. Foreigner talk shares features in common with caretaker speech, the language spoken to young children. Some of the most salient features of foreigner talk include: slow speech rate, loud speech, long pauses, simple vocabulary (e.g., few idioms, high frequency words), repetitions and elaborations, and paucity of slang.

Table 1. Examples of foreigner talk

NS speech	*Foreigner talk*
D'yu wanna go?	Do you want to go?
No, I can't.	No, I cannot.

Table 2. Summary of foreigner talk features

SLOW RATE = clearer articulation

    Final stops are released

    Fewer reduced vowels

    Fewer contractions

    Longer pauses

VOCABULARY

    High frequency vocabulary

        Less slang

        Fewer idioms

    Fewer pronoun forms

    Definitions

        Overtly marked (e.g., *This means X*)

        Semantic feature information (e.g., *a cathedral usually means a church, that's a very high ceiling*)

    Contextual information (e.g., *if you go for a job in a factory, they talk about a wage scale*)

    Gestures and pictures

SYNTAX

    Short and simple sentences

    Movement of topics to front of sentence

    Repetition and restatement

    New information at the end of the sentence

    NS grammatically repeats/modifies learners' incorrect utterances

    NS fills in the blank for learners' incomplete utterances

DISCOURSE

    NS gives reply within a question

    NS uses tag questions

    NS offers correction

Characteristics of foreigner talk are not always so obvious. Consider (1) and (2), which come from a survey on food and nutrition that NNSs conducted over the telephone (Gass and Varonis 1985):

(1)
NNS: How have increasing food costs changed your eating habits?
NS: Well, we don't eat as much beef as we used to. We eat more chicken, and uh, pork, and uh, fish, things like that.
NNS: Pardon me?
NS: We don't eat as much beef as we used to. We eat more chicken and uh, uh pork and fish ... We don't eat beef very often. We don't have steak like we used to.

(2)
NNS: There has been a lot of talk lately about additives and preservatives in food. In what ways has this changed your eating habits?
NS: I try to stay away from nitrites.
NNS: Pardon me?
NS: Uh, from nitrites in uh like lunch meats and that sort of thing. I don't eat those.

In these two examples, there was little indication of modified speech in the initial responses to the NNSs' questions. This is perhaps because the questions were scripted and rehearsed, and despite the obvious nonnativeness of the caller (Spanish in the first example and Arabic in the second), there was an appearance of fluency. However, once the NNS said *Pardon me?*, the NS in all likelihood realized the difficulty involved in the conversation and made modifications. In this case, the modification was not syntactic or phonological, as one typically expects with foreigner talk. Rather, the NS restated, repeated, and elaborated on the responses, the implication being that, given more information, the NNS would have an easier time understanding.

There are still other ways of modifying speech. From the same database come the following two examples:

(3)

NNS: How have increasing food costs changed your eating habits?

NS: Well, I don't know that it's changed THEM. I try to adjust.

NNS: Pardon me?

NS: I don't think it's changed MY EATING HABITS.

(4)

NNS: How have increasing food costs changed your eating habits?

NS: Oh, rising costs we've cut back on the more expensive things. GONE to cheaper foods.

NNS: Pardon me?

NS: WE'VE GONE to cheaper foods.

In (3), the NS specified the noun object more fully once the NNS indicated a lack of understanding. In (4), implicit grammatical information is made more explicit by adding the subject and the auxiliary verb.

What are the functions of foreigner talk in terms of language learning? Generally, one can claim that by hearing speech that has been simplified in the ways just described the second language learner will be better able to understand. It is a given that, without understanding the language, no learning can take place. Although understanding alone does not guarantee that learning will occur, it does set the scene for learning to take place. However, not all types of foreigner talk are created equal. Parker and Chaudron (1987) showed that simplifications resulting from discourse elaboration or modification of the conversational structure are more likely to aid comprehension than those simplifications which result from simplification at the linguistic level (i.e., foreigner talk).

H Types of Nonverbal Communication

Just as verbal language is broken up into various categories, there are also different types of nonverbal communication. As we learn about each type of nonverbal signal, keep in mind that nonverbals often work in concert with each other, combining to repeat, modify, or contradict the verbal message being sent.

Kinesics

Kinesics refers to body movements and posture and includes the following components:

① **Gestures** are arm and hand movements and include adaptors like clicking a pen or scratching your face, emblems like a thumbs-up to say "OK", and illustrators like bouncing your hand along with the rhythm of your speaking.

② **Head movements and posture** include the orientation of movements of our head and the orientation and positioning of our body and the various meanings they send. Head movements such as nodding can indicate agreement, disagreement, and interest, among other things. Posture can indicate assertiveness, defensiveness, interest, readiness, or intimidation, among other things.

③ **Eye contact** is studied under the category of **oculesics** and specifically refers to eye contact with another person's face, head, and eyes and the patterns of looking away and back at the other person during interaction. Eye contact provides turn-taking signals, signals when we are engaged in cognitive activity, and helps establish rapport and connection, among other things.

④ **Facial expressions** refer to the use of the forehead, brow, and facial muscles around the nose and mouth to convey meaning. Facial expressions can convey happiness, sadness, fear, anger, and other emotions.

Kinesthetics

Kinesthetics (also called **haptics**) refers to touch behaviors that convey meaning during interactions. Touch operates at many levels, including functional-professional, social-polite, friendship-warmth, and love-intimacy.

Vocalics

Vocalics refers to the vocalized but not verbal aspects of nonverbal communication, including our speaking rate, pitch, volume, tone of voice, and vocal quality. These qualities, also known as paralanguage, reinforce the meaning of verbal communication, allow us to emphasize particular parts of a message, or can contradict verbal messages.

Proxemics

Proxemics refers to the use of space and distance within communication. US Americans, in general, have four zones that constitute the personal space: the public zone (12 or more feet from our body), the social zone (4–12 feet from our body), the personal zone (1.5–4 feet from our body), and the intimate zone (from body contact to 1.5 feet away). Proxemics also studies territoriality, or how people take up and defend personal space.

Chronemics

Chronemics refers to the study of how time affects communication and includes how different time cycles affect our communication, including the differences between people who are past- or future-oriented and cultural perspectives on time as fixed and measured (monochronic) or fluid and adaptable (polychronic).

Personal presentation and environment

Personal presentation and environment refers to how the objects we adorn ourselves and our surroundings with, referred to as artifacts, provide nonverbal cues that others make meaning from and how our physical environment — for example, the layout of a room and seating positions and arrangements — influences communication.

Chapter 04 MindMap

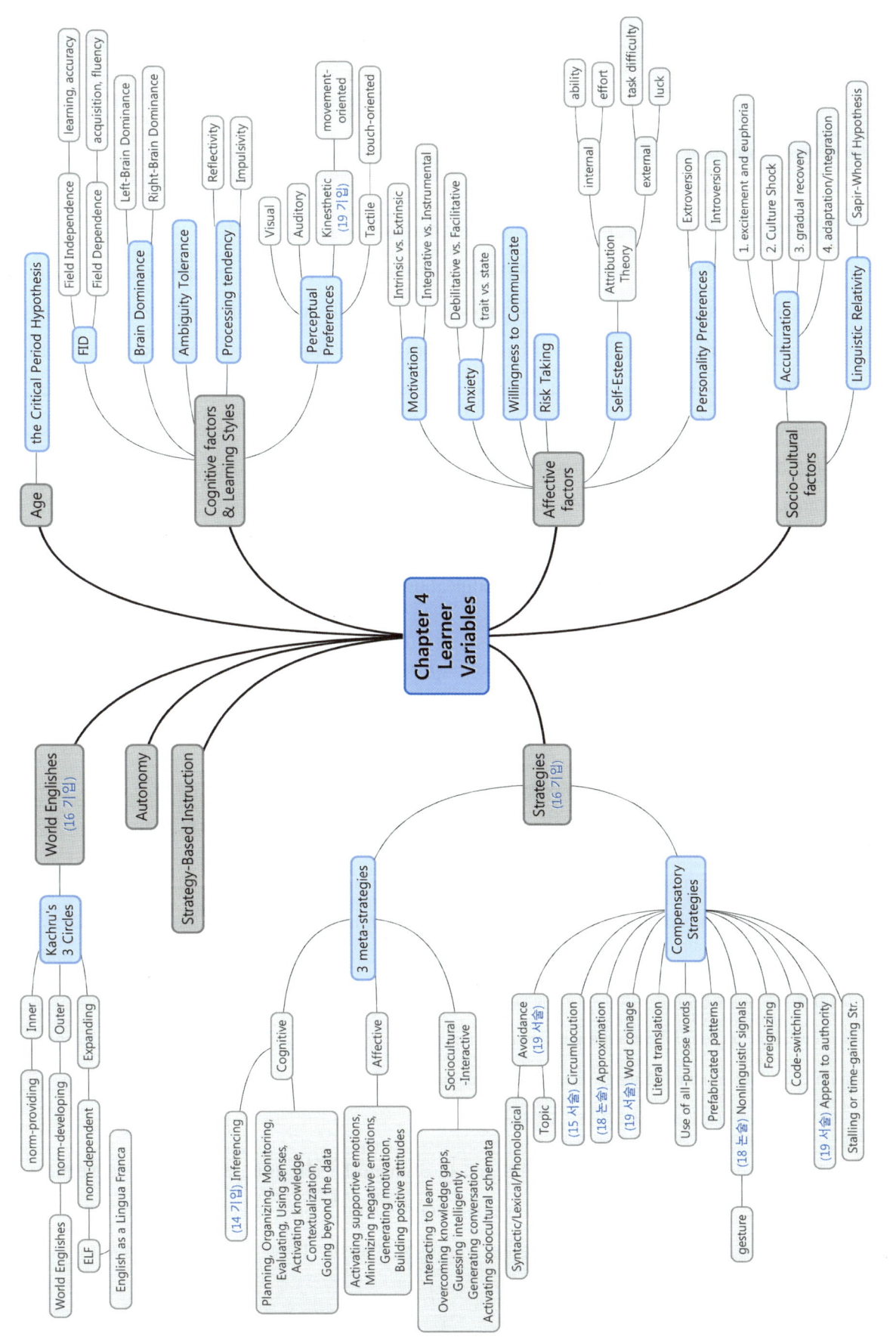

Chapter 04 Learner Variables

A. Age & the Critical Period Hypothesis

The **Critical Period** Hypothesis (CPH) means that animals, including humans, are genetically programmed to acquire certain kind of knowledge and skill at specific times in life. Beyond those 'critical periods', it is either difficult or impossible to acquire those abilities. With regard to language, the CPH suggests that children who are not given access to language in infancy and early childhood (because of deafness or extreme isolation) will never acquire language if these deprivations go on for too long. However, there certainly appear to be some potential advantages to an early age for SLA, but there is absolutely no evidence that an adult cannot overcome all of those disadvantages save one, accent, and the latter is hardly the quintessential criterion for effective interpersonal communication.

B. Cognitive factors & Learning Styles

B1. Field Independence vs. Field Dependence

Field Independence	step by step & with sequential instruction, more accurate learners
Field Dependence	when information is presented in context, more fluent learners

Field refers to a set of thoughts, ideas, or feelings from which your task is to perceive specific relevant subsets. There are two learning styles related to the field. **Field independence** is the tendency to learn most effectively step by step and with sequential instruction. Field independent learners are often more accurate language learners. **Field dependence** is, conversely, the tendency to learn best when information is presented in context. Field dependent learners are often more fluent language learners. Field dependence is synonymous with **field sensitivity**, a term that carries a more positive connotation.

A field independent (FI) style enables you to distinguish parts from a whole, to concentrate on something (like reading a book in a noisy train station), or to analyze separate variables without the contamination of neighboring variables. On the other hand, *too much* FI may result in cognitive 'tunnel vision': you see only the parts and not their relationship to the whole. Seen in this light, development of a field dependent (FD) style has positive effects: you perceive the whole picture, the larger view, the general configuration of a problem or idea or event. It is clear, then, that both FI *and* FD are necessary for most of the cognitive and affective problems we face.

Early research on FI/FS (Witkin & Goodenough 1981, Witkin 1962) found some interesting relationships. Affectively, persons who are more predominantly FI tend to be generally more independent, competitive, and self-confident. FS persons tend to be more socialized, to derive their self-identity from persons around them, and are usually more empathic and perceptive of the feelings and thoughts of others.

How does all this relate to second language learning? Two conflicting hypotheses have emerged. First, some studies concluded that FI closely related to classroom learning that involves analysis, attention to details, and mastering of exercises, drills, and other focused activities (Johnson, Prior, & Artuso 2000). The second hypothesis proposed that an FS style, by virtue of its association with empathy, social outreach, and perception of other people, yield successful acquisition of the *communicative* aspects of a second language.

Could FI and FS both be equally important? The two styles deal with two different kinds of language learning. One kind of learning implies natural, face-to-face communication, the kind of communication that occurs too rarely in the average language classroom. The second kind involves familiar classroom activities: drills, exercises, and tests. It is most likely that 'natural' language learning in the 'field', beyond the constraints of the classroom, is aided by an FS style, and the classroom learning is enhanced, conversely, by an FI style. Obviously, both styles are facilitative within appropriate contexts.

B2   Left-Brain Dominance vs. Right-Brain Dominance

Left- and **right-brain dominance** is a potentially significant issue in developing a theory of second language acquisition. As the child's brain matures, various functions become lateralized to the left or right hemisphere. The left hemisphere is associated with logical, analytical thought, with mathematical and linear processing of information. The right hemisphere perceives and remembers visual, tactile, and auditory images; it is more efficient in processing holistic, integrative, and emotional information. A compilation of a variety of characteristics of left-brain

(LB) and right-brain (RB) characteristics is listed in the table below.

Left-Brain Dominance	Right-Brain Dominance
Relies strongly on the intellect	Uses intuitive processes
Remembers names	Remembers faces
Responds to verbal instructions and explanations	Responds to demonstrated, illustrated, or symbolic instructions
Experiments systematically and with control	Experiments randomly and with less restraint
Makes objective judgments	Makes subjective judgments
Is planned and structured	Is fluid and spontaneous
Prefers established, certain information	Is comfortable with elusive, uncertain information
Reads analytically	Reads with synthesis
Relies on language in thinking and remembering	Relies on images in thinking and remembering
Is stronger in talking and writing, and verbal communication	Is stronger in drawing images and manipulating objects
Prefers multiple-choice tests	Prefers open-ended questions
Controls feelings	Is more free with feelings
Is not good at interpreting body language	Is good at interpreting body language
Uses empirical description	Uses metaphors and verbal imagery
Favors logical problem solving	Favors intuitive problem solving

The LB/RB construct helps to define another useful learning style continuum, with implications for L2 learning and teaching. Krashen, Seliger, and Hartnett (1974) found that LB dominant L2 learners preferred a deductive approach to teaching, while RB dominant learners were more successful in inductive techniques. Stevick (1982) concluded that LB dominant L2 learners are better at producing separate words, gathering the specifics of language, carrying out sequences of operations, and dealing with classification, labeling, and reorganization. RB dominant learners, on the other hand, appear to deal better with whole images, generalizations, metaphors, and emotional reactions, and artistic expressions.

B3 Ambiguity Tolerance

Ambiguity tolerance	cognitively willing to tolerate ideas and propositions that run counter to one's own belief system or structure of knowledge

Ambiguity tolerance refers to the degree to which one is cognitively willing to tolerate ideas and propositions that run counter to one's own belief system or structure of knowledge.

Some — those that are **ambiguity tolerant** (AT) — are relatively open-minded in at least entertaining ideologies, events, and fact that contradict their own views. Others — those that are **ambiguity intolerant** (AI) — are more closed-minded and dogmatic and tend to reject items that are contradictory or incongruent with their existing system; they wish to see every proposition fit into an acceptable place in their cognitive organization, and if they do not, they are rejected.

Advantages and disadvantages are present in each end of a continuum. The person who is AT is free to entertain a number of innovative and creative possibilities and not be cognitively or affectively disturbed by uncertainty. In second language learning a great amount of apparently contradictory information is encountered; words that differ from the native language, rules that not only differ but that are internally inconsistent because of certain exceptions, and sometimes a whole cultural system that is distant from that of the native culture. Successful language learning necessitates tolerance of such ambiguities, at least for interim periods or stages, during which time ambiguous items are given a chance to become resolved.

On the other hand, *too much* AT can have a detrimental effect. People can become 'wish-washy', adopting an 'anything goes' mentality, accepting virtually every proposition before them, and inefficiently subsuming necessary facts into their cognitive organizational structure. Grammatical rules and word definitions, for example, eventually need to be discarded — pruned — in favor of more-encompassing linguistic conceptualizations.

AI also has its advantages and disadvantages. An optimal level of intolerance enables one to guard against the wish-washiness referred to above, by closing off avenues of hopeless possibilities, rejecting contradictory material, and dealing with the reality of the system that one has built. On the other hand, AI can close the mind too soon, especially if ambiguity is perceived as a threat, and the result is a rigid, dogmatic, brittle mind that is too narrow to be creative. This may be particularly harmful in second language learning.

B4　Reflectivity vs. Impulsivity

Reflectivity	making a slow, more calculated decision to a problem
Impulsivity	making a quick or gambling guess to a problem

It is common for us to show in our personalities certain tendencies toward reflectivity sometimes and impulsivity at other times. **Reflectivity** is an approach in which a person tends to make a slow, more calculated decision to a problem, while **impulsivity** is an approach in which a person tends to make a quick or gambling guess at an answer to a problem.

B5 Perceptual Preferences (Sensory Preferences)

Visual	preferring reading & studying charts, drawings, and other graphic information
Auditory	preferring listening to lectures and audiotapes
Kinesthetic	movement-oriented, preferring demonstrations & physical activities
Tactile	touch-oriented

Sensory preferences can be broken down into four main areas: visual, auditory, kinesthetic (movement-oriented), and tactile (touch-oriented). Sensory preferences refer to the physical, perceptual learning channels with which the student is the most comfortable. **Visual** students like to read and obtain a great deal from visual stimulation. For them, lectures, conversations, and oral instructions without any visual backup can be very confusing. In contrast, **auditory** students are comfortable without visual input and therefore enjoy and profit from unembellished lectures, conversations, and oral instructions. They are excited by classroom interactions in role plays and similar activities. They sometimes, however, have difficulty with written work. **Kinesthetic** and **tactile** students like lots of movement and enjoy working with tangible objects, collages, and flashcards. Sitting at a desk for very long is not for them; they prefer to have frequent breaks and move around the room.

Most successful learners use a variety of modalities in learning, as would be expected. In this way they can accommodate to the various modes in which incoming information is processed.

C Affective factors

C1 Motivation

Intrinsic motivation	motivated by the activity itself
Extrinsic motivation	motivated by a reward from outside and beyond the self
Instrumental motivation	for practical goals
Integrative motivation	for social interchange

Motivation is undoubtedly the most frequently used catch-all term for explaining the success or failure of virtually any complex task. One of the earliest traditions of research on motivation is on the distinction between intrinsic motivation and extrinsic motivation. Edward Deci (1975) defined **intrinsic motivation** as expending effort "for which there is no apparent reward except the activity itself and not because it leads to an extrinsic reward." Intrinsically motivated behaviors are driven by internally rewarding consequences, namely, feelings of competence and self-determination, and are willingly engaged in through one's own volition. In contrast, **extrinsic motivation** is fueled by the anticipation of a reward from outside and beyond the self. Typical extrinsic rewards are money, prizes, grades, and even certain types of positive feedback. Behaviors initiated solely to avoid punishment are also extrinsically motivated. Which form of motivation is more powerful in SLA context? A stockpile of research strongly favors intrinsic orientations, especially for long-term retention.

Gardner and Lambert (1972) studied motivation in terms of a number of different kinds of attitudes. Two different clusters of attitudes were identified as instrumental and integrative orientations. An **instrumental** orientation referred to acquiring a language as a means for attaining practical goals such as furthering a career, reading technical material, or translation. An **integrative** orientation described learners who wished to integrate themselves into the culture of the second language group and become involved in social interchange in that group. Gardner and MacIntyre (1991) and Dörnyei (2001) later argued that instrumentality and integrativeness are not actually types of motivation, but rather, more appropriately forms of orientation. That is, depending on whether a learner's main focus or purpose is (1) academic or career related (instrumental), or (2) socially or culturally oriented (integrative), different needs might be fulfilled in learning an L2.

C2 Anxiety

helpful	Facilitative anxiety	Debilitative anxiety	harmful

Anxiety is associated with feelings of uneasiness, frustration, self-doubt, apprehension, or worry. The research on anxiety suggests that anxiety can be experienced at various levels. At the deepest, or global, level, trait anxiety is a more permanent predisposition to be anxious. At a more momentary, or situational, level, state anxiety is experienced in relation to some particular event or act. Yet another important insight to be applied to anxiety lies in the distinction between **debilitative** and **facilitative anxiety**, or what Oxford (1999) called 'harmful' and 'helpful' anxiety.

Several studies have suggested the benefit of facilitative anxiety in second language acquisition. So when your language students are anxious, you would do well to ask yourself if that anxiety is truly debilitative. It could well be that a little nervous tension in the process is a good thing. We find that a construct has an optimal point along its continuum: both too much and too little anxiety may hinder the process of successful second language learning.

C3 Willingness to Communicate

Willingness to communicate	the intention to initiate communication

Peter MacIntyre (2001) defined **Willingness to communicate** (WTC) as 'the intention to initiate communication, given a choice'. In an earlier study on WTC, MacIntyre et al. (1998) found that a number of factors appear to contribute to predisposing one learner to seek, and another learner to avoid, second language communication. Noting that a high level of communicative ability does not necessarily correspond with a high WTC, the researchers proposed a number of cognitive and affective factors that underlie WTC: motivation, personality, self-confidence, and intergroup climate. The latter, intergroup climate, was confirmed in Fushino's (2010) study of the relationship between beliefs about group work and WTC. Other studies of WTC generally confirm its relationship to self-efficacy and self-confidence (Yashima et al. 2004). And finally, MacIntyre and Legatto (2011) found WTC to be a 'dynamic system', one that varies considerably over time.

C4 Risk Taking

Risk taking	being able to gamble a bit and trying out hunches

Risk taking is important in second language acquisition, and learners have to be able to gamble a bit, to be willing to try out hunches about the language and take the risk of being wrong. Should L2 learners become *high* risk-taker? Not necessarily, as Beebe (1983) found, successful L2 learners are usually *moderate* risk-takers. The implications for teaching are important. In a few uncommon cases, overly high risk takers, as they dominate the classroom with wild gambles, may need to be 'tamed' a bit by the teacher. But most of the time our challenge as teachers will be to encourage students to guess somewhat more willingly than the usual student is prone to do, and to reward them for those risks.

C5 Self-Esteem / Attribution Theory & Self-Efficacy

Attribution theory	attributing to effort, not ability / task difficulty / luck

Self-esteem, self-confidence, knowledge of yourself, and **self-efficacy** is belief in your own capabilities to successfully perform that activity. Underlying the issues and questions about the role of self-esteem in language learning are the foundational concepts of attribution and self-efficacy. Based on the seminal work of psychologist Weiner (2000), **attribution theory** focuses on how people explain the causes of their own successes and failure. Weiner and others describes attribution theory in terms of four explanations for success and/or failure in achieving a personal objective: ability, effort, perceived difficulty of a task, and luck. Two of those four factors are internal to the learner: ability and effort; and two are attributable to external circumstances outside of the learner: task difficulty and luck.

According to Weiner, learners tend to ***attribute*** their success on a task using these four dimensions. Depending on the individual, a number of causal determinants might be cited. Thus, failure to get a high grade on a final exam in a language class might, for some, be judged to be due to their poor ability or effort, and by others to difficulty of exam, and perhaps others to just plain old bad luck!

This is where self-efficacy comes in. If a learner feels capable of carrying out a given task, in other words, a high sense of self-efficacy, an appropriate degree of effort is likely to be devoted to achieving success. Falling short of one's personal goals may then be attributable to not enough effort expended, but rarely, in the case of students with high self-efficacy, would an 'excuse' be made attributing the bad performance to something like bad luck. Conversely, a learner with low self-efficacy may quite easily attribute failure to external factors, a relatively unhealthy psychological attitude to bring to any task, one that creates a self-fulfilling sense of failure at the outset.

C6 Personality preferences

from other people	Extroversion	Introversion	within oneself

Extroversion is the extent to which a person has a deep-seated need to receive ego enhancement, self-esteem, and a sense of wholeness ***from other people*** as opposed to receiving that affirmation within oneself. **Introversion**, on the other hand, is the extent to which a person derives a sense of wholeness and fulfillment within oneself. Contrary to prevailing stereotypes, introverts can have an inner strength of character, be more attentive to thoughts and concepts, and be energized by concentration on the inner world. Introverts can be pleasantly conversational, but simply require more reflection, and possibly exercise more restraint in social situation. It is not clear that E/I helps or hinders the process of second language acquisition.

D Socio-cultural factors

D1 Acculturation and Culture Shock

L2 learning almost always involves the phenomenon of developing an identity. This creation of a new identity is at the heart of culture learning, or what has commonly been called **acculturation**. For an L2 learner, understanding a new culture can clash with a person's worldview, self-identity and systems of thinking, acting, feeling, and communication. When that disruption is severe, a learner may experience **culture shock**, a phenomenon ranging from mild irritability to deep psychological panic and crisis. It is common to describe culture shock as the second of four successive stages of culture acquisition:

① an initial period of excitement and euphoria

② culture stress or culture shock, erosion of self-esteem and security

③ gradual recovery, adjustment to new ways of thinking, feeling, and acting

④ a final stage of adaptation/integration, acceptance of a new identity

D2 Linguistic Relativity (Sapir-Whorf Hypothesis)

The principle of **linguistic relativity** holds that the structure of a language affects the ways in which its respective speakers conceptualize their world, i.e. their world view, or otherwise influences their cognitive processes. Popularly known as the Sapir-Whorf hypothesis, or Whorfianism, the principle is often defined to include two versions. The strong version says that language 'determines' thought, and that linguistic categories limit and determine cognitive categories, whereas the weak version says only that linguistic categories and usage 'influence' thought and certain kinds of non-linguistic behavior.

However, the usage of these terms has been criticized as a misnomer, since Sapir and Whorf did not in fact formulate a hypothesis for empirical research, and because it is unclear to what extent Sapir actually subscribed to the idea of language influencing thought. Currently, researchers prefer to use Whorf's own terminology, by referring to the principle of linguistic relativity.

The language teaching profession today has actually subscribed to a more moderate view of the Sapir-Whorf Hypothesis, only because of the mounting evidence of the interaction of language and culture. So, while some aspects of language seem to provide us with potential cognitive mind-sets, we can also recognize that through both language and culture, some universal properties bind us all together in one world. The act of learning to think in another language may require a considerable degree of mastery of that language, but a second language learner does not have to learn to think, in general, all over again. As in every other human learning experience, the second language learner can make positive use of prior experiences to facilitate the process of learning by retaining that which is valid and valuable for second culture learning and second language learning.

E Techniques in Teaching Culture

Hughes (1986) provided some techniques for teaching cultural awareness.

E1 Audiomotor unit or Total Physical Response

Primarily developed as a listening exercise, **Audiomotor unit** or Total Physical Response utilizes a carefully constructed list of oral commands to which the students respond. The commands are arranged in an order which will cause students to act out a cultural experience.

E2 Culture assimilator

Developed by social psychologists to facilitate adjustment to a foreign culture, the **culture assimilator** is a short description of a critical incident of cross-cultural interaction that could possibly be misunderstood by the students. The students are then presented with four possible explanations from which they are asked to choose the correct one. If the wrong choice is chosen, they are asked to seek further information that would lead them to the right conclusion.

E3 Culture capsule

The **culture capsule** is somewhat similar to culture assimilator, but cannot be assigned as a silent reading exercise. The teacher gives a brief presentation that shows one essential difference between a learner and a foreign custom, which is accompanied by visuals illustrating the difference, and a set of questions to stimulate class discussion.

E4 Cultural drama

The **cultural drama** is a technique especially useful for directly involving students in cross-cultural misunderstandings by having selected members act out a series of short scenes including a misinterpretation of something that happens in the target culture, and the cause of the problem is typically clarified in the final scene.

E5 Culture Island

In the classroom using the technique named the **culture island**, the teacher maintains a classroom atmosphere that is essentially a culture island through the use of posters, pictures, a frequently changing bulletin board to attract students' attention, elicit questions, and comment.

F World Englishes

The notions of World English and World Englishes are far from similar, although the terms are often mistakenly used interchangeably. **World English** refers to the **English language as a Lingua Franca** (a language in common, **ELF**) used in business, trade, diplomacy and other spheres of global activity, while **World Englishes** refers to the different varieties of English and English-based creoles developed in different regions of the world. Ferguson (1971) claimed that English has become a language of wider communication, or (in more recent terminology) what McKay (2012) calls English as an **international language** (**EIL**).

F1   Kachru's Three Circles of English

Inner Circle	UK, USA, Australia, New Zealand, Ireland, etc.	'norm-providing'
Outer Circle	(World Englishes) India, Nigeria, Pakistan, etc.	'norm-developing'
Expanding Circle	(ELF) Korea, China, Japan, Russia, Egypt, etc.	'norm-dependent'

The most influential early argument in favor of recognizing the existence of regional standards where English is used as an intranational and international language, rather than as a native language, comes from B. B. Kachru (1985). His well-known representation of three concentric circles of English makes the following distinctions:

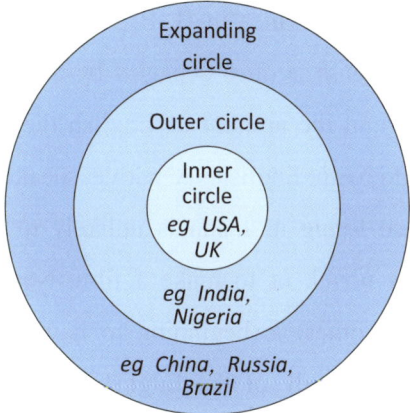

- the **inner circle** (the smallest circle at the center): the countries and regions where English is the native language of the majority

- the **outer circle** (the middle circle surrounding the inner circle): countries where English has had a long history of use and where local L2 varieties have developed and become codified through extensive use

- the **expanding circle** (the outermost circle): countries where English is a dominant foreign language used in limited domains but is beginning to become or has become a lingua franca

B. B. Kachru's major concern (and that of many of his colleagues) has been the varieties of English that have developed in outer circle countries — the various World Englishes. These are relatively stable varieties of English that can and have been described in terms of their grammar, lexicon, and phonology. The users of these varieties range in proficiency from expert to novice, generally depending on the user's level of education. The expert users have taken full possession of their variety of English and use it alongside their native language for many purposes, such as a medium of instruction in schools, a language of commerce, and a language for media (newspapers, television, movies, and Internet). The expert users not only write school assignments, reports, business letters, or news articles in their variety of English, they also use it to write literature (novels, plays, and poems). They have acquired full control of their variety of English and use it freely for communication and self-expression in most of the same ways that native speakers do. This is why B. B. Kachru and his colleagues have argued that these well-established World Englishes are fully legitimate varieties that deserve to be recognized alongside the native varieties of English.

When English is used as a lingua franca in B. B. Kachru's expanding circle, the situation is somewhat different. Although English is often deployed by these users for a variety of purposes, their range of uses for English and the amount of English they use does not match what the inner- and outer-circle users do with English. A native speaker of French living in France or a native speaker of Japanese living in Japan is unlikely to use English to converse with a colleague at work, to write a novel, or to make a film. Nevertheless, that they may often use ELF (e.g., to write to each other) is beginning to have an impact on the English that they do speak and write, and the study of the English used in ELF contexts has begun to be seriously studied.

Kachru classified the norms associated with the three circles in the following way. He considers inner circle varieties as 'norm providing', outer circle varieties as 'norm developing' and expanding circle varieties as 'norm dependent'. According to this classification, the inner circle varieties provide norms to the expanding circle varieties, whereas the outer circle varieties develop their own local norms. In other words, in expanding circle varieties, norms are external or 'exocentric' (being drawn from American or British English), whereas in outer circle varieties, norms are internal or 'endocentric'.

G Autonomy

Holec (1981) defined **autonomy** as 'the ability to take charge of one's own learning'. Until some of the 'designer' methods appeared in the 1970s, most of language teaching methodology was teacher centered. Students entered a classroom, sat down dutifully in their desks, and waited for the teacher to tell them what to do. Those directives might have been to translate a passage, to memorize a rule, or to repeat a dialogue. Then, the profession seemed to discover the value of learner autonomy in the form of allowing learners to do things like initiate oral production, solve problems in small groups, practice language forms in pairs, and practice using the language outside of the classroom.

The process of developing within learners a sense of autonomy required the use of strategies. The literature on the topic raises some caution flags. Schmenk (2005) appropriately described the nonuniversality of the concept of autonomy, and Pennycook (1997) warned us about the potential cultural imperialism involved in assuming that every culture equally values and promotes autonomy, especially in educational institutions. For language teaching in sub-Saharan Africa, Sonaiya (2002) questioned the global validity of the so-called autonomous method of language learning which has obvious origins in European and North American traditions of individualism. However, other studies are more encouraging. Schmenk recommended a 'glocalization' (a combination of both global and local considerations) of the concept of autonomy in non-Western cultures, one that involves 'a critical awareness of specific cultural backdrops and impacts'.

H Strategies

Cognitive strategies	constructing, transforming, and applying L2 knowledge
Affective strategies	employing beneficial emotional energy, forming positive attitudes, and generating and maintaining motivation
Sociocultural-Interactive strategies	generating and maintaining interactive communication within a cultural context
Compensatory strategies	making up for gaps in one's ability

Strategies are those specific actions that we take to solve a given problem, and that vary considerably *within* each individual. Oxford employed three broad categories (or **meta-strategies** — for general management and control) within which to consider strategic self-regulation

(S^2R): cognitive, affective, and sociocultural-interactive strategies.

Cognitive strategies

Cognitive strategies help the learner 'construct, transform, and apply L2 knowledge'. Included in this category are a number of subcategories, each of which includes specific **tactics**: 'specific manifestations of a strategy or meta-strategy by a particular learner in a given setting for a certain purpose'.

Affective strategies

Affective strategies help the learner to employ beneficial emotional energy, form positive attitudes toward the learning process, and generate and maintain motivation.

Sociocultural-Interactive strategies

Sociocultural-Interactive strategies, what others have called **communication** strategies, or **socioaffective** strategies, refer to the learner's tactics for generating and maintaining interactive communication within a cultural context. These strategies 'help the learner interact and communicate (despite knowledge gaps) and deal effectively with culture'.

Cognitive strategies and tactics	
Planning	Previewing, reviewing, setting schedules, deciding to attend to a specific aspect of language input, planning for and rehearsing linguistic components necessary to carry out an upcoming language task, deciding to postpone speaking
Organizing	Deciding to attend to specific aspects of language input or situational details that will cue the retention of language input, reordering, classifying, labeling items in the language
Monitoring	Correcting one's speech for accuracy in pronunciation, grammar, vocabulary, imitating a language model, including silent rehearsal, and self-checking
Evaluating	Checking the outcomes of one's own language learning against an internal measure of completeness and accuracy
Using senses	Creating visualizations and pictures to remember, noticing phonological sounds, acting out a word or sentence
Activating knowledge	Using the first language for comparison/contrast to remember words and forms, applying rules by deduction, using translation to remember a new word

Contextualization	Placing a word or phrase in a meaningful language sequence, relating new information to other concepts in memory	
Going beyond the data	Guessing meanings of new items, predicting words or forms from the context	
Affective strategies and tactics		
Activating supportive emotions	Encouraging oneself, making positive statements, making lists of one's abilities, rewarding oneself for accomplishments, noticing what one has accomplished to build self-confidence, writing a language learning diary	
minimizing negative emotions	Using relaxation to lower fear or anxiety, using positive self-talk to lower self-doubt, generating interesting charts, images, or dialogues to lower boredom, making a list of "to do" items to avoid feeling overwhelmed	
Generating motivation	Learning about the culture of a language, setting personal goals and monitoring their accomplishment, listing specific accomplishments, turning attention away from tests and toward what one can do with the language	
Building positive attitudes	Using relaxation to lower fear or anxiety, generating interesting activities to lower boredom, empathizing with others to develop cultural understanding	
Sociocultural-interactive strategies and tactics		
Interacting to learn	Cooperating with one or more peers to obtain feedback, pool information, or model a language activity	
Overcoming knowledge gaps	Asking a teacher or other native speaker for repetition, paraphrasing, explanation, and/or examples, questioning for clarification, using memorized chunks of language to initiate or maintain communication	
Guessing intelligently	Using linguistic clues in lexicon, grammar, or phonology to predict, using discourse markers to comprehend	
Generating conversation	Initiating conversation with known discourse gambits, maintaining conversation with affirmations, verbal and nonverbal attention signals, asking questions	
Activating socio-cultural schemata	Asking questions about culture, customs, etc., reading about culture (customs, history, music, art)	

H4　Compensatory strategies

It is of singular interest that many language learners who possess a "knack" for gaining communicative control of a second language have some special insights into what Dornyei (2009) and others have called **compensatory strategies**, which are designed to make up for gaps in one's ability.

Compensatory strategies	
Avoidance	Avoiding a topic, concept, grammatical construction, or phonological element that poses difficulty
Circumlocution	Describing or exemplifying the target object or action (e.g. *the thing you open bottles with* for *corkscrew*)
Approximation	Using an alternative term which expresses the meaning of the target lexical items as closely as possible (e.g. *ship* for *sailboat*)
Word coinage	Creating a nonexisting L2 word based on a supposed rule (e.g. *vegetarianist* for *vegetarian*)
Nonverbal signals	Mime, gesture, facial expression, or sound imitation
Prefabricated patterns	Using memorized stock phrases, usually for 'survival' purposes (e.g. *Where is the ____?*, *How much does this cost?*)
Code-switching	Using a L1 word with L1 pronunciation or a L3 word with L3 pronunciation while speaking in L2
Appeal to authority	Asking for aid from the interlocutor either directly (e.g. *What do you call ...?*) or indirectly (e.g. rising intonation, pause, eye contact, puzzled expression)
Keeping the floor	Using fillers or hesitation devices to fill pauses and to gain time to think (e.g. *well, now let's see, uh, as a matter of fact*)

H5 Strategies-based Instruction

Much of the work of researchers and teachers on the application of strategies to classroom learning has come to be known generically as **strategies-based instruction** (SBI), or as learner strategy training. As we seek to make the language classroom an effective milieu for learning, it has become increasingly apparent that "teaching learners how to learn" is crucial. Wenden (1985) was among the first to assert that learner strategies are the key to learner autonomy, and Chamot (2005) stressed the importance of including facilitation of that autonomy through explicit instruction.

It has been found that students will benefit from SBI if they (1) understand the strategy itself, (2) perceive it to be effective, and (3) do not consider its implementation to be overly difficult. (MacIntyre & Noels 1996) Therefore, our efforts to teach students some technical know-how about how to tackle a language are well advised.

The effective implementation of SBI in language classrooms involves several steps and considerations:

① identifying learners' styles and linking them with potential strategies

② incorporating SBI in communicative language courses and classrooms

③ providing extra-class assistance for learners

One way of accomplishing the first of these objectives is to administer a simple checklist to students, with a view to acquainting students with their own preferences in learning. You can use a **Styles Awareness Checklist** (SAC), a simple scaled questionnaire to familiarize students with their styles.

Then teachers can essentially be attuned to their role as facilitators of strategic action and there are several suggestions like the following: lower inhibitions, encourage risk taking, build self-confidence, develop intrinsic motivation, engage in cooperative learning, use right-brain processes, promote ambiguity tolerance, practice intuition, process error feedback, and set personal goals.

Finally, it is important to note that style awareness and strategic action are not and should not be limited to the classroom. Most successful learners reach communicative goals by virtue of their own self-motivated efforts to extend learning well beyond the confines of a classroom. Teachers can help learners to achieve this further step toward **autonomy** by helping learners to see that raising their awareness of styles and strategies aids them in the authentic use of language 'out there'.

최시원 전공영어 영어교육학
English Education Conceptual

Chapter 05 MindMap

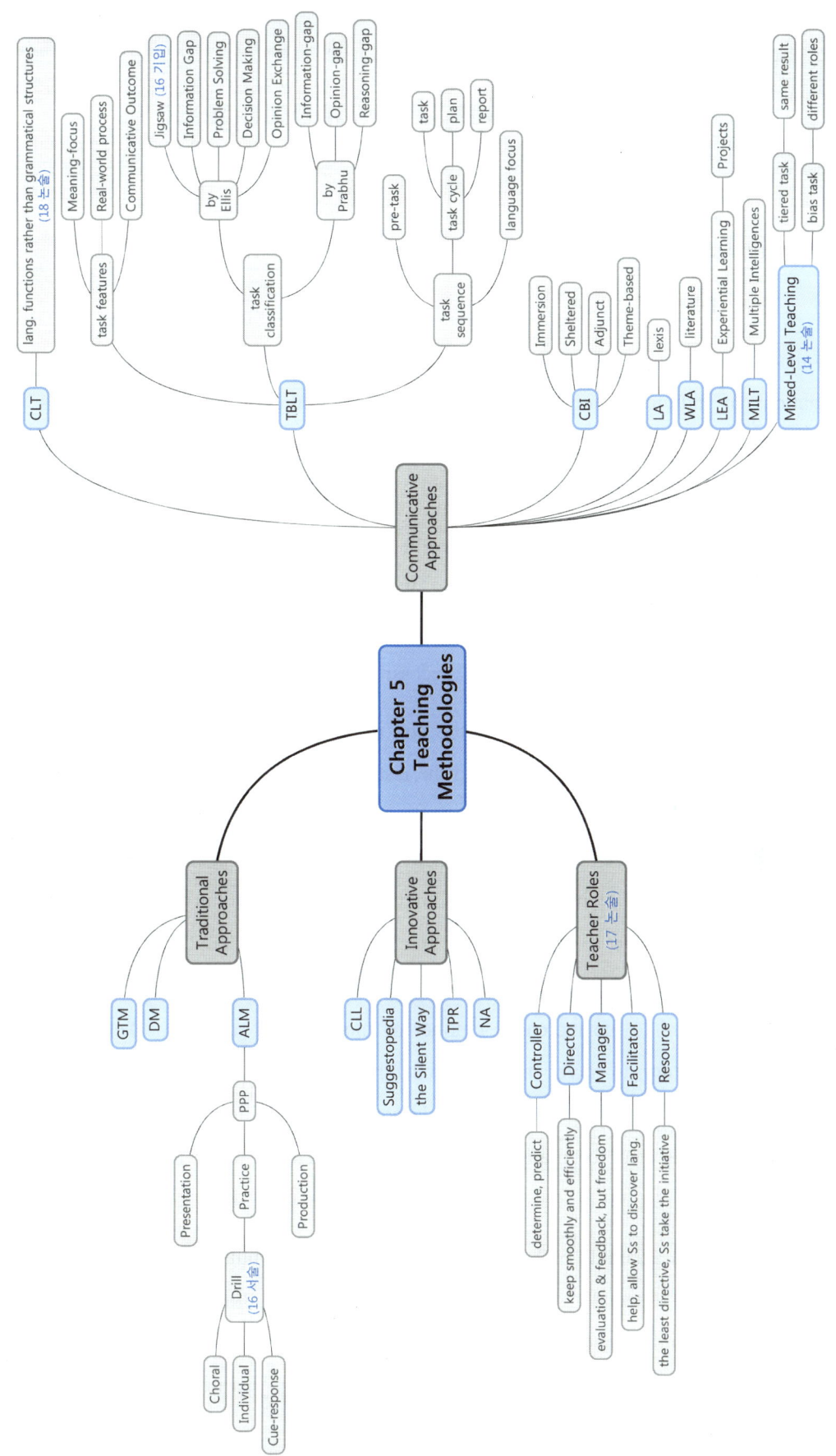

Chapter 05 Teaching Methodologies

A Traditional Approaches

A1 GTM, DM, & ALM

Typically, **Grammar-translation methods** did exactly what they said. Students were given explanations of individual points of grammar, and then they were given sentences which exemplified these points. These sentences had to be translated from the target language (L2) back to the students' first language (L1) and vice versa.

A number of features of the GTM are worth commenting on. In the first place, language was treated at the level of the sentence only, with little study, certainly at the early stages, of longer texts. Secondly, there was little if any consideration of the spoken language. And thirdly, accuracy was considered to be a necessity.

The **Direct method**, which arrived at the end of the nineteenth century, was the product of a reform movement which was reacting to the restrictions of GTM. Translation was abandoned in favor of the teacher and the students speaking together, relating the grammatical forms they were studying to objects and pictures, etc. in order to establish their meaning. The sentence was still the main object of interest, and accuracy was all important. Crucially (because of the influence this has had for many years since), it was considered vitally important that only the target language should be used in the classroom. This may have been against incessant translation, but, allied to the increased number of monolingual native speakers who started, in the twentieth century, to travel the world teaching English, it created a powerful prejudice against the presence of the L1 in language lessons. This position has shifted dramatically in the last few years, but for many decades L2-only methods were promoted all over the world.

When behaviorist accounts of language learning became popular in the 1920s and 1930s, the DM morphed, especially in the USA, into the **Audiolingual method**. Using the stimulus-response-reinforcement model, it attempted, through a continuous process of such positive reinforcement, to engender good habits in language learners.

Audiolingualism relied heavily on drills to form these habits; substitution was built into these drills so that, in small steps, the student was constantly learning and, moreover, was shielded from the possibility of making mistakes by the design of the drill.

The following example shows a typical Audiolingual drill:

Example 1	Example 2 (Backward build-up)
T: There's a cup on the table.... repeat.	T: Repeat please: "Good morning, Maria."
Ss: There's a cup on the table.	Ss: "Good morning, Maria."
T: Spoon.	T: "Where are you going?"
Ss: There's a spoon on the table.	Ss: "Where are you going?"
T: Book.	T: Good. "I'm going to the library."
Ss: There's a book on the table.	Ss: "I'm going to the library."
T: On the chair.	T: Listen: "I'm going to THE library."
Ss: There's a book on the chair. (etc.)	Ss: "I'm going to THE library."
	T: Listen again. "Li-BRA-ry." Rrr. "Librrrary."
	Ss: "Librrrary."
	T: "To the library."
	Ss: "To the library."
	T: "Going to the library."
	Ss: "Going to the library."
	T: "I'm going to the library."
	Ss: "I'm going to the library."
	T: Good! Now the next part.

Much Audiolingual teaching stayed at the sentence level, and there was little placing of language in any kind of real-life context. A premium was still placed on accuracy; indeed Audiolingual method does its best to banish mistakes completely. The purpose was habit-formation through constant repetition of correct utterances, encouraged and supported by positive reinforcement.

A2 Presentation, practice, and production

A variation on Audiolingualism is the procedure most often referred to (since the advent of CLT) as **PPP**, which stands for **presentation**, **practice**, and **production**. This grew out of structural-situational teaching whose main departure from Audiolingualism was to place the language in clear situational contexts. PPP represents an accuracy-to-fluency model of instruction.

In this procedure the teacher introduces a situation which contextualizes the language to be taught. The language, too, is then presented. The students now practice the language using accurate reproduction techniques such as **choral repetition** (where the students repeat a word, phrase or sentence all together with the teacher 'conducting'), **individual repetition** (where individual students repeat a word, phrase or sentence at the teacher's urging), and **cue-response drills** (where the teacher gives a cue such as *cinema*, nominates a student by name or by looking or pointing, and the student makes the desired response, e.g. ***Would you like to come to the cinema?***). Cue-response drills have similarities with the classic kind of Audiolingual drill we saw above, but because they are contextualized by the situation that has been presented, they carry more meaning than a simple substitution drill. Later, the students, using the new language, make sentences of their own, and this is referred to as production. The following elementary level example demonstrates the PPP procedure:

[Presentation]
The teacher shows the students the following picture and asks them whether the people in it are at work or on holiday to elicit the fact that they are on holiday.

The teacher points to the teenage boy and attempts to elicit the phrase, 'He's swimming.' by saying 'Can anybody tell me ... Jim ...?' or asking the question 'What's Jim doing ... anybody?'. The teacher then models the sentences (*He's swimming*) before isolating the grammar she wants to focus on (*he's*), distorting it (*he's ... he is ... he is*), putting it back together again (*he's ... he's*), and then giving the model in a natural way once more (Listen ... *He's swimming ... he's swimming*). She may accompany this demonstration of form rules by using some physical means such as bringing two hands (for *he* and *is*) together to show how the contraction works or by using the finger technique.

[Practice]

The teacher gets the students to repeat the sentence, 'He's swimming.' in chorus. She may then nominate certain students to repeat the sentence individually, and she corrects any mistakes she hears. Now she goes back and models more sentences from the picture (*Mary's reading a book, Paul and Sarah are playing cards*, etc.), getting choral and individual repetition where she thinks this is necessary. Now she is in a position to conduct a slightly free kind of drill than the Audio-Lingual one above:

> Teacher: Can anyone tell me? ... Mary? ... Yes, Sergio.
> Student: She's reading a book.
> Teacher: Good.

In this cue-response drill the teacher gives the cue (*Mary*) before nominating a student (Sergio) who will give the response (*She's reading a book*). By cueing before nominating she keeps everyone alert. She will avoid nominating students in a predictable order for the same reason. Usually the teacher puts the students in pairs to practice the sentences a bit more before listening to a few examples just to check that the learning has been effective.

[Production]

The end point of the PPP cycle is production, which some trainers have called 'immediate creativity'. Here the students are asked to use the new language (in this case the present continuous) in sentences of their own. For example, the teacher may get the students to think about what their friends and family are doing at this moment. They must now come up with sentences such as *My mother's working at the hospital, I think. My brother's lying on the beach. I'm sure. He's on holiday.*, etc.

B Innovative Approaches

Developed in the 1970s and 1980s, CLL, Suggestopedia, the Silent Way, and TPR are often considered together. While, individually, they are rarely used exclusively in 'mainstream' teaching, in different ways their influence is still felt today.

B1 CLL, Suggestopedia, and the Silent Way

In the classic form of **Community Language Learning**, a 'knower' stands outside a circle of students and helps the students say what they want to say by translating, suggesting or amending the students' utterances. The students' utterances may then be recorded so that they can be analyzed at a later date. Students, with the teacher's help, reflect on how they felt about the activities. CLL reminds us that teachers are in classrooms to facilitate learning and to help students with what they want to say.

Suggestopedia was developed by Georgi Lozanov and is concerned above all with the physical environment in which the learning takes place. Students need to be comfortable and relaxed so that their affective filter is lowered. Students take on different names and exist in a child-parent relationship with the teacher. Traumatic topics are avoided, and at one stage of a three-part procedure, the teacher reads a previously-studied dialogue to the accompaniment of music (preferably Baroque). During this phase there are also 'several minutes of solemn silence' and the students leave the room silently. Suggestopedia's insistence on lowering the affective filter reminds us how important affect is in language learning.

In **the Silent Way**, the teacher frequently points to different sounds on a phonemic chart, modeling them before indicating that students should say the sounds. The teacher is then silent, indicating only by gesture or action when individual students should speak (they keep trying to work out whether they are saying the sound correctly) and then showing when sounds and words are said correctly by moving on to the next item. Because of the teacher's silent non-involvement, it is up to the student — under the controlling but indirect influence of the teacher — to solve problems and learn the language. Typically, the Silent Way also gets students to use Cuisenaire rods (wooden blocks of different colors and sizes) to solve communication problems. To some, the Silent Way has seemed somewhat inhuman, with the teacher's silence acting as a barrier rather than an incentive. But to others, the reliance students are forced to place upon themselves and upon each other is exciting and liberating. It is students who should take responsibility for their learning; it is the teacher's job to organize this. Getting students to think about what they are learning and to rely on themselves matches our concern for cognitive depth, where close attention to language by individual students has a beneficial effect on the learning process.

B2 TPR

A typical **Total Physical Response** (**TPR**) lesson might involve the teacher telling students to 'pick up the triangle from the table and give it to me' or 'walk quickly to the door and hit it'. When the students can all respond to commands correctly, one of them can then start giving instructions to other classmates. James Asher believed that since children learn a lot of their language from commands directed at them, second-language learners can benefit from this, too. Crucially, in TPR students don't have to give instructions themselves until they are ready. There is no doubt about the appropriacy of getting students to move around in lessons of TPR. For students with a more kinesthetic inclination, this will be especially useful.

TPR and NA are **comprehension-based teaching**. Although Krashen has expressed his enthusiasm for TPR to teaching, it differs from his comprehensible input hypothesis in one important way. The comprehensible input hypothesis suggests that no structural grading is necessary but that teachers should modify their speech as needed to ensure students' comprehension. In TPR instruction, the vocabulary and structures learners are exposed to are carefully graded and organized. The material gradually increases in complexity so that each new lesson builds on the ones before.

B3 NA

The **Natural Approach** is designed to develop basic communication skills. The development stages are: (1) Comprehension (preproduction), (2) Early Production, and (3) Speech Emergence. This approach to teaching language has been proven to be particularly effective with limited English proficient students.

1) Comprehension stage

In order to maximize opportunities for comprehension experiences, NA instructors create activities designed to teach students to recognize the meaning in words used in meaningful contexts, and teach students to guess at the meaning of phrases without knowing all of the words and structures of the sentences. A typical activity in the Comprehension stage is Total Physical Response (TPR). The teacher gives commands to which the students react with their bodies as well as their brains.

2) Early Speech stage

In non-threatening environments, students move voluntarily into Stage 2. During the Early Speech stage, the instructor must give a meaningful and understandable input which will encourage the transition to Stage 3. Therefore, all student responses should be expanded if possible. Here is a sample exchange between the teacher and the class:

> Instructor: What do we see in this picture?
> Class: Woman.
> Instructor: Yes, there is a woman in this picture. Is there a man?
> Class: Yes.
> Instructor: Yes, there is. There are a man and a woman. Where is the man?
> Class: Car.
> Instructor: Yes, that's right. The man is in a car. Is he driving the car?
> Class: Yes.
> Instructor: Yes, he is. He's driving the car.

3) Speech Emergence stage

In the Speech Emergence stage, speech production will normally improve in both quantity and quality. The sentences that the students produce become longer, more complex and they use a wider range of vocabulary. Finally, the number of errors will slowly decrease. Students need to be given the opportunity to use oral and written language whenever possible. When they reach the stage in which speech is emerging beyond the two-word stage, there are many sorts of activities which will foster more comprehension and speech.

C Communicative Approaches

C1 CLT

Communicative language teaching (CLT) is best understood as an approach, rather than a method. It is therefore a unified but broadly based theoretical position about the nature of language and of language learning and teaching. Historically, CLT has been seen as a response to ALM, and as an extension or development of the notional-functional syllabus. Task-based language learning, a more recent refinement of CLT, has gained considerably in popularity.

Brown offers the following four interconnected characteristics as a definition of CLT.

① Classroom goals are focused on all of the components of communicative competence and not restricted to grammatical or linguistic competence.

② Language techniques are designed to engage learners in the pragmatic, authentic, functional use of language for meaningful purposes. Organizational language forms are not the central focus but rather aspects of language that enable the learner to accomplish those purposes.

③ Fluency and accuracy are seen as complementary principles underlying communicative techniques. At times fluency may have to take on more importance than accuracy in order to keep learners meaningfully engaged in language use.

④ In the communicative classroom, students ultimately have to use the language, productively and receptively, in unrehearsed contexts.

These four characteristics underscore some major departures from earlier approaches. While structurally (grammatically) sequenced curricula were a mainstay of language teaching for centuries, CLT suggests that grammatical structure might better be subsumed under various functional categories. In order to center on 'unrehearsed' communicative contexts, the mushrooming capability of technology (Internet, video, television, audio recordings, computer software) can come to the aid of teachers, especially novice teachers or nonnative speakers of the L2 being taught.

C2   TBLT

Task-based language teaching (TBLT) focuses on the use of authentic language and on asking students to do meaningful tasks using the target language. Some of its proponents present it as a logical development of CLT since it draws on several principles that formed part of the CLT movement from the 1980s.

Skehan (1998) describes a **task** as an activity in which (1) meaning is primary, (2) there is some communication problem to be solved, (3) there is some sort of relationship to comparable real-world activities, and (4) an objective that can be assessed in terms of an outcome.

The implication for TBLT is that if learners are provided with a series of tasks which involve both the comprehension and the production of language with a focus on meaning, language development will be prompted. The focus in TBLT is on process rather than product, and on how to learn rather than what to learn. According to Nunan (1989), task-based curriculum involves 'an integrated set of processes involving, among other things, the specification of both *what* and *how*'. According to Ellis (2003), various approaches to task-based teaching reflect the issues such as 'the role of meaning-based activity, the need for more learner-centered curricula, the importance of affective factors, the contribution of learner training, and the need for some focus-on-form'. Task-based pedagogy provides a way of addressing these various concerns and for this reason alone is attracting increasing attention.

Nunan (1991) mentions five features of task-based approach as follows:

1. An emphasis on learning to communicate through interaction in the target language.
2. Introducing authentic texts into the learning situation.
3. Providing opportunities for learners to focus not only on language but also on the process itself.
4. Enhancing learner's own personal experiences as important contributing elements to classroom learning.
5. Linking classroom language learning with language activation outside the classroom.

Nunan (2004) also draws a basic distinction between **real-world** or **target tasks**, and **pedagogical tasks**.

Target tasks	refer to uses of language in the world beyond the classroom.
Pedagogical tasks	are those that occur in the classroom.

(C2a) Criterial features of a task (Task vs. Exercise)

Widdowson would be critical of my own definition of a task:

1. The primary focus is on message.
2. There is some kind of gap.
3. Learners need to use their own linguistic and non-linguistic resources.
4. There is an outcome other than the display of language.

However, I (Rod Ellis) would argue that these criteria can effectively distinguish a 'task' from an 'exercise' and will illustrate how. In the two following activities (from Ellis 2010), there is a clear difference between the first (an exercise) and the second (a task).

> Look at Mary's shopping list. Then look at the list of items in Abdullah's store. Work with a partner. One person is Mary and the other person is Mr. Abdullah. Make conversations using 'any' and 'some'.
>
> Mary: Good morning. Do you have any flour?
> Abdullah: Yes, I have some *or* No, I don't have any.
>
> • Mary's shopping list
>
> 1. oranges   2. eggs   3. flour   4. powdered milk   5. biscuits   6. jam
>
> • Abdullah's store
>
> 1. bread 2. salt 3. apples 4. tins of fish 5. Coca Cola 6. flour 7. mealie meal flour
> 8. sugar 9. curry powder 10. biscuits 11. powdered milk 12. dried beans

In the exercise, learners are not required to produce their own messages; they simply substitute items in the model sentences given to them. There is no gap as the students can see the information contained in both Mary's shopping list and Abdullah's store. They do not need to use their own linguistic resources as model sentences and the vocabulary they need are given to them. Finally, there is clearly no outcome other than the display of correct language. This activity is a situational substitution exercise but not a task.

> Student A: You are going shopping at Student B's store. Here is your shopping list. Find out which items on your list you can buy.
>
> 1 oranges   2 eggs   3 flour   4 powdered milk   5 biscuits   6 jam
>
> Student B: You own a store. Here is a list of items for sale in your store. Find the items that Student A asks for that you do not stock.
>
> 1 bread   2 salt   3 apples   4 tins of fish   5 Coca Cola   6 flour   7 mealie meal flour
> 8 sugar   9 curry powder   10 biscuits   11 powdered milk   12 dried beans

The second activity is very different. Here learners have to create their own messages. There is an obvious gap as Student A cannot see Student B's information and vice-versa. The students are provided with some vocabulary, but they are not provided with any models to imitate. They will need to ask questions (e.g., 'Do you have oranges') and provide meaningful responses (e.g., 'Sorry, no') but how they formulate these messages is left to them. Finally, there is a clear outcome other than 'practising language' — the list of items that Student A was able to purchase and the list of items that Student A wanted but Student B did not stock. This is clearly a 'task' according to the criteria I have given. My purpose in comparing these two activities is not to claim that the 'task' is superior to the 'exercise'. Arguably, both have a place in language teaching, in accordance with my view that TBLT does not have to replace more traditional forms of teaching but can be used alongside them. However, if the aim is to create a context for more natural language use, then clearly the task is more likely to achieve this than the exercise.

(C2b) Classification of tasks 1 – psycholinguistic classification by Ellis

According to Ellis (2003), task classification is important because it ensures variety on a course by providing teachers with a selection of tasks. Ellis summarizes four approaches to classifying tasks: pedagogic; rhetorical; cognitive; and psycholinguistic. Among these different approaches, Ellis states that the psycholinguistic classification of tasks is based on how students are expected to interact in order to achieve the goals of the task. This allows opportunities for students to test their language use and work towards comprehension, and by doing so develop their language ability. Pica et al. (1993) proposed the following categories:

> 1. Interactant relationship (the responsibilities given to task participants to hold, request, and/or supply information needed to achieve the task goals)
> 2. Interaction requirement (the optional or obligatory requirements for information to be exchanged by participants in order to achieve the task goals)
> 3. Goal orientation (the convergent or divergent requirements of interactants in achieving the goals of the task)
> 4. Outcome options (the range of acceptable task outcomes available to interactants in attempting to meet task goals)

Using this framework, Pica et al. (1993) devised a typology of communication task types. The following table identifies the task types and their requirements:

	Interactant relationship	Interaction requirement	Goal orientation	Outcome options
Jigsaw	two-way	required	convergent	closed
Information gap	one-way or two-way	required	convergent	closed
Problem solving	one-way or two-way	optional	convergent	closed
Decision making	one-way or two-way	optional	convergent	open
Opinion exchange	one-way or two-way	optional	divergent	open

① **Jigsaw tasks**: These involve learners combining different pieces of information to form a whole. (e.g., three individuals or groups may have three different parts of a story and have to piece the story together.)

② **Information-gap tasks**: One student or group has one set of information and another student or group has a complementary set of information. They must negotiate and find out what the other party's information is in order to complete an activity.

③ **Problem-solving tasks**: Students are given a problem and a set of information. They must arrive at a solution to the problem. There is generally a single resolution of the outcome.

④ **Decision-making tasks**: Students are given a problem for which there are a number of possible outcomes and they must choose one through negotiation and discussion.

⑤ **Opinion exchange tasks**: Learners engage in discussion and exchange of ideas. They do not need to reach agreement.

From the five task types outlined by Pica et al. (1993), the curriculum developers felt the Jigsaw task type was the most conducive to facilitating interaction between students and thus provides opportunities for interactants to work towards comprehension. Based on the criteria of this type of task, an election task was devised whereby each student in a group would be given a different profile of a candidate for leader of an English Circle. Students would need to communicate with each other by describing their candidate's profiles and asking questions in order to decide which is the best candidate.

(C2c) Classification of tasks 2 – cognitive classification by Prabhu

Prabhu identifies three kinds of cognitive task types: information-gap, opinion-gap and reasoning-gap tasks.

An information-gap activity involves the exchange of information among participants in order to complete a task. For example, an information-gap activity might involve a student describing a picture for another student to draw or students drawing each others' family trees after sharing information.

An opinion-gap activity requires that students give their personal preferences, feelings, or attitudes in order to complete a task. For instance, students might be given a social problem, such as high unemployment and be asked to come up with a series of possible solutions. Another task might be to compose a letter of advice to a friend who has sought their counsel about a dilemma.

A reasoning-gap activity requires students to derive some new information by inferring it from information they have been given. For example, students might be given a railroad timetable and asked to work out the best route to get from one particular city to another or they might be asked to solve a riddle.

Prabhu (1987) feels that reasoning-gap tasks work best since information-gap tasks often require a single step transfer of information, rather than sustained negotiation, and opinion-gap tasks tend to be rather open-ended. Reasoning-gap tasks, on the other hand, encourage a more sustained engagement with meaning, though they are still characterized by a somewhat predictable use of language.

(C2d) TBLT framework (by Willis)

Jane Willis suggests three basic stages of task-based class procedure: the Pre-task, the Task cycle, and the Language focus.

In the **Pre-task** stage, the teacher explores the topic with the class and may highlight useful words and phrases, helping students to understand the task instruction. The students may hear a recording of other people doing the same task. During the **Task cycle** stage, the students perform the task in pairs or small groups while the teacher monitors from a distance. The students then plan how they will tell the rest of the class what they did and how it went, and they then report on the task either orally or in writing, and/or compare notes on what has happened. In the **Language focus** stage, the students examine and discuss specific features of any listening or reading text which they have looked at for the task and/or the teacher may conduct some form of practice of specific language features which the task has provoked.

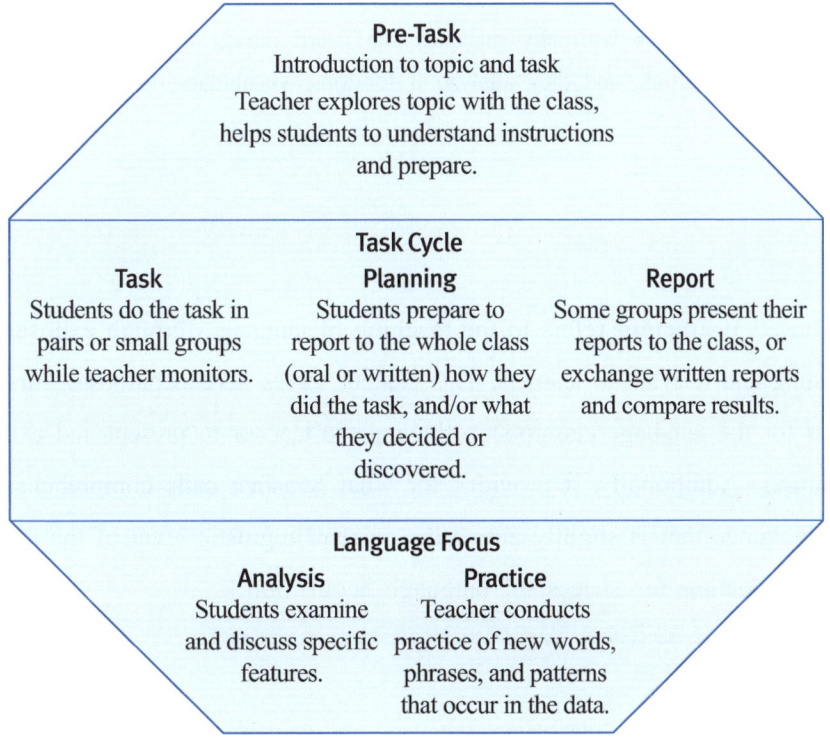

One of the examples that Jane Willis gives of such a procedure concerns a woman's phobia about spiders. The woman lived with her husband but could never be left alone because of her fear of spiders. Part of the procedure goes like this:

> [Pre-task]
> The teacher explains the woman's situation and asks students, in pairs, to brainstorm three consecutive steps they might take to help cure the woman of her phobia.

> [Task cycle]
>
> [Task] Pairs list possible ways to help the woman get over her phobia.
>
> [Planning] Pairs rehearse how to explain the steps they recommend, and justify the order they are in.
>
> [Report (and reading)] The pairs tell the class their proposals and justify them. The class listen and count how many ideas they come up with. The teacher lets the class decide and vote on which three steps might be similar to those in a newspaper report about the phobic woman's dilemma. She writes these on the board. The teacher gives out the text. She asks students to read to see whether their three steps were in the report. Finally, she asks which pair had the most steps that were similar.
>
> [Language focus]
>
> The teacher helps students with any mistakes she heard during the task. She then directs students back to the article and they analyze it for topic vocabulary, time expression, syntax elements, etc.

C3 CBI

Content-Based Instruction refers to the teaching of language through exposure to content that is interesting and relevant to learners. This content serves several purposes. First, it provides a rich context for the language classroom, allowing the teacher to present and explain specific language features. Additionally, it provides for what Krashen calls comprehensible input — challenging language that is slightly above the current linguistic level of the students which provides the foundation for successful language acquisition.

(C3a) Models of CBI

In a content-based language classroom, language and content are integrated in many different ways. Language and content are accorded equal weight in some cases. In other cases, content or language is the more significant. Various forms of instruction have made it flexible and feasible to apply the CBI approach to language teaching. Met (1999) proposes that CBI can be perceived as a continuum. A CBI course can either be content driven or language driven.

CONTENT DRIVEN			LANGUAGE DRIVEN
Immersion	Sheltered	Adjunct	Theme-based

① **Immersion**: Pupils attend specially designed content-area classes. All the students in a class speak the same native language and are at similar levels of proficiency in English. The teacher is not only certified in the regular content areas but also has some knowledge of the students' first language and culture. Immersion programs are found more commonly in EFL contexts than in ESL contexts.

② **Sheltered**: Content courses taught in the target language by a content specialist. Target language learners are sheltered from native-speaking students.

> English language learners enrolled in a sheltered seventh grade science class improve their English language skills while studying about the big bang theory of the origin of the universe. The science teacher in this class has received special training in working with L2 learners. Because the students are all still acquiring English as a second or additional language, she modifies her presentation style to help the students comprehend the material. The teacher's primary goal is for students to understand the content materials (in this case, about the origin of the universe). But she also spends some time helping students with language-related issues (e.g., academic vocabulary, reading skills) that pertain to the science unit they are studying. The exposure to higher-level language (through the content materials) and the explicit focus on language issues by the teacher set the stage for successful language acquisition.

③ **Adjunct**: Students are enrolled concurrently in two linked courses, a language course and a content course. Learners are sheltered in the language course, but integrated in the content course.

> University-level ESL students are enrolled in paired or 'adjuncted' English and psychology classes. Two separate instructors teach the classes — an English language instructor and a psychology instructor. Although the two classes meet and are graded separately, the two instructors meet regularly to coordinate their teaching objectives, and the English language instructor uses the psychology materials as content for the English language course. The instructional goals of these two classes differ since the main goal for the psychology class is for students to understand and learn the subject matter; the main goal for the English class, on the other hand, is for students to improve their English language skills. Students are able to achieve this goal through their exposure to challenging, yet comprehensible, input in the psychology class and through the language support and systematic language instruction that they receive in the English class.

④ **Theme-based**: The language class is structured around topics or themes, with the topics forming the backbone of the course curriculum.

> Beginning-level English language learners studying English at the fourth grade level work with the theme of friendship. Since the primary aim of this class is language acquisition, the English teacher uses this theme as a point of departure for instruction in reading, listening, speaking, and writing skills. The thematic content stretches over several weeks of instruction, providing rich input for lessons that are either language-based or skill-based.

(C3b) Differences of three CBI models (Theme-based, Sheltered, & Adjunct)

① **Population/setting**: Since theme-based instruction is the most generally applicable, it is appropriate at virtually any level of language learning and in a wide variety of settings. Sheltered and adjunct instruction, however, are more restricted in their applicability. Sheltered courses are typically found in middle schools and high schools where large populations of learners are receiving subject matter instruction in a language other than their first language. Finally, adjunct courses are typically found in settings where students are studying language as well as subject matter, such as high schools, colleges, and universities.

② **Lesson focus**: As can be seen from the above examples, the instructional focus in CBI may be on language (as in theme-based instruction), on content (as in sheltered instruction), or on both (as in adjunct instruction).

③ **Selection of content**: Because most CBI instruction occurs in schools, colleges, and universities, the content of the language class often overlaps with that of students' subject matter classes.

④ **Degree of faculty coordination**: Adjunct instruction is quite different from the other two models in this respect since it requires the systematic coordination of the language and content instructors. For example, these instructors typically meet before the course (and periodically throughout the course) to discuss curriculum and to coordinate objectives. They may also use this time to discuss the types of assignments they will set for the students. This is not true for sheltered and theme-based instruction, where the instructors do not coordinate in this fashion.

C4 LA

The **Lexical approach** is based on the assertion that 'language consists not of traditional grammar and vocabulary but often of multi-word prefabricated chunks' (Lewis 1997). These are the 'lexical phrases', 'lexical chunks' and other word combinations, i.e. the collocations, idioms, fixed and semi-fixed phrases which form such an important part of language. Lewis proposes that fluency is the result of acquisition of a large store of these fixed and semi-fixed pre-fabricated items which are 'available as the foundation for any linguistic novelty or creativity'. In short, a lexical approach is based on the belief that lexical competence comes simply from 'frequent exposure' and 'consciousness-raising'.

The Lexical approach would steer us away from an over-concentration on syntax and tense usage (with vocabulary slotted into these grammar patterns) towards the teaching of phrases which show words in combination, and which are generative in a different way from traditional grammar substitution tables. Thus, instead of teaching 'will' for the future, we might instead have students focus on its use in a series of 'archetypical utterances', such as 'I'll give you a ring, I'll be in touch, I'll see what I can do, I'll be back in a minute', etc.

In the area of methodology, word-order exercises can be adapted to focus on particular phrase components, as in this example for expression with 'get':

Example: 'Sentence anagrams' from "Implementing the Lexical Approach"

Rearrange these to make fixed expressions with the verb (get).

1. Things much can't worse get.
2. What we to there are supposed time get?
3. I you the very weren't happy impression got.
4. We've we as as the for can far moment got.
5. We be to don't anywhere seem getting.
6. What you I can get?

Which of these suggests: flying / offering a drink / frustration / despair

---

Elsewhere, however, Lewis suggests that exposure to enough suitable input, not formal teaching, is the 'key to increasing the learner's lexicon', and that 'most vocabulary is acquired, not taught'.

Suggesting that language should be taught in such a lexical approach is not without problems, however. In particular, we need to ask in what way a lexical approach differs from other accounts of language teaching since there are as yet no sets of procedures to exemplify such an approach to language learning. Despite this, the Lexical approach has certainly drawn our attention to facts about the composition of language; what it has not yet done is to make the leap from that to a set of pedagogic principles or syllabus specifications which could be incorporated into a method.

C5 WLA

Whole Language approach refers to a literacy philosophy which emphasizes that children should focus on meaning and strategy instruction. It is often contrasted with phonics-based methods of teaching reading and writing which emphasize instruction for decoding and spelling. The Whole Language movement is strongly opposed to these approaches to teaching reading and writing and argues that language should be taught as a 'whole'. Whole Language instruction was originally developed to help children learn to read, and has also been extended to secondary schools and to the teaching of ESL. The Whole Language approach emphasizes learning to read and write naturally with a focus on real communication and reading and writing for pleasure. In language teaching it shares a philosophical and instructional perspective with CLT since it emphasizes the importance of meaning and meaning making in teaching and learning. It also relates to NA since it is designed to help children and adults learn a second language in the same way that children learn their first language. The major principles of WLA are as follows:

① the use of authentic literature and a focus on real and natural events

② reading for the sake of comprehension and for a real purpose

③ writing for a real audience and as a process through which learners explore and discover meaning

④ the use of student-produced texts rather than teacher- or other-generated texts

⑤ integration of reading, writing, and other skills

⑥ student-centered learning in partnership with other learners

⑦ encouragement of risk taking and exploration and the acceptance of errors as signs of learning rather than of failure.

The following involves activities built around the use of 'Parallel Texts'. Two English translations of the same short story is an example of Parallel Texts. Study of the two translations highlights the range of linguistic choices open to the writer (and translator) in the contrast of linguistic choices made by the translators and the responses made to these choice by the students as readers. Students present and interpret them in pairs.

Parallel Texts: Opening sentences from two translations of a Korean short story.

1a. *Cranes* by Hwang Sun-Won (translated by Kevin O'Rourke)

"The village on the northern side of the 38th Parallel frontier was ever so quiet and desolate beneath the high, clear autumn sky. White gourds leaned on white gourds as they swayed in the yard of an empty house."

1b. *The Cranes* by Hwang Sun-Won (translated by Kim Se-young)

"The northern village at the border of the 38th Parallel was ever so snug under the bright high autumn sky. In the space between the two main rooms of the empty farm house, a white empty gourd was lying against another white empty gourd."

Examples of student activities based on parallel texts:

1. Think of the village as described in 1a and 1b as two different villages. Which one would you choose to live in? Why?
2. Write an opening sentence of a short story in which you briefly introduce the village of 1a as it might appear in winter rather than autumn.

C6 Experiential Learning & Project-Based Learning

Experiential learning, also known as project-based learning, highlights giving students *concrete experiences* in which they must use language in order to fulfill the objectives of a lesson. Both models include activities that contextualize language, integrate skills, and point toward authentic, real-world purposes, as in the following examples:

- hands-on projects (e.g., constructing a diorama)
- field trips and other on-site visits (e.g., to a factory or museum)
- research projects (e.g., the value of solar power)
- extra-class dinner groups (e.g., learning about Vietnamese cuisine)
- creating a video advertising a product (e.g., organic fruit)

Experiential learning emphasizes the psychomotor aspects of language learning by involving learners in physical actions into which language is subsumed and reinforced. Through action, students are drawn into a utilization of multiple skills. The educational foundations of experiential learning lie in the advantages of 'learning by doing', discovery learning, and inductive learning.

A specialized form of experiential learning that is still used in some circles is the **Language Experience Approach** (**LEA**), an integrated-skills approach initially used in teaching native language reading skills, but more recently adapted to second language learning context. With widely varying adaptations, students' personal experiences (a trip to the zoo, a movie, a family gathering at a park, etc.) are used as the basis for discussion, and then students, with the help of the teacher, write about the 'experience'. which is preserved in the form of a 'book'. The benefit of the LEA is in the intrinsic involvement of students in creating their own stories rather than being given other people's stories. As in other experiential techniques, students are directly involved in the creative process of fashioning their own products, and all four skills are readily implied in carrying out a project.

For learners of all ages, but perhaps especially for younger learners who can greatly benefit from hands-on approaches to language, certain projects can be rewarding indeed. Example:

> You are pursuing an environmental awareness theme in your class. Small groups are assigned to do different things: Group A creates an environmental bulletin board for the rest of the school; Group B develops fact sheets; Group C makes a three-dimensional display; Group D puts out a newsletter for the rest of the school; Group E develops a skit and presents it.

As learners get absorbed in purposeful projects, both receptive and productive language is used meaningfully.

C7 MILT

Related work by psychologist H. Gardner on **multiple intelligences** has been influential in language teaching. Teachers who recognize the multiple intelligences of their students acknowledge that students bring with them specific and unique strengths, which are often not taken into account in classroom situations. Gardner has theorized that individuals have at least eight distinct intelligences that can be developed over a lifetime. The eight are:

1. Logical/mathematical – the ability to use numbers effectively, to see abstract patterns, and to reason well
2. Visual/spatial – the ability to orient oneself in the environment, to create mental images, and a sensitivity to shape, size, color
3. Body/kinesthetic – the ability to use one's body to express oneself and to solve problems
4. Musical/rhythmic – the ability to recognize tonal patterns and a sensitivity to rhythm, pitch, melody
5. Interpersonal – the ability to understand another person's moods, feelings, motivations, and intentions
6. Intrapersonal – the ability to understand oneself and to practice self-discipline
7. Verbal/linguistic – the ability to use language effectively and creatively
8. Naturalist – the ability to relate to nature and to classify what is observed.

One way to teach from a multiple intelligence is to think about the activities that are frequently used in the classroom and to categorize them according to intelligence type. Christison and Armstrong give us examples of activities that fit each type of intelligence:

1. Logical/mathematical – puzzles and games, logical, sequential presentations, classifications and categorizations
2. Visual/spatial – charts and grids, videos, drawing
3. Body/kinesthetic – hands-on activities, field trips, pantomime
4. Musical/rhythmic – singing, playing music, jazz chants
5. Interpersonal – pair work, project work, group problem solving
6. Intrapersonal – self-evaluation, journal keeping, options for homework
7. Verbal/linguistic – note-taking, storytelling, debates
8. Naturalist – collecting objects from the natural world; learning about them.

A second way to teach from a multiple intelligence perspective is to deliberately plan lessons so that the different intelligences are represented. Here is one lesson plan:

> Step 1 : Give students a riddle and ask them to solve it in pairs: I have eyes, but I see nothing. I have ears, but I hear nothing. I have a mouth, but I cannot speak. If I am young, I stay young; if I am old, I stay old. What am I? [Answer: A person in a painting or photograph.] (Intelligences: interpersonal, verbal/linguistic)

Step 2 : Guided imagery: Tell students to close their eyes and to relax; then describe a picture of a scene or a portrait. Ask them to imagine it. Play music while you are giving the students the description. (Intelligences: spatial/visual, musical)

Step 3 : Distribute to each person in a small group a written description of the same picture they have just heard described. Each description is incomplete, however, and no two in the group are quite the same. For example, one description has certain words missing; the others have different words missing. The students work together with the other members of their group to fill in the missing words so that they all end up with a complete description of the picture. (Intelligences: interpersonal, verbal/linguistic)

Step 4 : Ask the groups to create a tableau of the picture by acting out the description they have just completed. (Intelligence: body/kinesthetic)

Step 5 : Show the students the picture. Ask them to find five things about it that differ from their tableau or from how they imagined the painting to look. (Intelligence: logical/mathematical)

Step 6 : Ask students to identify the tree in the painting. (Intelligence: naturalist)

Step 7 : Reflection: Ask students if they have learned anything about how to look at a picture. Ask them if they have learned anything new about the target language. (Intelligence: intrapersonal)

D Roles of the Interactive Teacher

directive					non-directive
	Controller	Director	Manager	Facilitator	Resource

Teachers can play many roles in the course of teaching.

(1) The teacher as controller

A role that is sometimes expected in traditional educational institutions is that of 'master' controller, always in charge of every moment in the classroom. Master controllers determine what the students do, when they should speak, and what language forms they should use. They can often predict virtually all student responses because everything is mapped out ahead of time, with no leeway for going on tangents. In some respects, such control may sound admirable. But for interaction to take place, the teacher must create a climate in which spontaneity can thrive, in which unrehearsed language can be performed, and in which the freedom of expression given over to students makes it impossible to predict everything that they will say and do.

(2) The teacher as director

Some interactive classroom time can legitimately be structured in such a way that the teacher is like a conductor of an orchestra or a director of a drama. As students engage in either rehearsed or spontaneous language performance, it is your job to keep the process flowing smoothly and efficiently. The ultimate motive of such direction, of course, must always be to enable students eventually to engage in the real-life drama of improvisation as each communicative event brings its own uniqueness.

(3) The teacher as manager

This metaphor captures your role as one who plans lessons and modules and courses, one who structures the larger, longer segments of classroom time, but who then allows each individual player to be creative within those parameters. Managers of successful corporations, for example, retain control of certain larger objectives of the company, keep employees pointed toward goals, engage in ongoing evaluation and feedback but give freedom to each person to work in their own individual areas of expertise. A language class should not be markedly different.

(4) The teacher as facilitator

A less directive role might be described as facilitating the process of learning, of making learning easier for students, helping them to clear away roadblocks, to find shortcuts, to negotiate rough terrain. The facilitating role requires that you step away from the managerial or directive role and allow students, with your guidance and gentle prodding here and there, to find their own pathways to success. A facilitator capitalizes on the principle of intrinsic motivation by allowing students to discover language through using it pragmatically rather than telling them about language.

(5) The teacher as resource

Here you take the least directive role. In fact, the implication of the resource role is that the student takes the initiative to come to you. You are 'there' for advice and counsel when the student seeks it. It is of course not practical to push this metaphor to an extreme where you would simply walk into a classroom and say something like "Well, what do you want to learn today?" Some degree of control, of planning, of managing the classroom is essential. But there are appropriate times when you can literally take a back seat and allow the students to proceed with their own linguistic development.

As an interactive teacher, you should be able to assume all five of the above roles on this continuum of directive to nondirective teaching. But the key to interactive teaching is to play toward the upper, nondirective end of the continuum, gradually enabling our students to move from their roles of total dependence (upon you, the class activities, the textbook, etc.) to relatively total independence.

Chapter 06 MindMap

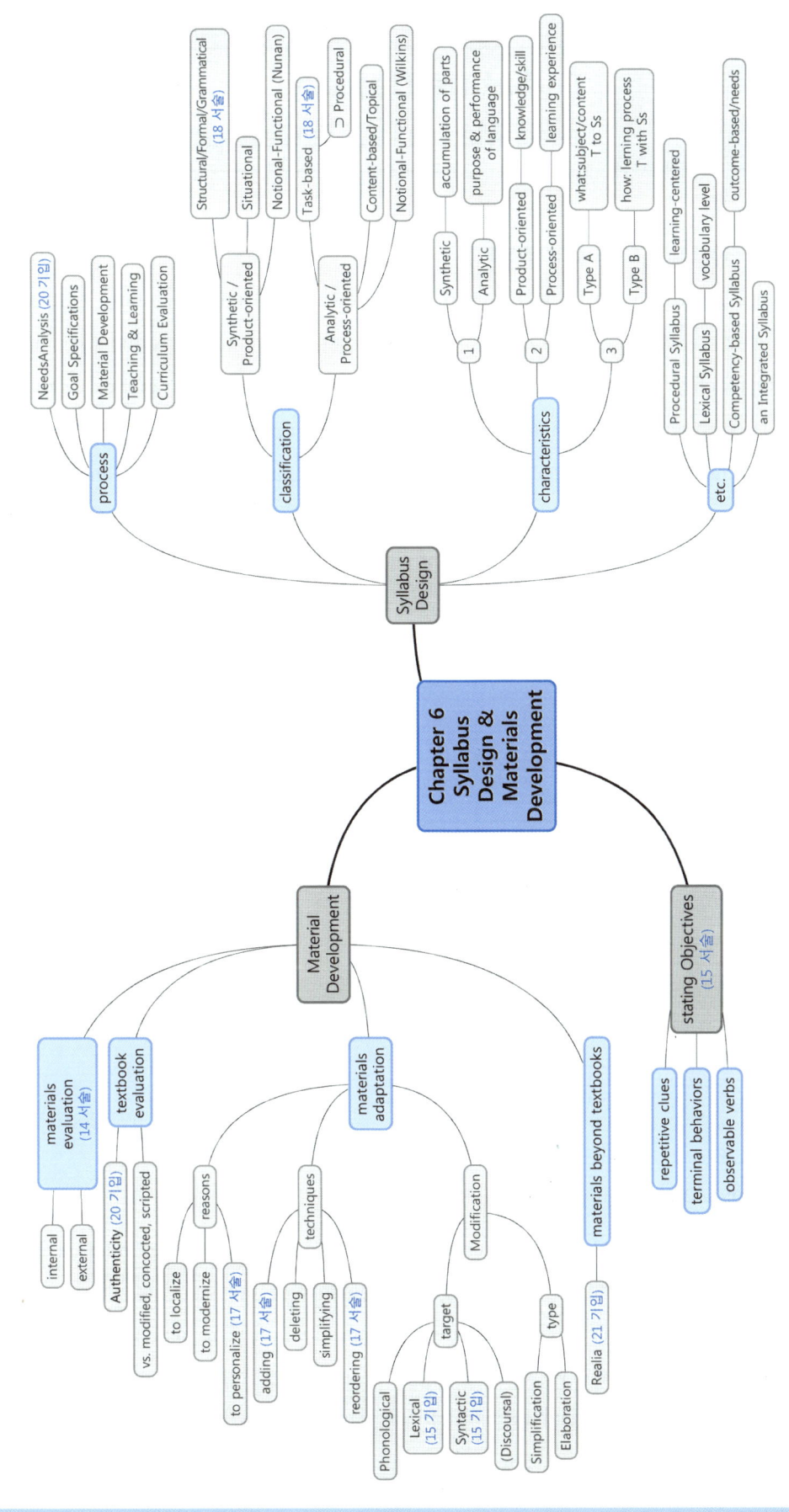

Chapter 06 Syllabus Design and Material Development

A Curriculum components

The model shown in the figure (adapted from Brown 1989) not only draws on the language teaching literature but also fits the more general models used to describe long established systems approaches to curriculum design. This model is meant to be applicable to language programs, yet complete and consistent with the widely accepted systems approach used in educational technology and curriculum design circles, particularly that of Dick and Carey (1985). As shall become evident the model provides both a set of stages for logical program development and a set of components for the improvement and maintenance of an already existing language program. The model is also meant to provide for a continuing process of curriculum development and maintenance while accounting for possible interaction among the various components of the design.

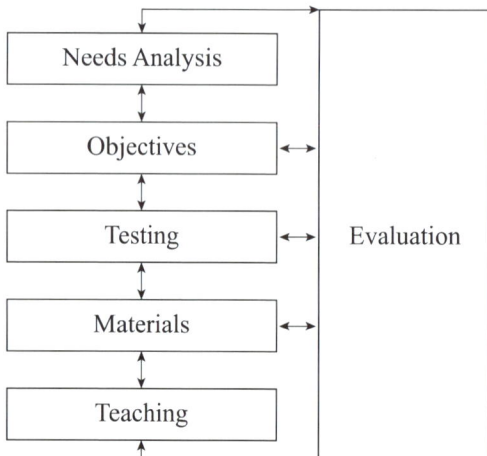

A1 Needs Analysis

Needs analysis is defined as the systematic collection and analysis of all relevant information necessary to satisfy the language learning requirements of the students within the context of the particular institutions involved in the learning situation. The analytical focus is on the learners, and their needs are viewed in linguistic terms. In truth, it is logical to make the learners the focus of any sound needs analysis. Learners are, in a sense, clients and their needs should be served. But at the same time, teachers, administrators, employers, institutions, societies, and even whole nations have needs that may also have a bearing on the language teaching and learning situation.

A2 Goals and Objectives

A logical outcome of determining the needs of a group of language students is the specification of goals, that is, general statements about what must be accomplished in order to attain and satisfy students' needs. Objectives, on the other hand, are precise statements about what content or skills the students must master in order to attain a particular goal. The specification of objectives and the process of thinking through what is involved in achieving the program goals will lead to analyzing, synthesizing, and clarifying the knowledge and skills necessary to meet the students' language needs. Since the difference between goals and objectives clearly hinges on level of specificity, the dividing line between the two is not always clear. Nonetheless, the distinction will prove useful in planning and maintaining language programs.

A3 Language Testing

The next logical step in curriculum development is the development of tests based on a program's goals and objectives. The processes of developing and refining tests is by no means magical nor is it particular easy. Nonetheless, sound tests can be used to unify a curriculum and give it a sense of cohesion, purpose, and control. Test can be used to drive a program by shaping the expectations of the students and their teacher. In short, tests are a very crucial element in the curriculum development process.

A4 Materials Development

With at least preliminary sets of needs analyses, objectives, and tests in hand, curriculum planners are in the unusual position of being able to deal rationally with the problem of materials. It is relatively easy to adopt, develop, or adapt materials for a program that is well defined in terms of needs analyses, objectives, and tests. In fact, the decision as to which strategy to use (adopt, develop, or adapt) in putting materials in place is itself made easier.

A5   Language Teaching

Given a reasonably high level of program support, the teacher can be left alone to concentrate on the most effective means for teaching the courses at hand. The teacher and only the teacher should make judgments about the particular students in a given class. These judgments can be very important as the teacher deals with the myriad cognitive, affective, and personal variables that will be interacting for the particular students at a particular time to form the unique characteristics of a given class.

A6   Program Evaluation

Program evaluation is defined as the ongoing process of information gathering, analysis, and synthesis, the entire purpose of which is to constantly improve each element of a curriculum on the basis of what is known about all of the other elements, separately as well as collectively. Such a continuing process of evaluation makes possible the assessment of the quality of a curriculum once it is put in place as well as the maintenance of that curriculum on an ongoing basis.

B   Classification of Syllabus

Syllabus is a sequential list of objectives, topics, situations, skills, and forms to be taught. Virtually applied linguists have distinguished six types of syllabi throughout the literature: Synthetic and Analytic syllabi, Product-oriented and Process-oriented syllabus, Type A and Type B syllabi.

Synthetic syllabus	(by Wilkins)	Analytic syllabus
accumulation of parts		purpose + performance of language
Product-oriented syllabus	(by Nunan)	Process-oriented syllabus
knowledge / skills		learning experience
Type A syllabus	(by White)	Type B syllabus
what: subject or content / T to Ss		how: learning process / T with Ss

B1 Synthetic vs. Analytic Syllabus

Wilkins (1976) separates language syllabi into **synthetic syllabi** and **analytical syllabi**. A synthetic language teaching strategy is one in which different parts of language are taught separately and gradually (step by step). Here acquisition is regarded as a process of gradual accumulation of the parts until the whole structure of language is built up. The learners' job is to synthesize the language that has been taken apart and presented to them in fragments. In contrast, analytical syllabuses are organized in terms of the purposes for which people intend to learn the language and the kinds of language performance that are necessary to fulfill those objectives. The analytical syllabus is a semantic, meaning-based syllabus, which aims at developing the learners' communicative competence. There is no orderly presentation of linguistic items, one after the other. In this process of learning, to communicate, the learner uses his/her capabilities to understand discrete items in language.

B2 Product-oriented vs. Process-oriented Syllabus

Nunan (1988) explains that **product-oriented syllabi** are those in which the focus is on the knowledge and skills which learners should gain as a result of instruction, while **process-oriented syllabi** are those which focus on the learning experiencing them. The product-oriented syllabus is also known as synthetic approach and the process-oriented syllabus as analytic approach. Synthetic/product-oriented syllabi focus on what the learners will know as a result at the end of instruction session. The grammatical, lexical, situational, and notional-functional are the examples of these syllabi. On the other hand, analytical/process-oriented syllabi operate in terms of the purposes for which people are learning language and the kinds of language performance that are necessary to meet those purposes (Wilkins 1976). It is a process rather than a product. Hence, in this process focus is on the specification of learning tasks and activities that learners will undertake during the course, not on what the student will have accomplished on the completion of the program. Procedural, process and task syllabuses are examples of analytic/process-oriented syllabi.

Synthetic/Product-oriented syllabuses	Analytic/Process-oriented syllabuses
- Structural/formal syllabus - Situational syllabus - Notional-functional syllabus (Widdowson 1979)	- Task-based syllabus - Procedural syllabus - Content-based syllabus - Notional-functional syllabus (Wilkins 1976)

B3 Type A vs. Type B syllabus

White (1988), from another perspective explains that all current syllabuses come under two categories — Type A and Type B. Type A syllabi deal with what should be learned in a second language classroom. They don't consider who the learner may be or how languages are acquired. The emphasis is only upon subject and content. They determine a series of objectives and they 'pre-package' the language by dividing it into small, discrete units. The teacher is the authority and main research person for the students. The teacher decides what items the students must master and how they will be evaluated. In this process things are done to the learner. Hence all synthetic syllabi are considered Type A syllabi. On the contrary, Type B syllabi are concerned with how the language is learned and how this language is integrated with learner's experiences. The emphasis is upon the learning process. The elements of the syllabus come out from a process of negotiation between learners and teachers. Objectives are decided during the course and based upon the needs of the learners. In this process things are done with the learner.

C Types of Syllabus

C1 Grammatical (Structural/Formal) syllabus

The structural syllabus is, doubtless, the most familiar of syllabus types. The underlying assumption behind grammatical syllabus is that language is a system which consists of a set of grammatical rules; learning language means learning these rules and applying them to practical language use. The learner is expected to master each structural step and add it to his/her grammar collection. These syllabi introduce one item at a time and require mastery of that item before moving on to the next.

C2 Situational syllabus

The situational syllabus appeared as an alternative to the grammatical syllabus. Palmer and Hornby believed that a grammatical or structural syllabus was neither efficient, nor effective for language learning since this model offers language sample outside their social and cultural contexts which makes transfer of learning from the classroom to the real world quite difficult.

It is based on the view that language always occurs in a social context and the teaching of language should not be isolated from its context. With this type of syllabus, the essential component of organization is a non-linguistic category i.e. the situation. The situation usually includes several participants who are involved in some activity in a particular setting. The language used in the situation comprises a number of functions combined into a plausible part of available discourse.

C3 Notional-functional syllabus

The notional-functional syllabus appeared in the early 1970s as an alternative to minimize the difficulties of both the grammatical and situational syllabus. In notional-functional syllabus, the input is selected and graded according to communicative functions (such as requesting, complaining, suggesting, agreeing etc.) that language learners need to perform at the end of language program. The notional-functional approach draws on theories and descriptions of language that emphasize the functional and social aspects of competence. This syllabus introduces two elements to syllabus designing — the first is notional or conceptual aspect such as time, space, movements, cause, and effect, and the second is a functional aspect which describes the intentional or purposive use of language. Widdowson argues, these syllabuses deals with 'items' not 'strategies', with 'components of discourse' not the 'process of creation'.

C4 Task-based syllabus

Prabhu defines a task as 'an activity which requires to arrive at an outcome from given information through some process of thought, and which allows teachers to control and regulate that process'. Prabhu recognizes that the acquisition of a linguistic structure is not 'an instant, one step procedure', and claims with Krashen that language form is acquired subconsciously through 'the operation of some internal system of abstract rules and principles' when the teacher's attention is focused on meaning i.e. task-competence, not language (Prabhu 1987).

A task-based syllabus supports tasks and activities to encourage learners to make the language communicative so as to achieve a purpose. It indicates that a language is a skill best perfected through interaction and practice. Nunan (2001) asserts that task-based syllabus offers a specific realization of communicative language teaching and differs from the previously proposed syllabuses like structural and functional-notional syllabus on the ground that task-based syllabuses start with needs analysis.

C5   Procedural syllabus

The procedural syllabus is based on a 'learning centered' approach to language teaching. The syllabus was proposed by Prabhu (1980) in the 'Bangalore Project' in India. His work is based on the principles that the learning is best carried out when attention is concentrated on meaning. The focus shifts from the linguistic aspect to the pedagogical one focusing learning or the learner. The Bangalore Communication Teaching Project comprises a list of graded activities based on cognitive tasks which deal with topics of everyday conversation. The learners are expected to solve problems and complete their tasks by using English. In due course, it is supposed that the grammatical system of the language will be covered through a meaningful interaction between the teacher and the learners. The procedural syllabus is a task-based syllabus. These tasks are not innovative, but they are claimed to be so in the way the material is used.

C6   Content-based (Topical) syllabus

Krahnke (1987) defines content-based syllabus as the teaching of content or information in the language being learned with little or no direct or explicit effort to teach the language itself separately from the content being taught. Content-based syllabus is considered as a sub-category of process-oriented and an analytic syllabus (Nunan 1988). While Ellis (2003) believes that content-based instruction is a kind of task-based approach, Nunan (1988) maintains that in content-based syllabuses unlike task-based syllabuses which are based on linguistic criteria, the experiential content is derived from subject area.

This content may come from other subjects on the school curriculum, such as science, history, environmental studies, or it might be generated from an analysis of students' interests and needs (Nunan 2004). Snow et al. (1988) believe that the rationale behind the integration of language and content is that language is learned most effectively for communication in meaningful, purposeful social and academic contexts. In real life, people use language to talk about what they know and what they want to know more about, not to talk about language itself. Another underlying rationale is that the integration of content with language instruction provides a substantive basis for language teaching and learning. Content can provide both a motivational and a cognitive basis for language learning. Nunan sees the followings as the advantages of content-based syllabuses:

- Content-based syllabuses enjoy a logical and coherent selection and grading content.
- It shares the advantages of analytical syllabuses.
- Learners learn other aspects of school learning alongside language itself.
- It integrates all the four language skills.
- It actively involves students in the phase of learning.
- It utilizes authentic tasks.
- For all these reasons, it can raise motivation and heighten the engagement of the learner in his or her own learning process.

D Material Development

Objectives of adaptation	Personalization, Localization, Modernization
Techniques for adaptation	Adding, Deleting, Simplifying, Reordering, Replacing

D1 Objectives of materials adaptation

With adapting materials, teachers may have some objectives to realize. These objectives go parallel with the reasons of adapting materials. Islam and Mares (2003) utter having a clear objective is a necessary starting point for adapting any materials. Clear adaptation objective(s) for the materials or knowing what works for one's class will help decide the appropriate content or language choice.

(1) Personalization

By adapting materials, teachers may aim at personalizing English lessons. They can do this by adapting materials in order to appeal the learning styles of the learners. With the help of Multiple Intelligences, learners' personalities may be involved. The interests and motivations of the learners may be juxtaposed with adapted activities and this lets the personalities involved into the lesson.

(2) Localization

With the omission of the extreme cultural information, the course books can be localized. By supplying texts, mentioning an event or giving a piece of news from the society that the teaching takes place may be helpful for localization of activities and materials. Human being has a learning system reading from local to universal, easy to hard, close to far, and known to unknown.

(3) Modernization

The method, the authenticity, the context, the order, and the balance of skills may need adaptation according to the needs of learners. By adapting materials, teachers may reflect the latest methods to the materials in-use. Modernization of the materials may also include the technological support; namely, PowerPoint Presentation (PPT), OHP slides and so forth.

D2   Techniques for Materials Adaptation

After recognizing a gap (mismatch or non-congruence) between published teaching materials and the needs and objectives of the classroom, the teacher has to address the practicalities of adapting the material to meet her class objectives more closely. McDonough & Shaw (1993) and Cunningsworth (1995) offer lists of techniques that may be used when adapting materials better to 'fit' a specific class. These techniques are: Adding; extending and expanding / Deleting; subtracting and abridging / Simplifying / Reordering / Replacing.

(1) Adding; Extending and Expanding

When adding to published materials the teacher is supplementing the existing materials and providing more material. The teacher can do this by either extending or expanding.

Extending: When extending an activity the teacher supplies more of the same type of material, thus making a quantitative change in the material. For example, an activity may practise a particular grammar point by asking the learner to complete a sentence with the missing verb in the correct form, such as the simple past. The coursebook may have provided ten sentences for this treatment, but the teacher may value this type of activity for her particular class and adapt the coursebook by adding five more sentences with missing verbs.

Expanding: Expanding classroom material is different from extending in that it adds something different to the materials; the change is qualitative. For instance, the teacher may feel her students need to be made aware of the different sounds of verb endings when used in the simple past but the coursebook does not address this phonetic issue. Consequently, she may add an activity or series of activities that deal with the phonetics of the past simple. The teacher may want to draw students' attention to the fact that, when pronouncing the verbs ***visited***, ***played***, and ***worked***, the endings (-ed) are pronounced /id/, /d/, and /t/ respectively. Other expansions could involve including a discussion to contextualize and personalize the topic of a particular unit of study, or including a TPR phase to make difficult language items in a reading or listening text more comprehensible. It is important to note that additions to materials can come at the beginning, at the end or in the middle of the materials being adapted.

(2) Deleting; Subtracting and Abridging

As with the technique of adding, material can be deleted both quantitatively (subtracting) or qualitatively (abridging). When subtracting, for example, a teacher can decide to do five of the questions practising the simple past tense instead of the ten in the coursebook. When abridging, however, the teacher may decide that focusing attention on pronunciation may inhibit the learner's fluency and decide not to do any of the pronunciation exercises in a coursebook.

(3) Simplifying

When simplifying, the teacher could be rewording instructions or text in order to make them more accessible to learners, or simplifying a complete activity to make it more manageable for learners and teachers. It is worth pointing out here that there is a distinct danger of distorting language when attempting to simplify a text and thus making the text inauthentic.

(4) Reordering

When reordering, the teacher has decided that it makes more pedagogic sense to sequence activities differently. An example is beginning with a general discussion before looking at a reading passage rather than using the reading as a basis for discussion.

(5) Replacing

When replacing material a teacher may decide that a more appropriate visual or text might serve an activity better than the ones presented in the published material. This is often the case with culturally specific or time-specific activities. A teacher may decide to replace an illustration for one that students could identify with more closely or use information concerning a popular figure with whom the students are familiar rather than the one presented in the published materials. Teachers may also decide to replace a whole activity depending on the goals, for example, a listening activity instead of a reading activity.

D3 Types of Materials

Just as with listening materials, reading materials can be classified as authentic or constructed. Nunan gave us a definition of authentic material like the following: '**authentic materials** are usually defined as those which have been produced for purposes other than to teach language' (1988). Language teachers often wonder whether constructed or authentic materials are better for developing their students' language proficiency. **Constructed materials** have the advantage of using words and structures that are familiar to learners so that students have a feeling of recognition and a sense of accomplishment when they read. These materials can also be used to introduce and reinforce new grammar and vocabulary. On the other hand, constructed materials are seldom as inherently interesting to students as authentic materials and they do less to prepare students for real world reading. In addition, constructed materials typically do not contain the inherent meaning support typically found in authentic materials. Ironically, just as with constructed listening materials, constructed reading materials often have less built-in redundancy than authentic materials and can actually be more difficult for learners than well-chosen authentic materials. Both authentic and constructed materials can be used for intensive reading activities, but teachers generally prefer authentic materials for extensive reading.

D4 Input Modification (Adapting Materials)

Authentic	Modified (= Constructed, Scripted, Concocted)	
not for teaching	for teaching purposes	
	Simplified	Elaborated
	by removing complex structures	by adding redundant info. to the text

There have been a number of studies that investigated the comprehensibility of different types of texts. Yano et al. (1994) compared three versions of a written text:

- **authentic** (e.g., "Because he had to work at night to support his family, Paco often fell asleep in class.");

- **simplified** (e.g., "Paco had to make money for his family. Paco worked at night. He often went to sleep in class.");

- **elaborated** (e.g., "Paco had to work at night to earn money to support his family, so he often fell asleep in class the next day during his teacher's lesson.").

Their subjects found the authentic version the most difficult. Incidentally, there was little difference in foreign language students' comprehension of the simplified and the elaborated versions.

When one discusses the role of input modification, it is useful to keep in mind two different criteria that can be paraphrased into two questions: (a) What is modified? (target of modification); and (b) How is it modified? (type of modification).

With regard to the first question, studies have investigated modifications at different linguistic levels, i.e., phonology, lexicon, syntax, and discourse. To name a few examples, NSs are found to speak more slowly to NNSs with longer pauses (phonological modification), and speak in shorter utterances to lower proficiency learners (syntactic modification). Modification at the discourse level is also referred to as interactional modification, and forms an independent area of SLA research.

The other question, How is input modified?, can be addressed to modifications of lexicon and syntax. There are two types of modifications: (a) simplification, and (b) elaboration. **Simplification** has widely been used in many commercially published L2 reading materials under the belief that the use of controlled vocabularies and short simple sentences will facilitate L2 reading comprehension. Most of the readability formulas are also based on the lexical and syntactic complexity, such as ratio of low-frequency words or sentence lengths. Though simplified texts are generally easier to understand, some researchers argue against the use of simplification. In L2 reading study, Blau (1982) demonstrated that simple sentences only do not necessarily aid comprehension.

In terms of language learning, even if simplification may facilitate L2 comprehension, it has a crucial weakness in that comprehension is achieved by removing items that L2 learners need to learn. To quote Yano et al. (1994):

> ... removal of possibly unknown linguistic items from a text may facilitate comprehension but will simultaneously deny learners' access to the items they need to learn. Linguistic simplification can be self-defeating to the extent that the purpose of a reading lesson is not the comprehension of a particular text, which learners are unlikely ever to encounter again outside the classroom, but the learning of the language in which the text is written and/or the development of transferable, non-text-specific, reading skills.

An alternative technique of text modification is **elaboration**, or **elaborative modification**. A text can be modified for easier comprehension not by removing complex structures as simplification does, but by adding redundant information to the text through the use of repetition, paraphrases, and appositionals (Long 1996).

E Lesson Objectives

Objectives may entail levels from general to specific, or 'terminal' (the ultimate aim) to 'enabling' (steps that support the learner in getting to the final goal). A simple way of thinking about objectives is to imagine what students will be able to do at the end of the class that they could not do when they walked in. Instead of "improve in reading," define a specific objective such as "students will defend their answers to comprehension questions by referring back to the text." Instead of "practice pronunciation," define a specific objective such as "students will use rising intonation for *would you like* questions in the context of offering hospitality to a guest." Another useful way to think about objectives and activities is with this framework: "If the students engage in X activity, then they will be able to do Y with the target language."

E1 Useful action verbs for writing objectives related to ESL classes

1. related to the main skills: ***read, write, speak, listen to, pronounce***

2. related to specific skills: ***predict, scan, proofread, summarize, take notes, revise, participate in***

3. related to specific assignments or activities: ***copy, complete, fill in, translate, correct, edit*** (however, these tend to focus on things students do in class rather than on things they need to do in the real world)

4. ***produce*** (sentences, paragraphs, essays, presentations)

5. ***use*** (words, patterns)

6. ***identify*** (ideas), ***analyze*** (texts), ***interpret*** (message)

7. ***comprehend*** (texts), ***recognize*** (errors)

8. ***organize, outline*** (ideas, essays)

9. ***apply*** (rules, strategies)

E2 Useful specification

texts at _____ level

TEXTS of __#__ words

_____ kinds of texts/tasks

topics related to _____, for _____ purposes, by means of _____

with _____% accuracy

so that errors do not interfere with comprehension

using the words _____, _____, and _____

including _____ and _____ features

E3 Typical weaknesses in writing objectives

Students will be able to comprehend short texts. How do we know the students have comprehended? → *Students will comprehend short texts as demonstrated by means of multiple choice questions.*

Students will learn how to write an essay. How do we know they know they have learned? → *Learn* is not a strong verb for objectives.

Students will write an essay. What kind of essay? According to what standards? → *Students will write an essay following format and including thesis/supporting ideas and with fewer than errors per page.*

Students will practice the simple present tense. Why? What will they be able to do with it after they practice? → *Practice* is not a strong verb for objectives.

최시원 전공영어 영어교육학
English Education Conceptual

Chapter 07 MindMap

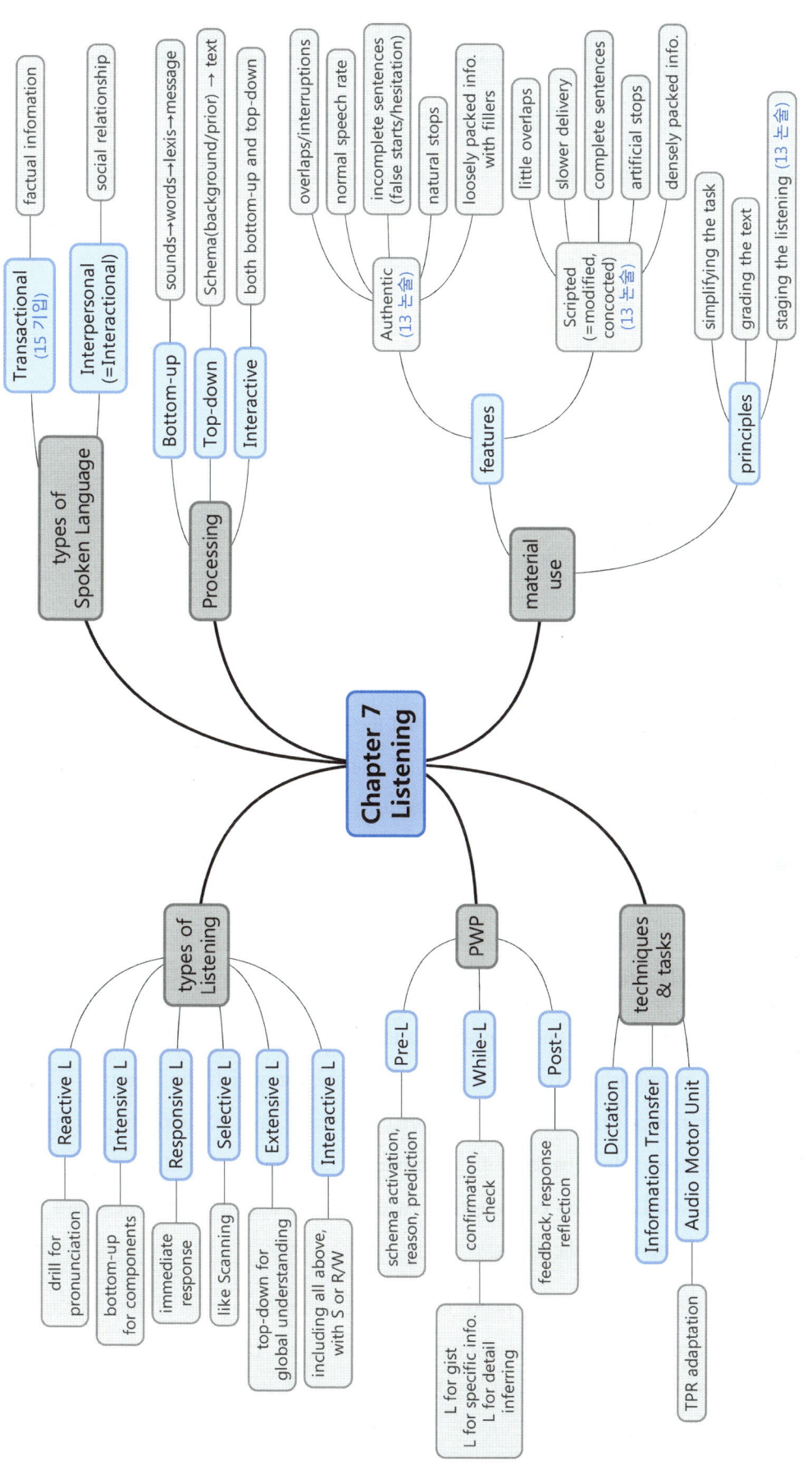

Chapter 07 Teaching Listening

A Types of Spoken Language (L/S)

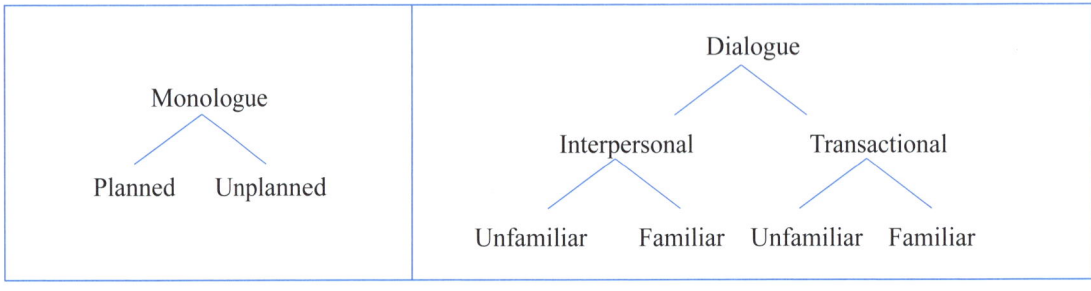

Interactional (Interpersonal)	promoting social relationships
Transactional	conveying propositional or factual information

In monologues, when one speaker uses spoken language for any length of time, as in speeches, lectures, readings, news broadcasts, and the like, the hearer must process long stretches of speech without interruption — the stream of speech will go on whether or not the hearer comprehends. Planned, as opposed to unplanned, monologues differ considerably in their discourse structures. Planned monologues usually manifest little redundancy and are therefore relatively difficult to comprehend. Unplanned monologues exhibit more redundancy, which makes for ease in comprehension, but the presence of more performance variables and other hesitation can either help or hinder comprehension.

Dialogues involve two or more speakers and can be subdivided into those exchanges that promote social relationships (**interpersonal**) and those for which the purpose is to convey propositional or factual information (**transactional**). In each case, participants may have a good deal of shared knowledge (background information, schemata); therefore, the familiarity of the interlocutors will produce conversations with more assumptions, implications, and other meanings hidden between the lines.

Remember these categories are really not discrete, mutually exclusive domains; rather, each dichotomy, as usual, represents a continuum of possibilities. If each category, then, is viewed as an end point, you can aim your teaching at appropriate ranges in between.

B Bottom-up vs. Top-down Processing (L/R)

Bottom-up processing	sounds → words → lexis → a final message
Top-down processing	schema (background/prior knowledge) → text
Interactive processing	both bottom-up and top-down

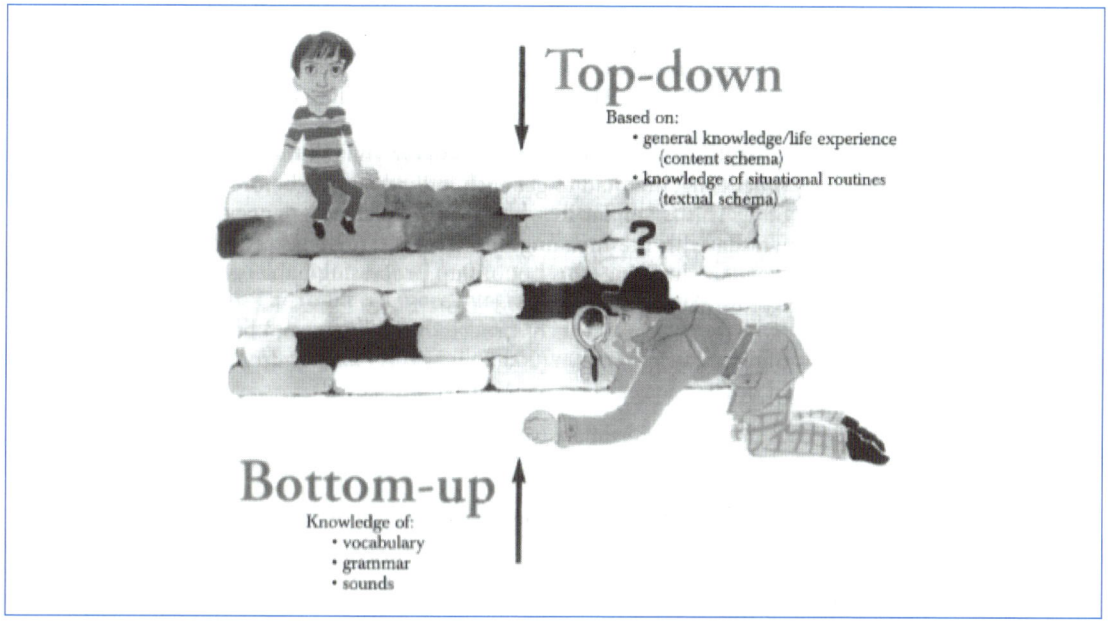

Bottom-up processing proceeds from sounds to words to grammatical relationships to lexical meanings, etc., to a final 'message', while top-down processing is evoked from 'a bank of prior knowledge and global expectations' and other background information (schemata) that the listener brings to the text. It is not possible to replace bottom-up with top-down, and it wouldn't be desirable to do so even if we could. We need to help learners integrate the two. In my case, this top-down/bottom-up integration happened by accident. In the classroom, prelistening activities are a good way to make sure it happens. Before listening, learners can, for example, brainstorm vocabulary related to a topic or invent a short dialogue relevant to functions such as giving directions or shopping. In the process, they base their information on their knowledge of life (top-down information) as they generate vocabulary and sentences (bottom-up data). The result is a more integrated attempt at processing. The learners are activating their previous knowledge. This use of the combination of top-down and bottom-up data is also called interactive processing.

B1 Background problems in listening

The obvious answer to the question 'What causes the comprehension problems that foreign learners have and native speakers don't?' is 'the language'. But this really only scratches the surface. It makes two assumptions: (1) that what L2 learners are doing is learning a language and no more; (2) that native speakers do not experience comprehension problems comparable with those of L2 listeners. Both assumptions need to be questioned.

Let us take the first assumption. When we learn a foreign language, we do more than learn a linguistic system, we acquire some degree of familiarity with the foreign cultural system. Language is the means used by a community to express facts, ideas, beliefs, rules, and so on — in short, to express its culture. So gaps in our knowledge of the L2 culture, of the associations and references available to native users, can present obstacles to comprehension.

Sample Task 1

Here are three spoken headlines from the BBC 1 *Six o'clock News* of 26 November 1986:

1. 'If you drink and drive, you're a menace' — the Government's message this Christmas.
2. Higgins is told 'Play on for the moment'. Police are investigating allegations of assault.
3. President Reagan's Attorney General says he believes more people could be involved in the arms scandal.

Which took longest to understand? Why? What did you need to do in order to interpret the meanings?

Secondly, L2 learners underestimate the native user's comprehension problems. Although foreign learners are naturally only too aware of their own misunderstandings of the L2, it is also the case that native users of the same language may fail to understand each other. Misunderstandings can arise if a speaker wrongly assumes that the listener shares their background knowledge.

Equally, what works as perfectly adequate communication for the people involved may be incomprehensible to an eavesdropper who happens to be an outsider, either in terms of language or culture. We will illustrate this point with a short conversation extract, based on real life. You are unlikely to find any words in it that you have not encountered before, whether you are a native reader of English or not; but the meaning may well remain unclear, if you are an outsider to the sub-culture relevant to the conversation.

> ### Sample Task 2
>
> Please follow these instructions exactly. Take a piece of paper and cover up the whole extract below. Then read it slowly and carefully, uncovering only a single line at a time. After each of speaker B's turns, make a note of what you think A and B are talking about. All you need to know at this stage is that they are colleagues at work.
>
> > A: What's it like, then?
> > B: Not bad. It's got a good short menu, which saves quite a bit of time.
> > A: It doesn't have a mouse, does it?
> > B: No, not at that price, no.
> > A: Anything else special?
> > B: Well, it's got a thing to stop you having to worry about widows and orphans.
> > A: So you're happy with it, then?
> > B: So far, yes.
> > A: Did you get the 512, in the end?
> > B: No, the 256.

In that particular case the words 'menu', 'mouse', 'widow', and 'orphan' are unlikely to have been new to you. But you may have been unfamiliar with their specialized meanings in the context of the topic that A and B were discussing; features of a word processor that A knew B had recently bought. So one source of misunderstanding or non-comprehension, for both native and foreign readers and listeners, may be the unfamiliar use of a familiar word or phrase.

Background knowledge is crucial to the way we understand language. It is often the absence or incompleteness of such information that results in the sort of non-comprehension that the foreign listener experiences: where the language element in fact presents no obstacle, but where it is the lack of shared schematic or contextual information that makes comprehension difficult or impossible.

C Features of authentic materials in Listening

Widdowson states that authenticity is something to do with the purpose of the text and the quality of response it elicits. One way to define authenticity may be to say that if the text exists for a communicative purpose other than teaching language, then it is authentic. Below is a list of common differences between authentic and scripted speech.

Authentic	Scripted
Overlaps and interruptions between speakers	Little overlap between speakers
Normal rate of speech delivery	Slower (maybe monotonous) delivery
Relatively unstructured language	Structured language, more like written English
Incomplete sentences, with false starts, hesitation, etc.	Complete sentences
Background noise and voices	No background noise
Natural stops and starts that reflect the speaker's train of thought and the listener's ongoing response	Artificial stops and starts that reflect an idealised version of communication (in which misunderstandings, false starts, etc. never occur)
Loosely packed information, padded out with fillers	Densely packed information

Compare a scripted dialogue and an authentic dialogue about similar topics.

W: What type of exercises are you keen on?

M: I'm keen on running.

W: Do you do it regularly?

M: Er … three or four times a week.

W: Where do you run?

M: In the park.

M = man, W = woman

M: Are you in, are you in fairly good shape? Do you still keep … keep fit?

W: [pause] I think so, yeah. In my opinion, yeah.

M: Well, what do you do exactly? To, to stay fit?

W: Mmm. Keep a routine, a routine like going … doing something every day.

M: Uh huh ‖

W: ‖ It doesn't matter what it is but

M: (Wh) But ‖

W: ‖ What I do more is going to the gym, lifting weights ‖ and

M: ‖ Uh huh

W: (Wh ⋯?)

M: But you do something, one of these, every day, one or two of these every day. Is it ⋯?

W: No, I do it, I do it every day.

M: One or two of those every day, one or two of those exercises?

W: No, no, I do both of them ‖ but

M: ‖ Ah, right.

W: For example, when the gym is closed on ‖

M: ‖ Yeah.

W: I do something every day. I have to do something every day.

W: Ah, right, right, OK.

M = man, W = woman

Features of the authentic dialogue include overlapping sentences (this is what the ‖ symbol means); much repetition (***every day*** occurs seven times in 20 seconds); misunderstanding and negotiation of meaning (the man wasn't sure how many exercises the woman did every day); false starts (***like going ⋯ doing something***); backchannel devices (***uh huh***) which show that you are listening; non-standard forms (***What I do more is*** ⋯); and a far longer conversation than in the scripted dialogue, which is 'cleaned up' of most of these elements.

We need, however, to evaluate the scripted conversation on its own terms. It isn't there as genuine listening practice; it's there to exemplify a grammar point, and it serves its purpose: it provides a clear model of the rules of question forms in the present simple. It is both easily understood, with little to distract the listener, and economical in terms of time and space.

Ultimately, then, much depends on what we wish to teach. If we want our students to practice listening, and we want to teach discourse markers and useful chunks (***in good shape, keep fit, keep a routine, lifting weights,*** etc.), the authentic dialogue will be more useful. If we want to teach question forms, we will choose the first dialogue.

C1　Using authentic materials in listening

There is a conservative view that the proper place for authentic recording in foreign language listening class is with the advanced learners. The early-stage learners had better start with simplified materials, since self-confidence and motivation are very important for them. This view sounds rational and reasonable, but it denies the early-stage learners the opportunity of hearing what the target language really sounds like. If we limit the listeners' experience to what has been graded to fit their language level, then they will not be equipped to cope if and when they come face to face with the target language in the outside world. (Field 2008) There are some ways in which a teacher can ensure that an authentic recording falls within the listening competence of the learners.

1) Simplifying the task

Teachers may counter-balance the increased linguistic difficulty of the text by simplifying the requirements of the task. It is not necessarily the language that makes a piece of listening difficult. Difficulty may also arise from the task that is set. It is possible to use a listening passage which is well beyond the learners' level, provided that what is demanded of the learner is correspondingly simple. If one notches up the text, one notches down the task. (Field 2008)

2) Grading the text

As a teacher, if you prepare to use authentic recording with your students, you should have a large enough collection of recording samples, then you can grade authentic recording in accordance with the proficiency level of your learners. You should bear the following in your mind when doing the grading: more frequent vocabulary; simple syntax; simpler and less dense ideas and facts; a degree of redundancy, with ideas/facts expressed more than once; a degree of repetition, with the same form of words repeated; a very specific context or genre of communication which to some extent pre-determines how participants behave. (Field 2008)

3) Staging the listening

With a piece of authentic recording, teachers may design many tasks. In the classroom, they should begin with very simple tasks, and progress to the tasks that are more demanding.

In all, we can find every reason that foreign language teachers should introduce authentic listening materials to the learners at all levels to increase their exposure to the real target language in use. Quite a lot of evidence shows that learners feel more comfortable and motivated with authentic listening materials. There are a lot of ways to help us to achieve this without demanding too much of the learners.

D Types of Listening Performance

Reactive L	drill for pronunciation
Intensive L	bottom-up for language components
Responsive L	immediate response to short stretches of teacher talk
Selective L	specific information in longer texts (like scanning in R)
Extensive L	top-down for global understanding
Interactive L	including all above, with S or R/W

1) Reactive Listening

The role of the listener as merely a 'tape recorder' (Nunan 1991) is very limited because the listener is not generating meaning. About the only role that reactive listening can play in an interactive classroom is in brief choral or individual drills that focus on pronunciation.

2) Intensive Listening

Techniques whose only purpose is to focus on components (phonemes, words, intonation, discourse markers, etc.) of discourse may be considered to be intensive in their requirement that students single out certain elements of spoken language. They include the bottom-up skills that are important at all levels of proficiency.

- Students listen for cues in certain choral or individual drills.
- The teacher repeats a word/sentence several times to 'imprint' it in the students' mind.
- The teacher asks students to listen to a sentence or a longer stretch of discourse and to notice a specified element, such as intonation, stress, a contraction, etc.

3) Responsive Listening

A significant proportion of classroom listening activity consists of short stretches of teacher language designed to elicit immediate responses. The students' task in such listening is to process the teacher talk immediately and to fashion an appropriate reply.

- asking questions ("How are you today?", "What did you do last night?")
- giving commands ("Take a sheet of paper and a pencil.")
- seeking clarification ("What was that word you said?")
- checking comprehension ("So, how many people were in the elevator at that time?")

4) Selective Listening

The purpose of selective listening performance is not to look for global or general meanings, necessarily, but to be able to find important information in a field of potentially distracting information. Selective listening differs from intensive listening in that the discourse is in relatively long lengths such as speeches, media broadcasts, stories and anecdotes, and conversations in which learners are 'eavesdroppers'.

[Techniques promoting selective listening skills could ask students to listen for]
- names / dates / facts or events / location or situation / main ideas or conclusion

5) Extensive Listening

Unlike intensive processing, extensive listening performance aims to develop a top-down, global understanding of spoken language. Extensive performance could range from listening to lengthy lectures, to listening to a conversation and deriving a comprehensive message or purpose. Extensive listening may require the student to invoke other interactive skills (e.g., note taking and/or discussion) for full comprehension.

6) Interactive Listening

Interactive listening performance can include all five of the above types as learners actively participate in discussions, debates, conversations, role plays, and other pair and group work. It must be intricately integrated with speaking (and perhaps other) skills in the authentic give and take of communicative interchange.

E Process Listening (PWP)

Current thinking suggests that listening sequences should usually be divided into three parts: pre-listening, while-listening and post-listening. Here is a summary of the sequence:

Pre-listening	1. Schemata Activation: What do I know? 2. Reason: Why listen? 3. Prediction: What can I expect to hear?
While-listening	1. Monitor (1): Are my expectations met? 2. Monitor (2): Am I succeeding in the task?
Post-listening	1. Feedback: Did I fulfill the task? 2. Response: How can I respond?

1) Pre-listening

This stage helps our students to prepare for what they are going to hear, and this gives them a greater chance of success in any given task. The first stage of pre-listening usually involves activating schemata in order to help students to predict the content of the listening passage. The second stage is setting up a reason to listen. Maybe there is an information gap that needs to be filled or an opinion gap or pre-set questions, or perhaps the students have asked questions based on things they would hope to hear.

2) While-listening

The students hear the input once, probably listening for gist, although of course there may be occasions when they need to listen for specific information or listen in detail. They check their answers in pairs or groups. This is to give them confidence and to open up any areas of doubt. They then listen a second time, either in order to check or to answer more detailed questions. It is important that the students should be required to do different tasks every time they listen.

3) Post-listening

The whole class checks answers, discusses difficulties such as unknown vocabulary, and responds to the content of the passage, usually orally, sometimes, in writing. This may be done in plenary (with the whole class) or in pairs or groups. A final stage may involve the 'mining' of the recording for useful language, a particular grammatical structure, vocabulary or discourse markers (*you know, I think, well,* etc.), for example.

F. Listening Exercises

1) For beginning level listeners

Bottom-up Exercises	- discriminate between intonation contours in sentences - discriminate between phonemes - selective listening for morphological endings - select details from the text (word recognition) - listen for normal sentence word order
Top-down Exercises	- discriminate between emotional reactions - get the gist of a sentence - recognize the topic
Interactive Exercises	- build a semantic network of word associations - recognize a familiar word and relate it to a category - follow directions

2) For intermediate level listeners

Bottom-up Exercises	- recognize fast speech forms - find the stressed syllable - recognize words with reduced syllables - recognize words as they are linked in the speech stream - recognize pertinent details in the speech stream
Top-down Exercises	- analyze discourse structure to suggest effective listening strategies - listening to identify the speaker or the topic - listen to evaluate themes and motives - find main ideas and supporting details - make inferences
Interactive Exercises	- discriminate between registers of speech and tones of voice - recognize missing grammar markers in colloquial speech - use knowledge of reduced forms to clarify the meaning of an utterance - use context to build listening expectations - listen to confirm your expectations - use context to build expectations, use bottom-up processing to recognize missing words / compare your predictions to what you actually heard - use incomplete sensory data and cultural background information to construct a more complete understanding of a text

3) For advanced level listeners

Bottom-up Exercises	- use features of sentence stress and volume to identify important information for note taking - become aware of sentence-level features in lecture text - become aware of organizational cues in lecture text - become aware of lexical and suprasegmental markers for definitions - identify specific points of information
Top-down Exercises	- use the introduction to the lecture to predict its focus and direction - use the lecture transcript to predict the content of the next section - find the main idea of a lecture segment
Interactive Exercises	- use incoming details to determine the accuracy of predictions about content - determine the main ideas of section of a lecture by analysis of the details in that section - make inferences by identifying ideas on the sentence level that lead to evaluative statements - use knowledge of the text and the lecture content to fill in missing information - use knowledge of the text and the lecture content to discover the lecturer's misstatements and to supply the ideas that he or she meant to say

G Listening Techniques and Tasks

G1 Dictation (→ Teaching Writing section 'Imitative Writing')

In its simplest form, dictation refers to a person reading some text aloud so that the listener(s) can write down what is being said. When used in the language classroom, the aim has traditionally been for students to write down what is said by the teacher, word for word, later checking their own text against the original and correcting the errors made. While this certainly has its uses, there are countless variations that can make it more interesting and learner-centred. Instead of the standard formula of the teacher dictating the text, there are a number of ways of taking the focus off the teacher and onto the students themselves. Using the students as the 'dictators' has the added benefit of focusing on students' pronunciation and, in a multilingual class, giving students further exposure to different non-native accents.

G2 Dictation with a difference

Dictation as it is usually done presents some problems because it is almost completely bottom-up — students need to catch every word. In our native language we don't process every word. So dictation is often asking students to do something in a foreign language that is unnatural and very difficult even in the first language. A related problem is that, since dictation is a 'word level' exercise, the learners don't need to think about overall meaning. The following exercise attempts to deal with those problems.

> **Step 1**
>
> A road went through a forest. A woman was walking down the road. Suddenly she saw a man. He was wearing a shirt, pants, and a hat. He smiled and said something.

In class, students hear the passage and imagine the story. Then they listen again, but this time, at several points, they hear a bell. As they listen, they fill in a cloze (fill in the blanks) dictation sheet. Each time they hear the bell, they write any word that fits the story as they imagined it. The imagined words go in the parentheses.

> Listen again. Write the missing words on the lines. When you hear the bell, write any word in the circle that makes sense.
>
> A (   ) road went ____ a (   ) ____ . A (   ) ____ was ____ down the ____ . Suddenly she ____ a (   ) ____ . He was ____ a (   ) ____ , (   ) ____ , and a (   ) ____ . He ____ and ____ , " ____ ."

The script, as they hear it this time is as follows. The dots (•) show the points where the learners hear the bell.

> **Step 2**
>
> A • road went through a • forest. A • woman was walking down the road. Suddenly she saw a • man. He was wearing a • shirt, • pants, and a • hat. He smiled and said, • .

While the students have the accuracy work of the dictation — writing the missing words (*forest, woman, walking,* etc.) — they are also getting the top-down experience of imagining the story and describing their version of it. Since everyone's image of the story will be somewhat different, it provides a good reason for them to compare stories after they finish their writing. This, of course, means they continue listening — this time to their partners.

G3 Dicto-comp (→ Teaching Writing section 'Intensive Writing')

G4 Dictogloss (→ Teaching Grammar section 'Dictogloss')

G5 Information Transfer

Information transfer is one of the while-listening activities. The students complete a diagram or drawing based on what they hear. Here is a simple, low-level information transfer activity: the students each have an illustration of an empty plate. In pairs, they take turns to describe what they ate for lunch that day while their partner attempts to draw the food on the plate.

A higher-level activity might be to get the students to describe an average day in terms of time spent on activities. For example, a student might say, 'I sleep for eight hours. Of the other sixteen hours, I spend about two hours a day eating, and about an hour travelling …', etc. Their partner listens carefully and draws a pie chart of the speaker's average day. A pie chart is a circle divided into slices, like a pie. The size of the slices, which are labelled 'sleeping', 'eating', 'travelling', etc, depends on the time spent doing each activity.

G6 Audio Motor Unit (TPR adaptation)

The **audio-motor unit** is a special type of demonstration that is very effective in teaching listening comprehension. The teacher prepares a script of about twenty sentences in the target language. The sentences should be centered around a single topic, such as 'getting ready for class', and should contain new as well as already familiar vocabulary and structures. The sentences are then taped on a cassette, preferably by a native speaker. In class, the teacher plays the tape once while pantomiming the sentences. The tape is played a second time while students join the teacher in acting out the script. This step may be repeated over a series of several classes, if necessary, but many times students are ready to 'solo' at this point. Finally, the tape is played and students pantomime the sentences alone. At this time, the teacher may want to make an informal check of comprehension and vocabulary by giving words and phrases in the target language and having students provide the English gist or translation. Because of the visual and motor impact of the activity, learners' attention and retention rates are usually high.

최시원 전공영어 영어교육학
English Education Conceptual

Chapter 08 MindMap

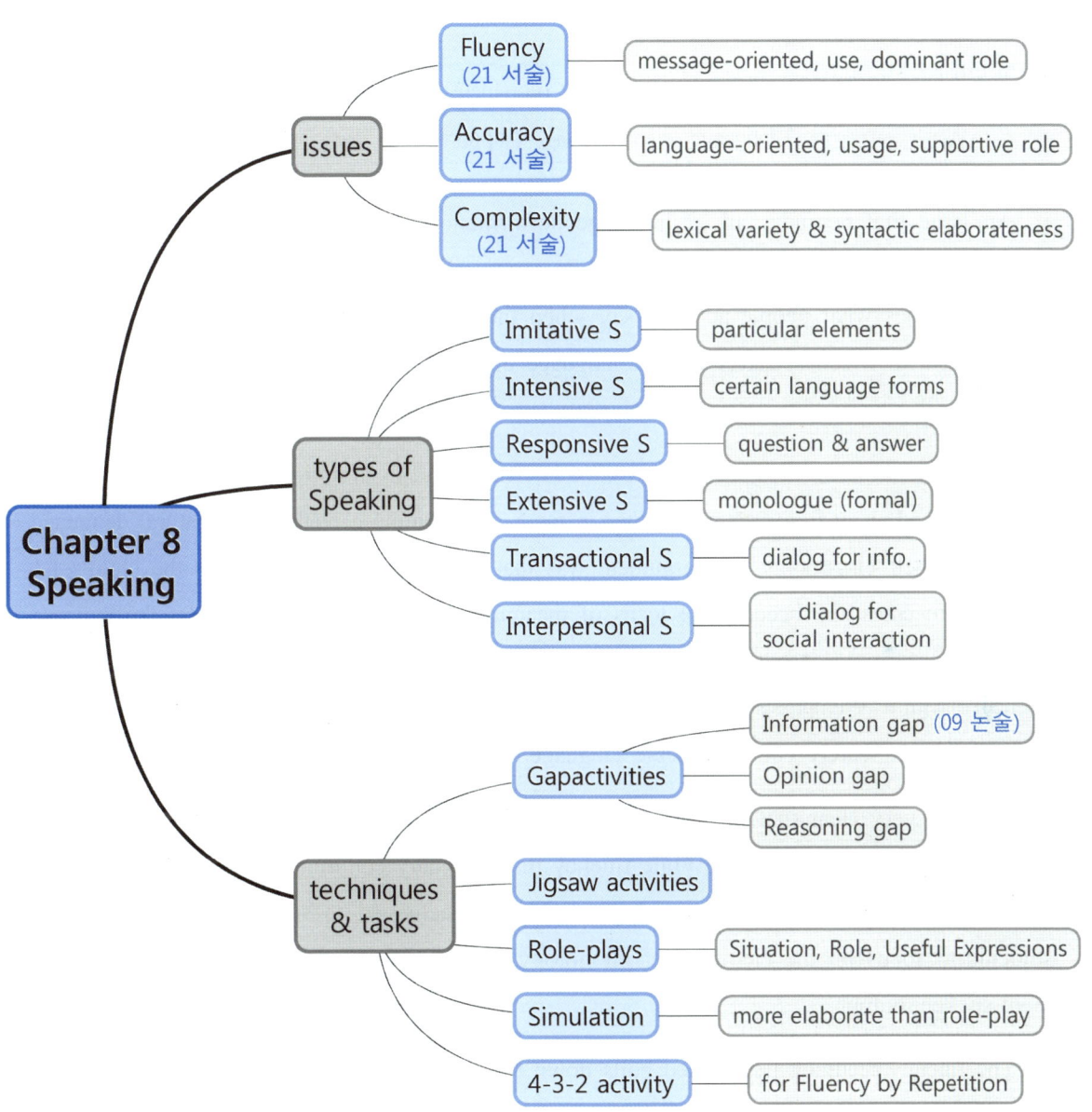

Chapter 08　Teaching Speaking

A Fluency vs. Accuracy issues

Fluency	message-oriented; use (dominant)
Accuracy	language-oriented; usage (supportive)

An issue that pervades all of language performance centers on the distinction between accuracy and fluency (Lazaraton 2014). While **accuracy** refers to the extent to which students' speech matches what people actually say when they use the target language, **fluency** refers to the extent to which speakers use the language quickly and confidently, with few hesitations or unnatural pauses, false starts, word searches, etc.

In the mid to late 1970s, egged on by a somewhat short-lived anti-grammar approach, some teachers turned away from accuracy issues in favor of providing a plethora of 'natural' language activity in their classrooms. The argument was that adult SLA should simulate the child's L1 learning processes and become the locus of meaningful language involvement (at the expense of focus on forms). Unfortunately, such classrooms so strongly emphasized the importance of fluency—with a de-emphasis on grammar and phonology—that many students managed to produce fairly fluent but barely comprehensible language. Something was lacking.

It's now very clear that fluency and accuracy are both important goals to pursue in CLT and/or TBLT (Lazaraton 2014). While fluency may in many communicative language courses be an *initial* goal in language teaching, accuracy is achieved to some extent by allowing students to focus on the elements of phonology, grammar, morphosyntax, and discourse in their spoken output.

The fluency/accuracy issue often boils down to the extent to which our techniques should be message oriented (or, as some call it, teaching language *use*) as opposed to language oriented (also known as teaching language *usage*). Current approaches to language teaching lean strongly toward message orientation, with language usage offering a supporting but important role.

(A1) Complexity

Complexity	lexical variety and syntactic elaborateness

A related issue that has garnered some attention recently is the extent to which L2 tasks can be graded by **complexity** which generally refers to the lexical variety and syntactic elaborateness of the learner's linguistic system. Both grammatical and lexical complexity must be taken into account, but the task design itself may fall into a range of cognitive, strategic, and interpersonal complexity. The extent to which a task involves pre- and within-task planning has been found to be a major contributor to complexity, and subsequently to both fluency and accuracy of learners' oral production. Complexity also varies according to cognitive operations, abstract thinking, quantity of information, negotiation of meaning, and time pressure, among other factors, all of which could account for accuracy, fluency, and successful completion of a task.

B   Types of Speaking Performance

Imitative S	particular elements of language form
Intensive S	beyond imitative S, certain language forms
Responsive S	question & answer, not into longer dialogues
Transactional S	(dialogue) information, extended from responsive S
Interpersonal S	(dialogue) social interaction
Extensive S	(monologue) extended, formal, deliberative

1) Imitative Speaking

A very limited portion of classroom speaking time may legitimately be spent generating 'human tape recorder' speech, where, for example, learners practice an intonation contour or try to pinpoint a certain vowel sound. Imitation of this kind is carried out not for the purpose of meaningful interaction, but for focusing on some particular element of language form.

2) Intensive Speaking

Intensive speaking goes one step beyond imitative to include any speaking performance that is designed to practice some phonological or grammatical aspect of language. Intensive speaking can be self-initiated, or it can even form part of some pair work activity, where learners are 'going over' certain forms of language.

3) Responsive Speaking

Responsive speaking refers to short replies to teacher- or student-initiated questions or comments. These replies are usually sufficient and do not extend into dialogues.

---

(1) T: How are you today?
　　S: Pretty good, thanks, and you?
(2) T: What is the main idea in this essay?
　　S: The United Nations should have more authority.
(3) S1: So, what did you write for question number one?
　　S2: Well, I wasn't sure, so I left it blank.

---

4) Transactional Speaking (dialogue)

Transactional language is an extended form of responsive language. Conversations, for example, may have more of a negotiative nature to them than does responsive speech.

T: What is the main idea in this essay?
S: The United Nations should have more authority.
T: More authority than what?
S: Than it does right now.
T: What do you mean?
S: Well, for example, the UN should have the power to force certain countries to destroy its nuclear weapons.

---

5) Interpersonal Speaking (dialogue)

Interpersonal dialogue is carried out more for the purpose of maintaining social relationships than for the transmission of facts and information. These conversations are a little trickier for learners because they can involve some or all of the following factors: a casual register, colloquial language, emotionally charged language, slang, ellipsis, sarcasm, hidden meanings that require understanding 'between the lines'.

> Amy: Hi, Bob, how's it going?
>
> Bob: Oh, so-so.
>
> Amy: Not a great weekend, huh?
>
> Bob: Well, far be it from me to criticize, but I'm pretty miffed about last week.
>
> Amy: What are you talking about?
>
> Bob: I think you know perfectly well what I'm talking about.
>
> Amy: Oh, that ... How come you get so bent out of shape over something like that?
>
> Bob: Well, whose fault was it, huh?
>
> Amy: Oh, wow, this is great. Wonderful. Back to square one. For crying out loud, Bob, I thought we'd settled this before. Well, what more can I say?

6) Extensive Speaking (monologue)

Extensive speaking refers to giving extended monologues in the form of oral reports, summaries, or perhaps short speeches. Here the register is more formal and deliberative. These monologues can be planned or impromptu.

C Speaking Techniques and Tasks

C1 Information gap

Information gap is a useful activity in which one person has information that the other lacks. They must use the target language to share that information. For instance, one student has the directions to a party and must give them to a classmate. Another natural information gap task — especially if the students don't know each other well — is to have one learner describe his family to another, while his partner draws a family tree diagram and labels it with names and information about the speaker's family. This activity promotes a great deal of negotiation for meaning, as one student asks another, "Wait, who lives in Madrid? Your aunt or, how you say, your cousin?"

C2 Jigsaw

Jigsaw is a bidirectional or multidirectional information gap. Each person in a pair or group has some information the other persons need. For example, one student could have a timetable for train travel in Canada. Another could have a map of Canada. Without showing each other the information, they must speak English to plan a one-week trip.

C3   Role-plays

Role-plays are excellent activities for speaking in the relatively safe environment of the classroom. In a role-play, students are given particular roles in the target language. For example, one student plays a tourist telephoning the police to report his wallet stolen. The other plays the role of a police officer trying to help the tourist file a report. Role-plays give learners practice speaking the target language before they must do so in a real environment.

C4   Simulations

Simulations are more elaborate than role-plays. In a simulation, props and documents provide a somewhat realistic environment for language practice. So for instance, in a language lesson about the grocery store, a teacher might bring in 'products' for the students to buy (a box of crackers, coffee, a jar of jam) and even play money for making their purchases. A check-out counter would be set up for the students to practice transactional speaking with the cashier.

C5   4-3-2 activity

Speaking fluency activities involve speaking on very familiar topics with some pressure to speak faster as in a 4/3/2 activity where the learners speak to one listener for four minutes on a topic, then give exactly the same talk to a different listener but in three minutes, and then to a different listener in two minutes. In this pair work format, the objective is to retell a story or monologue within a time limit that decreases at each retelling, thereby encouraging greater automaticity.

Students are also paired and take it in turns to do a monologic speaking task, e.g. recounting a story or explaining a process, based on picture prompts, or summarizing a text they have each read. For the first 'telling' each speaker is allowed four minutes. The second time round they have to achieve the same degree of detail but in only three minutes, and the task can be repeated a third time, but in two minutes. (The timings can vary according to the nature of the task and the degree of challenge that is desirable. 4-2-1, for example, may be more appropriate for more fluent speakers.)

Chapter 09 MindMap

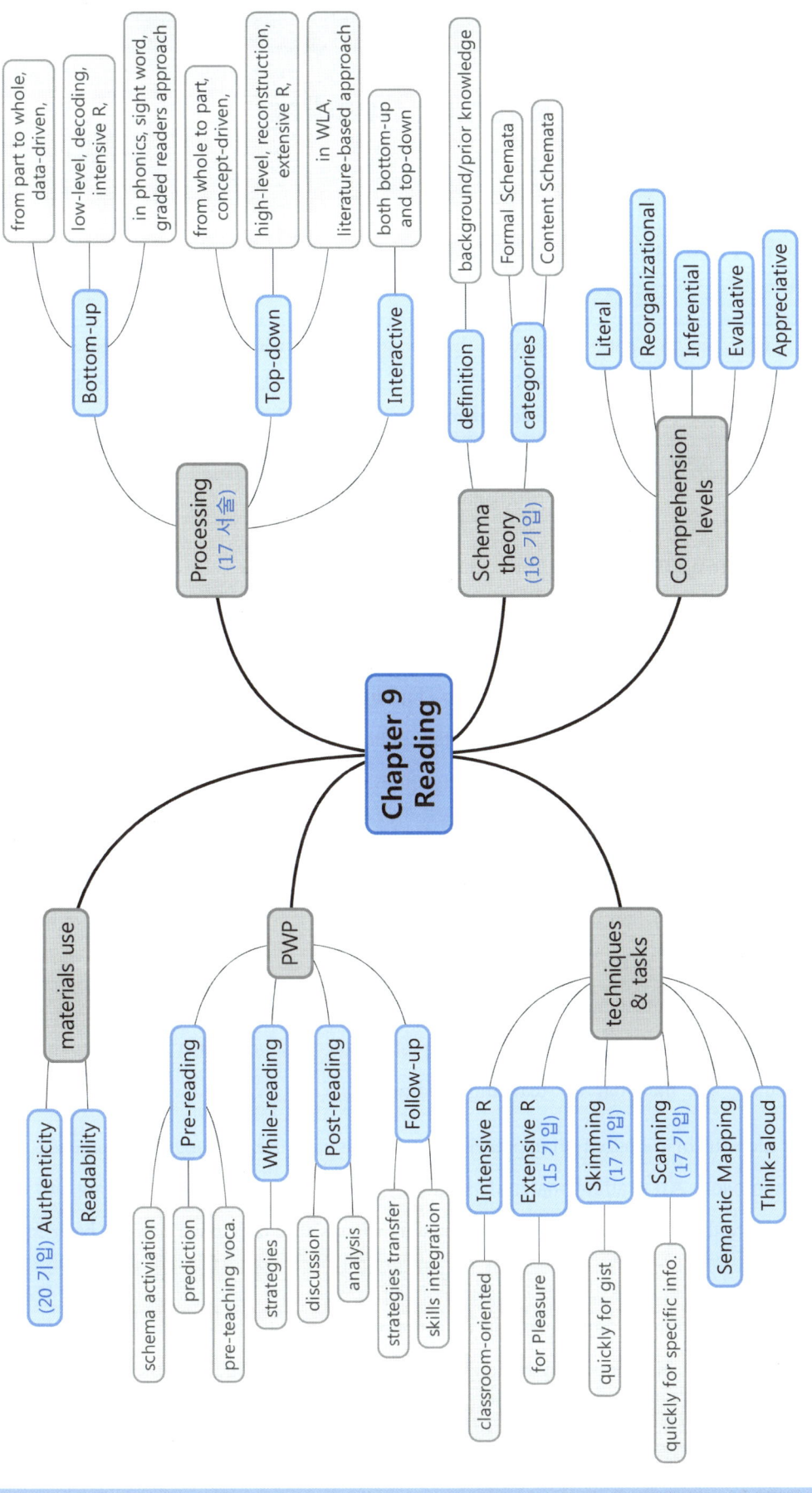

Chapter 09   Teaching Reading

A   Bottom-up vs. Top-down Process

Bottom-up	Top-down
from part to whole, data-driven, low-level, decoding, intensive R, in phonics, sight word, graded reader approach	from whole to part, concept-driven, high-level, reconstruction, extensive R, in WLA, literature-based approach
Interactive	
bottom-up & top-down	

1) Bottom-up models

Bottom-up models typically consist of lower-level reading processes. Students start with the fundamental basics of letter and sound recognition, which in turn allows for morpheme recognition followed by word recognition, building up to the identification of grammatical structures, sentences, and longer texts. Letters, letter clusters, words, phrases, sentences, longer text, and finally meaning is the order in achieving comprehension.

A phonics approach to teaching reading supports a bottom-up model. This approach is used in many reading series. Many teachers and researchers suggest that for readers to be successful they must be able to break a word down into its smallest parts, the individual sounds. When a reader comes to an unknown word he or she can sound out the word because of the knowledge of the individual units that make up the word. The blending together of the various sounds allows the reader to then move toward comprehension. Teachers must remember that phonics is a method, not the goal for teaching reading.

One element of a bottom-up approach to reading is that the pedagogy recommends a graded reader approach. All reading material is carefully reviewed so that students are not exposed to vocabulary that is too difficult or that contains sounds that they have not yet been introduced to.

Figure 1 is a graphic representation of a bottom-up approach to reading. The reader begins with the smallest elements and builds up to comprehension of what is being read.

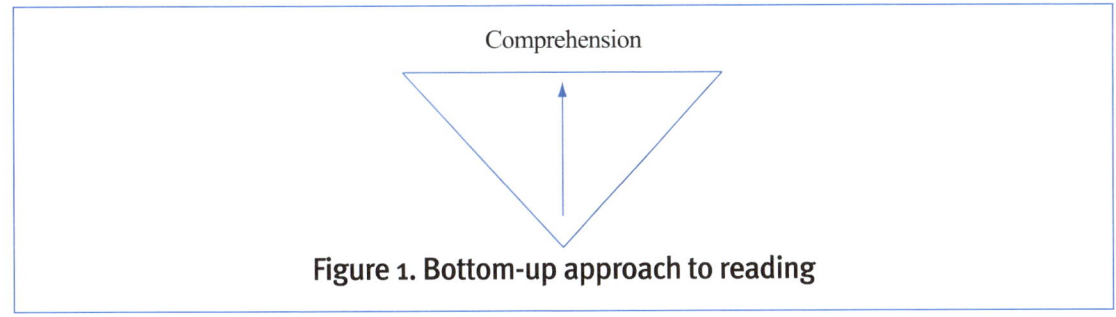

Figure 1. Bottom-up approach to reading

Within a bottom-up approach to reading, the most typical classroom focus is on what we call intensive reading. **Intensive reading** involves a short reading passage followed by textbook activities to develop comprehension and/or a particular reading skill. Most textbooks used to teach first and second language reading using an intensive reading approach.

2) Top-down models

Top-down models, on the other hand, begin with the idea that comprehension resides in the reader. The reader uses background knowledge, makes predictions, and searches the text to confirm or reject the predictions that are made. A passage can thus be understood even if all of the individual words are not understood. Within a top-down approach to reading the teacher should focus on meaning generating activities rather than on mastery of word recognition.

A meaning-based approach of a whole language approach to reading is supportive of top-down models of reading. Four key features highlight a meaning-based or whole language approach to teaching reading. First, it is a literature-based approach. Books are used which contain authentic language. Readers are exposed to a wide range of vocabulary. Next, whole language is student-centered; the focus is on the individual reader choosing what he or she wants to read. Third, reading is integrated with writing. Classes work on both skills simultaneously. Finally, emphasis is on constructing meaning. The focus should be on meaning and keeping the language whole, as opposed to breaking it down into smaller units. Whole language is a method, not the goal.

Figure 2 is a graphic representation of a top-down approach to reading. The reader begins with the largest elements and works down towards smaller elements to build comprehension of what is being read.

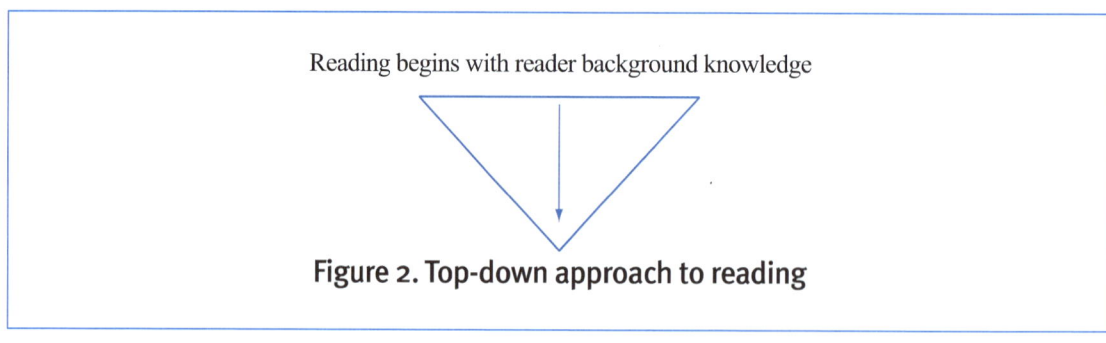

Figure 2. Top-down approach to reading

Extensive reading plays a key role in top-down approaches to reading. Extensive reading can be contrasted with intensive reading. **Extensive reading** means reading many books (or longer segments of text) without a focus on classroom exercises that may test comprehension skills.

3) Interactive models

Interactive models combine elements of both bottom-up and top-down models assuming 'that a pattern is synthesized based on information provided simultaneously from several knowledge sources'. These models are accepted as the most comprehensive description of the reading process. Murtagh (1989) stresses that the best second language readers are those who can 'efficiently integrate' both bottom-up and top-down processes.

Figure 3 is a graphic representation of an interactive approach to reading. The reader combines elements of both bottom-up and top-down models of reading to reach comprehension.

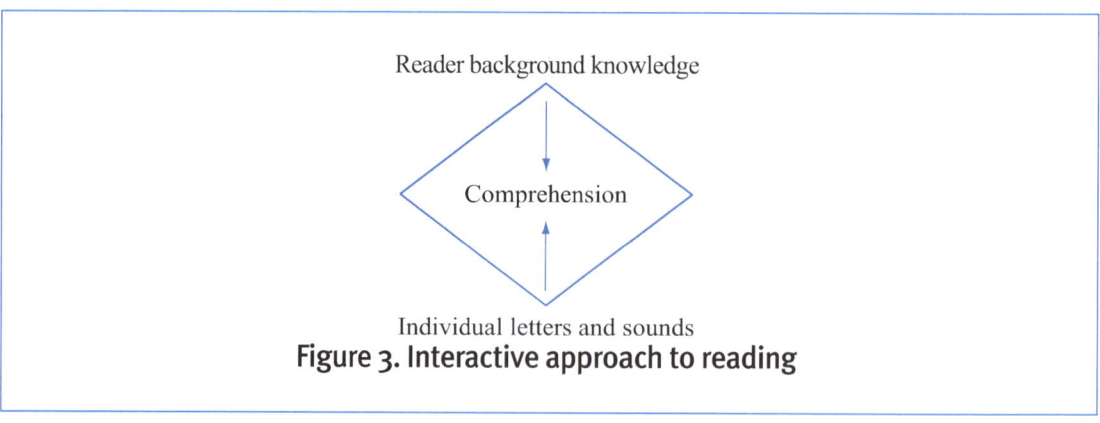

Figure 3. Interactive approach to reading

An interactive approach to reading would include aspects of both intensive and extensive reading. We need to provide learners with shorter passages to teach specific reading skills and strategies explicitly. We also need to encourage learners to read longer texts without an emphasis on testing their skills. Extensive reading provides opportunities to practice strategies introduced during intensive reading instruction.

B Schema Theory

Schema(ta)	
background/previous/prior knowledge	
Content schema(ta)	Formal schema(ta)
our knowledge about people, the world, culture, and the universe	our knowledge about language and discourse structure

Schema theory is the hallmark of which is that a text does not by itself carry meaning. The reader brings information, knowledge, emotion, experience, and culture — that is, schemata (plural) — to the printed word. Research has shown that reading is only incidentally visual. More information is contributed by the reader than by the print on the page. That is, readers understand what they read because they are able to take the stimulus beyond its graphic representation and assign it membership to an appropriate group of concepts already stored in their memories. The skill in reading depends on the efficient interaction between linguistic knowledge and knowledge of the world.

A full understanding of a text requires that the reader know two categories of schemata: content and formal schemata. **Content schemata** include what we know about people, the world, culture, and the universe, while **formal schemata** consist of our knowledge about language and discourse structure.

C Comprehension Level

Literal	focusing on information explicitly stated in the text
Reorganizational	organizing information explicitly stated in the text
Inferential	going beyond the immediate text
Evaluative	making judgements
Appreciative	responding emotionally and aesthetically

We often use Barrett Taxonomy's five levels of comprehension:

1) **Literal comprehension**

Literal comprehension focuses on information which is explicitly stated in the text. As you can imagine, there is a danger that this need not involve true understanding at all; it can be no more than a demand for the mechanical repetition of what is plainly in the text.

2) **Reorganizational comprehension**

At this level, the student has to organize for himself some of the information explicitly expressed. He may have to summarize information or handle it in a different sequence. For instance, if he has been told that B happened after A, he may be asked what happened before B.

3) **Inferential comprehension**

Here the student is required to go beyond the immediate text. He has to make use of his own experience and intuition, and possibly predict outcomes. A question set at this level might begin something like this: 'From what you have read do you think that Mr. Smith really wants to sell the house, or is he possibly being forced into it?'

4) **Evaluative comprehension**

This level of response requires the student to make judgements. These may require him to make use of his own knowledge of a particular subject. An appropriate question might begin: "To what extent do you think the writer has provided adequate support for his conclusion that ...?"

5) **Appreciative comprehension**

At this advanced level of response to a text the student has to be emotionally and aesthetically sensitive to what he is reading. It also requires some appreciation of literary techniques.

D Authenticity vs. Readability issues in Choosing Text

By now, the importance of authentic language should be more than clear. But in teaching reading, one issue that has invited some controversy is the advisability of what are called '**simplified text**', in which an otherwise authentic text is edited to keep language within the proficiency level of a set of students. In order for you to make a decision on this issue, it is important to distinguish between (a) simple texts and (b) simplified texts and to understand sources of complexity in reading material.

Authentic simple texts can either be devised or located in the real world. From ads to labels to reports to essays, texts are available that are grammatically and lexically simple. Simplifying an existing potential reading selection may not be necessary. Yet if simplification must be done, it is important to preserve the natural redundancy, humor, wit, and other captivating features of the original material.

Second, you might ask yourself what 'simplicity' is and then determine if a so-called simplified text is really simpler than its original. Sometimes simplified texts remove so much natural redundancy that they actually become difficult. And what you perceive as textual complexity may be more a product of background schemata than of linguistic complexity. Richard Day and Julian Bamford (1998), in warning against 'the cult of authenticity and the myth of simplification', contended that our CLT approach has overemphasized the need for so-called authenticity, and that there is indeed a place for simplified texts in reading instruction.

Christine Nuttall (1996) offered three criteria for choosing reading texts for students:

Suitability of content	Material that students will find interesting, enjoyable, challenging, and appropriate for their goals in learning English
Exploitability	A text that facilitates the achievement of certain language and content goals, that is exploitable for instructional tasks and techniques, and that is integratable with other skills (listening, speaking, writing)
Readability	A text with lexical and structural difficulty that will challenge students without overwhelming them

The benefit of simplified readers is that students are likely to encounter a reasonable number of new words.

E Process Reading (PWP)

Pre-reading tasks	drawing Ss' attention, making predictions by schema activation
While-reading tasks	reading with strategies by focusing on decoding skills
Post-reading tasks	expanding the knowledge by discussion and analysis of the text content
Follow-up	transferring strategies to other texts & integrating with other skills

1) Pre-reading

Pre-reading activities introduce students to a particular text, elicit or provide appropriate background knowledge, and activate necessary schemata. Previewing a text with students should arouse their interest and help them approach the text in a more meaningful and purposeful manner as the discussion compels them to think about the situation or points raised in a text. The pre-reading phase helps students define selection criteria for the central theme of a story or the major argument of an essay. Pre-reading activities include: discussing author or text type, brainstorming, reviewing familiar stories, considering illustrations and titles, skimming and scanning.

2) While-reading

While-reading exercises help students develop reading strategies, improve their control of the foreign language, and decode problematic text passages. Helping students to employ strategies while reading can be difficult because individual students control and need different strategies. Nevertheless, the teacher can pinpoint valuable strategies, explain which strategies individuals most need to practice, and offer concrete exercises in the form of 'guided reading' activity sheets. Such practice exercises might include guessing word meanings by using context clues, word formation clues, or cognate practice; considering syntax and sentence structure by noting the grammatical functions of unknown words, analyzing reference words, and predicting text content; reading for specific pieces of information; and learning to use the dictionary effectively.

3) Post-reading

Post-reading exercises first check students' comprehension and then lead students to a deeper analysis of the text, when warranted. Because the goals of most real world reading are not to memorize an author's point of view or to summarize text content, but rather to see into another mind, or to mesh new information into what one already knows, foreign language reading must go beyond detail-eliciting comprehension drills to help students recognize that different strategies are appropriate with different text types. For example, scanning is an appropriate strategy to use with newspaper advertisements whereas predicting and following text cohesion are effective strategies to use with short stories. By discussing in groups what they have understood, students focus on information they did not comprehend, or did not comprehend correctly. Discussions of this nature can lead the student directly to text analysis as class discussion proceeds from determining facts to exploring deeper ramifications of the texts.

4) Follow-up

Follow-up exercises take students beyond the particular reading text in one of two ways: by transferring reading skills to other texts or by integrating reading skills with other language skills (Phillips 1985). Transferable reading strategies are those that readers can assimilate and use with other texts. Exercises that emphasize the transfer of skills include beginning a new text similar to a text for which effective strategies have already been taught, i.e., giving students the front page of a newspaper to read after they have learned to read the table of contents of a journal. Integrative activities use text language and ideas in foreign language listening, speaking, and/or writing. Integrative skills exercises include such activities as students reacting to texts with summaries, new endings, or pastiches; reenacting text; carefully listening for key words or phrases in authentic video or audio tapes; and creating role-play situations or simulations of cultural experiences.

F Reading Techniques and Tasks

Intensive R	classroom-oriented activity (shorter text)
Extensive R	pleasure reading (longer text)
Skimming	quick reading to get the gist (main idea)
Scanning	quick reading to locate specific information
Semantic Mapping	grouping ideas into meaningful clusters
Think-aloud	verbalizing the thinking for inferences

F1 Intensive reading

Intensive reading is usually a classroom-oriented activity in which students focus on the linguistic or semantic details of a passage. Intensive reading calls students' attention to grammatical forms, discourse markers, and other surface structure details for the purpose of understanding literal meaning, implication, rhetorical relationships, etc.

F2 Extensive reading

Extensive reading is carried out to achieve a general understanding of a usually somewhat longer text. Most extensive reading is performed outside of class time. Pleasure reading is often extensive. Technical, scientific, and professional reading can, under certain special circumstances, be extensive when one is simply striving for global or general meaning from longer passages. Extensive reading can sometimes help learners get away from their tendency to overanalyze or look up words they don't know, and read for understanding.

F3 Skimming

Skimming refers to quickly running one's eyes across a whole text for its gist. Skimming gives readers the advantage of being able to predict the purpose of the passage, the main topic, or message, and possibly some of the developing or supporting ideas. This gives them a head start as they embark on more focused reading. You can train students to skim passages by giving them, say, 30 seconds, to look through a few pages of material, close their books, and then tell you what they learned.

F4 Scanning

Scanning refers to quickly searching for some particular piece or pieces of information in a text. Scanning exercises may ask students to look for names, or dates, to find a definition of a key concept, or to list a certain number of supporting details. The purpose of scanning is to extract specific information without reading through the whole text. For academic English, scanning is absolutely essential. In vocational or general English, scanning is important in dealing with genres like schedules, manuals, forms, etc.

F5 Semantic Mapping

The strategy of **semantic mapping**, or grouping ideas into meaningful clusters, helps the reader to provide some order to the chaos. Making such semantic maps can be done individually, but they make for a productive group work technique as students collectively induce order and hierarchy to a passage.

F6   Think-aloud

The teacher reads aloud to students and verbalizes the thinking he or she is doing in order to make inferences that help the teacher comprehend the text. Specifically:

1. Locate the evidence (stated facts) in the text from which one can reason.
2. Think out loud, showing students how to put together prior knowledge and the facts from the text to answer the question.
3. Model the inferencing procedure until the students can begin to take over the necessary steps, finally reasoning successfully on their own.

By modeling this skill, normally invisible thought processes are made clear to students. For example, the teacher reads the following text:

"Grizzly bears are found in western Canada and in Alaska, living in forests on mountain sides. They have shaggy fur, humped shoulders, sharp teeth and long, sharp claws ... Grizzlies usually live alone. Each bear has its own area of land, called a home range. It leaves scents on the bark of trees all the way around its home range to let other bears know where it lives."
[Wood, J. (1989). My first book of animals (p. 34). Boston, MA: Little, Brown.]

A portion of the teacher's **think-aloud** might be as follows:

"Humped shoulders? Hmmm. What do they mean by that? Oh, maybe when they're down on all fours; yeah, their backs are kind of like a hump then, okay, I get it!"

최시원 전공영어 영어교육학
English Education Conceptual

Chapter 10 MindMap

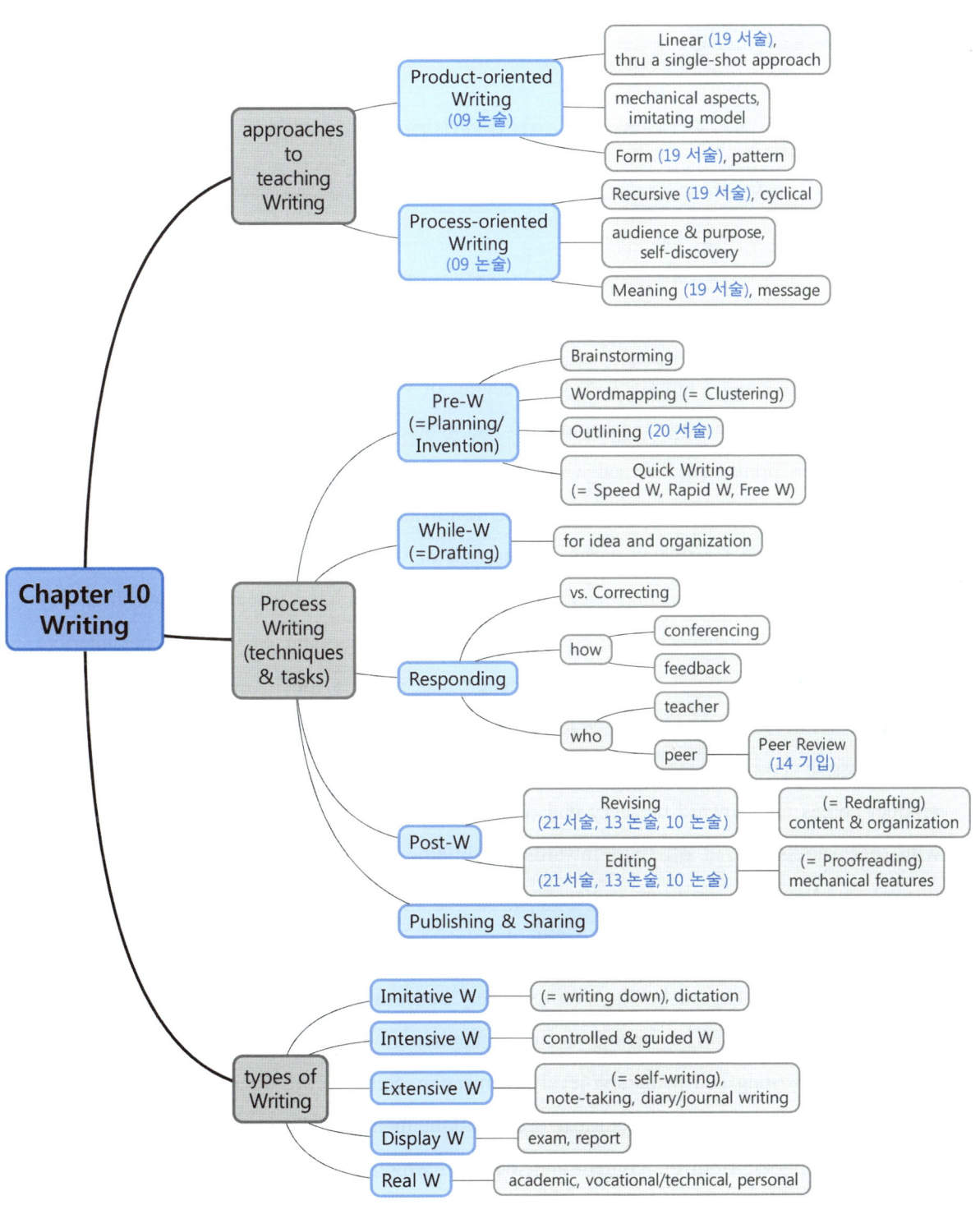

Chapter 10　Teaching Writing

A　Product- vs. Process-oriented Writing

Product-oriented Writing	Process-oriented Writing
linear, thru a single-shot approach mechanical aspects, imitating models form, pattern	cyclical, recursive audience & purpose, self-discovery meaning, message

The **product-oriented approach** to the teaching of writing emphasizes mechanical aspects of writing, such as focusing on grammatical and syntactical structures and imitating models. This approach is primarily concerned with 'correctness' and form of the final product. Moreover, this approach fails to recognize that people write for an audience and for a purpose and that ideas are created and formulated during the process of writing. However, the **process-oriented approach** emphasizes that writing itself is a developmental process that creates self-discovery and meaning. While the mechanical aspects of writing are important, they should not interfere with the composing process. This composing process requires much revision and rewriting. The teacher intervenes and guides students during the composing process but initially does not emphasize 'correctness' and the final product; the emphasis on 'correctness' and the final product comes only toward the very end of the writing process (and, often, a major concern with 'correctness' is put off until towards the middle or even end of the writing course). Instead of worrying about form, students concentrate on conveying a written message. Hence the product of writing will improve with the discovery involved in composing.

Product-oriented approaches to writing largely concern the forms of the written products that students compose. The writing exercises applied in this approach typically deal with sentence-level writing and paragraph-level organization. Students are often given a framework which illustrates a pattern of rhetorical organization; then, they are asked to fit their ideas into this framework. Both the content and the form which the students deal with are largely controlled by the teacher. Since the main focus of these approaches is on written form, grammar is emphasized and a particular effort is made to avoid errors.

Process-oriented approaches concern the process of how ideas are developed and formulated in writing. Writing is considered a process through which meaning is created. Student writers engage in their writing tasks through a cyclical approach rather than through a single-shot approach. In other words, these activities serve to encourage brainstorming, drafting, writing, feedback, revising, and editing in a cyclical fashion. This approach focuses on how clearly and efficiently a student can express and organize his ideas, not on correctness of form. The assumption is that what the student as a writer is going to say will become clearer through these processes. Students are also taught writing devices used in marking the organization and in making the general coherence clearer.

B Process Writing (PWP; Writing Techniques and Tasks)

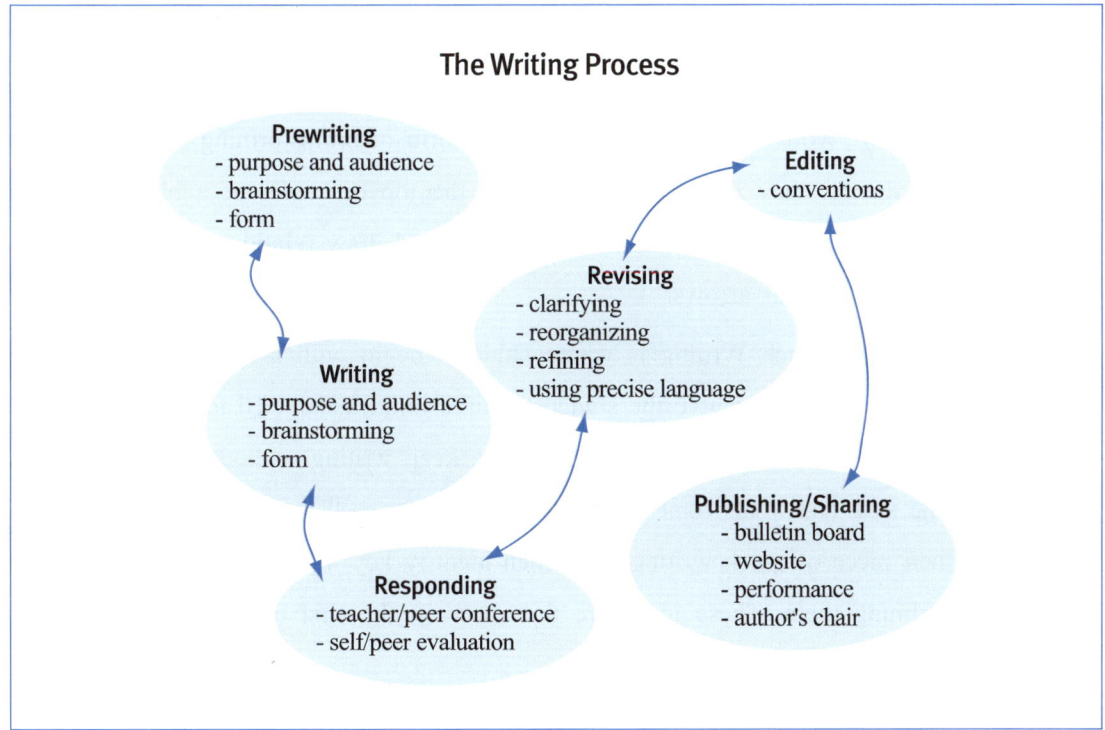

Pre-W	(= Planning / Invention)	Brainstorming
		Wordmapping (= Clustering), Outlining, …
		Quick Writing (= Speed W, Rapid W, Free W)
While-W	(= Drafting)	for ideas and organization
Responding (vs. Correcting) - conferencing & feedback / teacher & peer		
Post-W	Revising	(= Redrafting) for content & organization
	Editing	(= Proofreading) for mechanical features
Publishing & Sharing		

1) Pre-writing (Planning / Invention)

① **Brainstorming**: Brainstorming can be done individually or in pairs or groups of students. In a brainstorming session, students list all the ideas they can think of related to a topic, either in writing or aloud, quickly and without much planning. If no topic is given, then the student can brainstorm possible topics.

② **Wordmapping**: Wordmapping is a more visual form of brainstorming. When students create wordmaps, they begin with an idea at the top or center of a blank piece of paper. They then think of related ideas or words and draw relationships with a series of boxes, circles, and arrows.

③ **Quick Writing**: Quick Writing is where students begin with a topic, but then write rapidly about it. You can give the students a time limit, usually 10 to 15 minutes, and instruct them not to erase or cross out text, to keep writing without stopping, and to just let the ideas and words come out without concern for spelling, grammar, or punctuation. From their piece of quick writing, they then identify key ideas or interesting thoughts by underlining them. These ideas are then used in the first draft of their essays.

2) Writing (Drafting)

After students have developed their topics and ideas, it is time for them to write their first draft. Ample time should be given for the first draft, and students should be reminded that at this point, they need to focus on the development of ideas and the organization of those ideas more than the development of perfect grammar, punctuation, or spelling.

3) Responding

After the draft is handed in, the instructor can make comments, but only in keeping with the instructions given to students; make comments more on the ideas and organization than on the grammar and spelling. At this point, the instructor can also utilize peer feedback. Students exchange papers and provide each other with comments on the paper's contents. If peer commentary is used, it is best to use some kind of structured feedback form like the following.

Peer Comment written by _____ for _____

Read your partner's paper. Answer these questions:
1. Is the introduction effective? Explain your answer.
2. What is the author's main idea? Restate it here:
3. Does the writer support that idea with evidence? What is that evidence?
4. What evidence is missing, or incomplete?
5. What questions do you have about this writing?
6. Is the conclusion effective? How would you improve it?
7. Do you notice any grammar or word choice errors? Underline them.

Give this sheet back to your partner, and then discuss your answers.

---

4) Revising (Redrafting)

After students have received feedback, they then begin the process of revising their papers. Note that students often mistake the idea of revision with 'correcting mistakes', so you should spend time talking about the process of reorganization, developing ideas, and so forth, as separate from editing for grammar or spelling.

5) Editing (Proofreading)

Before the final draft is turned in for evaluation, students should, of course, read for mistakes in spelling, grammar, punctuation, and so forth. Students can help each other to proofread and edit, although the instructor should keep his/her involvement to a minimum. In developing independent writers, it is important that students learn to proofread and edit on their own as much as possible. And a teacher should not correct a student's draft by supplying all the correct forms of words, punctuation, and so forth. Students are often overwhelmed by the large amount of teacher's writing on their papers, and feel paralyzed by what looks like an immense number of 'errors'.

B1 Responding vs. Correcting

Responding	concerned with the content and design	conferencing: face to face
		feedback: thru paper
Correcting	concerned with the accuracy	

When responding to our students' work we are not only concerned with the accuracy of their performance but also — and this is crucial — with the content and design of their writing. We might respond, for example, to the order in which they have made their points ("Why did you start with the story about the bus that was late? You could have begun, instead, with the problem of public transport in general."). We might respond by saying how much we enjoyed reading their work — and then recommend that the student have a look at a book or website which has more information about the same topic. When responding, we are entering into a kind of affective dialogue with the students. That is, we are discussing their writing rather than judging it.

Correcting, on the other hand, is the stage at which we indicate when something is not right. We correct mistakes in the students' written performance on issues such as syntax (word order), concord (grammatical agreement between subjects and verbs), collocation (words which live together), or word choice.

B2 Peer Review

Peer review has the advantage of encouraging students to work collaboratively, something which, in a group, we want to foster. It also gets round the problem of students reacting too passively to teacher responses. Although there are occasions where teacher correction and feedback may be extremely useful, still we want to develop our students' ability to edit and revise when they are on their own.

Peer review, therefore, is less authoritarian than teacher review, and helps students to view both colleagues and teachers as collaborators rather than evaluators. However, in order for it to be successful, students will need guidance from their teacher so that they know what to look at when they read their classmates' work.

Peer review is not problem-free, however. In the first place, some students who rely on the teacher's approval may resent it, valuing their colleagues' opinions much less than their teacher's. Secondly, not all students work well together; the success of peer review may depend on exactly who is the reviewer and whose work is being reviewed. Finally, if students are not focused on the task, the quality of the feedback they have to offer may be questionable. Nevertheless, despite these dangers, getting students to help each other in the editing process can be extremely useful when handled in a sensitive and encouraging way.

C Types of Writing Performance

Imitative W	(= mechanical writing), dictation
Intensive W	controlled & guided writing, dicto-comp
Extensive W	(= self-writing), note-taking, diary/journal writing
Display W	exam, report
Real W	academic, vocational/technical, personal

1) Imitative or Mechanical Writing

At the beginning level of learning to write, students will simply 'write down' English letters, words, and possibly sentences in order to learn the conventions of the orthographic code. Several types of classroom techniques such as recognition techniques, copying, sound-spelling practice, and dictation.

One effective technique for practicing sound-spelling correspondences as well as reinforcing grammatical and discourse features is dictation. Dictations typically involve the teacher reading (aloud) a short passage, rereading it in segments, pausing for students to write what they hear, reading it through a third time, and then checking written responses for accuracy.

2) Intensive (Controlled) Writing

Writing is sometimes used as a production mode for learning, reinforcing, or testing grammatical concepts. This intensive writing typically appears in controlled, written grammar exercises. This type of writing does not allow much, if any, creativity on the part of the learner.

A common form of controlled writing is to present a paragraph to students in which they have to alter a given structure throughout. So, for example, they may be asked to change all present tense verbs to past tense; in such a case, students may need to alter other time references in the paragraph.

Guided writing loosens the teacher's control but still offers a series of stimulators. For example, the teacher might get students to tell a story just viewed on a videotape by asking them a series of questions: *Where does the story take place? Describe the principal character. What does he say to the woman in the car?*

Yet another form of controlled writing is a **dicto-comp**. Here, a paragraph is read at normal speed, usually two or three times; then the teacher asks students to rewrite the paragraph to the best of their recollection of the reading. In one of several variations of the dicto-comp technique, the teacher, after reading the passage, puts key words from the paragraph, in sequence, on the chalkboard as cues for the students.

3) Self-writing

A significant proportion of classroom writing may be devoted to self-writing, or writing with only the self in mind as an audience. The most salient instance of this category in classrooms is note taking, where students take notes during a lecture for the purpose of later recall. Other note taking may be done in the margins of books, through digital notes and highlights, as portfolio entries, and simply on notepaper filed for easy access later on.

Diary or journal writing also falls into this category. However, in many circumstances a **dialogue journal**, in which a student records thoughts, feelings, and reactions and which an instructor reads and responds to, while ostensibly written for oneself, has two audiences.

4) Display Writing

Writing within the school curricular context is a way of life. For all language students, short-answer exercises, essay examinations, and even research reports will involve an element of display. For academically bound ESL students, one of the academic skills that they need to master is a whole array of display writing techniques.

5) Real Writing

While virtually every classroom writing task will have an element of display writing in it, some classroom writing aims at the genuine communication of messages to an audience in need of those messages. The two categories of real and display writing are actually two ends of a continuum, and in between the two extremes lies some combination of display and real writing. Three subcategories illustrate how reality can be injected:

a. **Academic**: Group problem-solving tasks, especially those that relate to specific disciplinary themes along with personally relevant topics, may have a writing component in which information is genuinely sought and conveyed. Peer-editing work adds to what would otherwise be an audience of one (the instructor) and provides real writing opportunity. In many academic courses, students may exchange new information (that they have written about) with each other, and/or present findings from written work to the rest of the class, adding the reality of an audience.

b. **Vocational/technical**: Quite a variety of real writing can take place in classes of students studying an L2 for advancement in their occupation. Real letters can be written; genuine directions for some operation or assembly might be given; and actual forms can be filled out. These possibilities are even greater in workplace language courses, where an L2 is offered within companies and corporations.

c. **Personal**: In virtually any L2 class, diaries, letters, post cards, notes, personal messages, and other informal writing can take place, especially within the context of an interactive classroom. While certain tasks may be somewhat contrived, nevertheless the genuine exchange of information can happen.

최시원 전공영어 영어교육학
English Education Conceptual

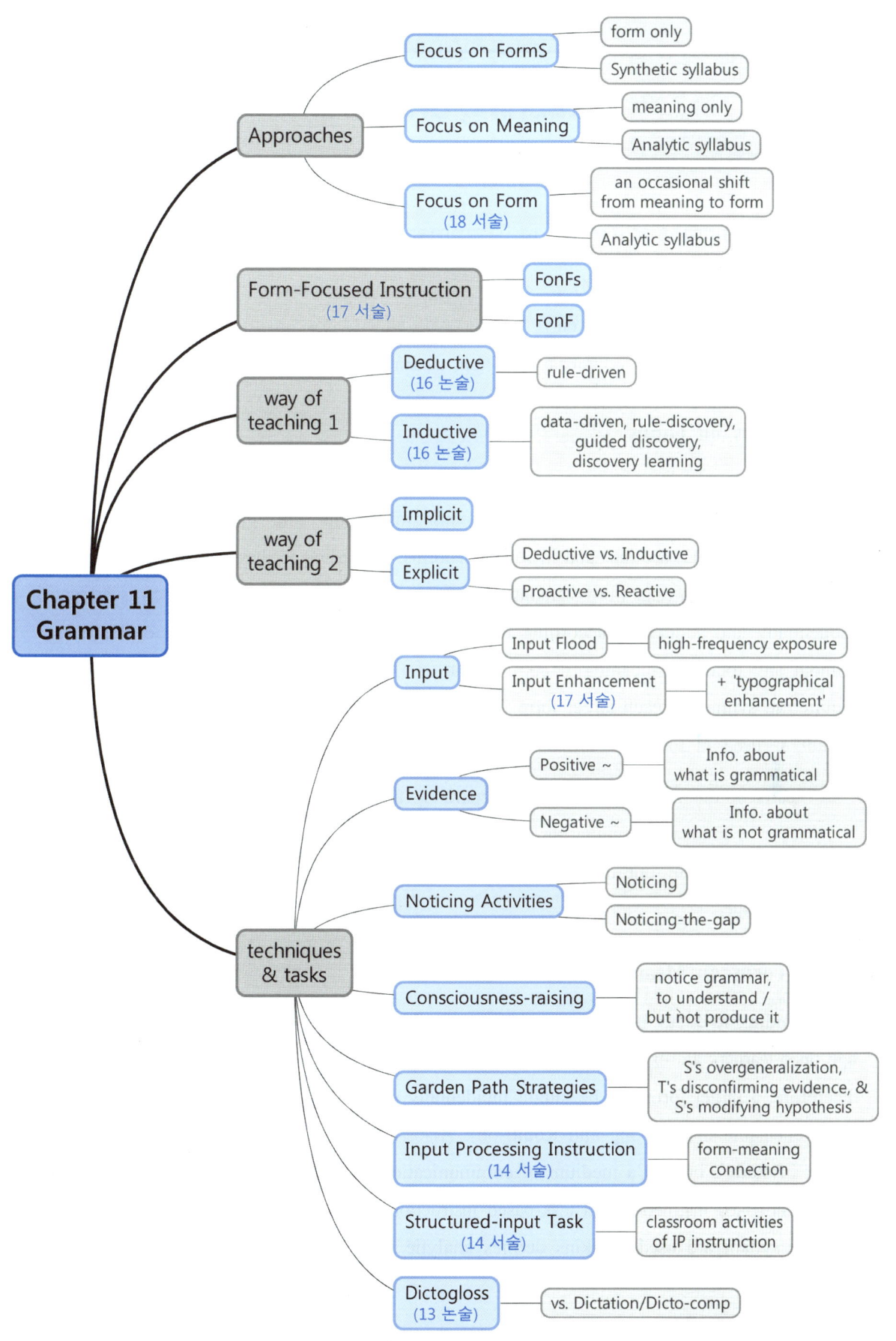

Chapter 11 Teaching Grammar

A Approaches to Teaching Grammar & FFI

Focus on Forms	form only
Focus on Meaning	meaning only
Focus on Form	an occasional shift from meaning to form

→ FFI

A1 Focus on Forms

Focus on forms refers to the traditional approach in which only linguistic forms are taught explicitly without communication and meaningful input. The grammar-translation and audio-lingual methods are included in focus on forms. According to these traditional approaches, a discrete target form (e.g. words, grammar rules, intonation and stress patterns, etc.) is presented sequentially and additively, according to 'such criteria as valence, difficulty, or frequency' without any focus on meaningful communication (Long and Robinson). Then, learners are required to synthesize each target form for communication by themselves; therefore, synthetic syllabi, is used in focus on forms. Wilkins defines synthetic syllabi as follows:

> ⋯ parts of the language are taught separately and step by step so that acquisition is a process of gradual accumulation of parts until the whole structure of language has been built up ⋯ At any one time the learner is being exposed to a deliberately limited sample of language.

A2 Focus on Meaning

According to **focus on meaning**, however, a L2 can be acquired naturally regardless of age once learners are exposed to sufficient comprehensible input like first language acquisition. Therefore, a target form can be taught incidentally and implicitly with the help of repetitive comprehensible input (Long and Robinson). Also, a language should not be treated 'as an object of study', but 'as a medium of communication' as found in CLT methodologies such as content-based instruction and task-based instruction. For this reason, unlike focus on forms, analytic syllabi are used. Wilkins defines analytic syllabi as follows:

… prior analysis of the total language system into a set of discrete pieces of language that is a necessary precondition for the adoption of a synthetic approach is largely superfluous. Analytic approaches … are organized in terms of the purposes for which people are learning language and the kinds of language performance that are necessary to meet those purposes.

> ### Problems Associated with Focus on Forms and Focus on Meaning
> Nassaji and Fotos argue that both focus on forms and focus on meaning are problematic. In focus on forms, learners are only required to accumulate discrete grammar items without using a language for communication; therefore, they fail to improve communicative competence. On the other hand, in focus on meaning, learners can improve fluency through verbal interaction and meaningful input. However, learners cannot improve accuracy because of reduced or absent attention to linguistic forms they receive during a class. In addition to these insufficiencies, the results of the Canadian immersion studies show that learners often used fossilized forms of a language even though they did not have difficulty expressing their overall intentions. In short, Doughty and Williams assert, "Neither forms-based instruction nor meaning-based instruction alone can lead to complete SLA".

A3   Focus on Form

In order to solve the problems, Michael Long introduced the **focus on form** approach in order to maintain the strength of focusing on meaning while dealing with the limitations of the traditional focus on forms approach and CLT's focus on meaning (Long and Robinson). According to Long, the distinguishing factor in focus on form is that '[focus on form] overtly draws students' attention to linguistic elements as they arise incidentally in lessons whose overriding focus is on meaning or communication'. This focus on form definition was redefined by Long and Robinson as follows:

> Focus on form often consists of an occasional shift of attention to linguistic code features — by the teacher and/or one or more students — triggered by perceived problems with comprehension or production. … The usual and fundamental orientation is to meaning and communication.

Long explains focus on form as follows, "A syllabus with a focus on form teaches something else — biology, mathematics, workshop practice, automobile repair, the geography of the country where the foreign language is spoken, the cultures of its speakers, and so on." Therefore, focus on form adopts analytic syllabi, and task-based instruction and content-based instruction are included in focus on form (Long and Robinson).

Focus on form has been explained and referred to differently by scholars. According to Long, most of the grammatical features can be naturally acquired through exposure to meaningful input (Doughty and Williams). Therefore, he believes focus on form should be applied when learners only make 'repetitive', 'pervasive', and 'remedial' errors as 'a reaction to linguistic problems that occur during communicative activities' (Long, 'Focus on Form'). In short, Long's focus on form is considered 'reactive focus on form'. On the other hand, Doughty and Williams suggest a proactive focus on form which is in contrast with Long's reactive focus on form. Proactive focus on form means that a teacher expects the learners' possible language problems and prepares pedagogical materials or methods before a class (Doughty and Williams).

A4   FFI

Rod Ellis, moreover, presents a broader perspective on focus on form by introducing **form-focused instruction** (FFI). He explains form-focused instruction as follows:

> FFI is used to refer to any planned or incidental instructional activity that is intended to induce language learners to pay attention to linguistic form ⋯ Thus, FFI includes both traditional approaches to teaching forms based on structural syllabi and more communicative approaches, where attention to form arises out of activities that are primarily meaning-focused ("Investigating Form-Focused").

In summary, Ellis' form-focused instruction contains not only focus on form but also focus on forms. He also accepts the importance of proactive focus on form like Doughty and Williams.

B Deductive vs. Inductive teaching

Deductive teaching	rule-driven
Inductive teaching	data-driven, rule-discovery, guided discovery, discovery learning

A **deductive teaching** starts with the presentation of a rule and is followed by examples in which the rule is applied, while an **inductive teaching** starts with some examples from which a rule is inferred.

In the deductive classroom, the teacher gives a grammatical explanation or rule followed by a set of exercises designed to clarify the grammatical point and help the learners master the point. In deductive teaching, you work from principles to examples. Inductive procedures reverse this process. In inductive teaching, you present the learners with samples of language and through a process of **guided discovery**, get them to work out the principle or rule for themselves.

So, which is better, deductive or inductive teaching? The answer is — it depends. It depends on the grammar point being taught, and the learning style of the student. For example, the disadvantage of an inductive approach is that it takes more time for learners to come to an understanding of the grammatical point in question than with a deductive approach. However, inductive techniques appear to result in learners retaining more of the language in the long term. In place of terms deductive and inductive, it may be easier to use the terms **rule-driven learning** and **discovery learning** respectively.

C Techniques and Tasks in teaching grammar

C1 Input Flood(ing) vs. Input Enhancement & Positive vs. Negative Evidence

Input flood	high-frequency exposure to a particular form w/o grammar teaching
Input enhancement	'typographical enhancement' added to input flood

Positive evidence	Information about what is grammatical in the L2
Negative evidence	Information about what is not grammatical in the L2

(C1a) Input flood

In **input flood**, efforts have been made to draw second language learners' attention to language forms in the input, for example, by providing high-frequency exposure to specific language features without teaching grammar points or any error correction. In this technique, students simply read the passages and complete a variety of comprehension activities based on them.

Although learners benefited from this exposure to specific features, their learning was incomplete (Trahey & White 1991). It is found that the input flood could help them add something new to their interlanguage, but did not lead them to get rid of an error based on their L1. White argued that although exposure to language input provides learners with **positive evidence** (information about what is grammatical in the second language), it fails to give them **negative evidence** (information about what is not grammatical). Positive evidence is not enough to permit learners to notice the absence in the target language of elements that are present in their interlanguage (and their L1). Thus, more explicit information about what is not grammatical in the L2 may be necessary for learners' continued development.

(C1b) Input enhancement

Michael Sharwood Smith (1993) coined the term '**input enhancement**' to refer to a variety of things that might draw learners' attention to features in the second language, thus increasing the chances that they would be learned. The major difference between the two is that typographical enhancement was added. In input enhancement, the text was in bold type, underlined, italicized, or written in capital letters. White compared the performance of learners who had read the typographically enhanced passages with that of learners who read the same texts without enhancement. She found that learners made more progress when they were given a simple rule and then worked together to find the correct possessive determiners like in the following example.

> (For third person singular possessive determiner)
> Once upon a time there was a king. *He* had a beautiful young daughter. For *her* birthday, the king gave *her* a golden ball that *she* played with every day. The king and *his* daughter lived near a dark forest. ...

C2 Noticing activities

The noticing hypothesis suggests that unless learners notice the way language is used, their grammatical proficiency will not develop. Noticing can be the focus of activities such as the following:

> An example of a guided noticing activity is for the teacher to give out extracts from texts (e.g. magazine or newspaper articles) and to ask students to see how many examples they can find of a particular form or grammatical pattern. These are then examined more closely to observe the functions they perform at both the sentence and text level.

C3 Consciousness-raising tasks

Consciousness-raising activities are designed to get learners to notice a particular grammatical feature or principle. However, learners are not required to produce the target structures. Instead, students are made aware of the target grammatical item through discovery-oriented tasks.

> Study the following examples, and work out the rule for the correct order of direct and indirect objects in English.
>
> We took a gift for the teacher.
> We took the teacher a gift.
> He recited a poem for his girlfriend.
> He recited his girlfriend a poem.

C4 Garden Path Strategies

Garden path strategies could be considered rather cruel. In order to encourage students to process the target structure somewhat more deeply than they might otherwise do, the task is set up to get students to overgeneralize. It thus leads them into error. This is a technique based on inductive learning. Students study examples of the language and come to a hypothesis or generalization. The generalization is too broad. They are given disconfirming evidence and then have to modify their hypothesis.

> T: Look at these examples for forming superlative adjectives. (Writes on the board: cute → the cutest; grand → the grandest.) Now make superlatives out of 'beautiful', 'outrageous', 'expensive'... OK, now, what have you written? Sonia?
>
> S: Beautifulest, outrageousest, expensivest.
>
> T: No, for these words, the superlative forms are 'the most beautiful', 'the most outrageous', and 'the most expensive'. Now, I want you to get into groups and figure out the rule. ...... Who thinks they have the answer? Jose's group.
>
> S: It's about how big the word is. If it's a big word, you use 'most'.
>
> T: Big. Hmm. How do we measure the size of words?
>
> S: The number of syllables.
>
> T: The number of syllables. OK. And how many syllables do 'beautiful', 'outrageous', and 'expensive' have?
>
> S: Three.
>
> T: Three. OK. So, who can state the rule?
>
> S: Adjectives with three syllables form the superlative with 'most'.

C5 Input Processing Instruction & Structured-input Task

VanPatten (1996) argued that the main goal in IP approach 'is to alter the processing strategies that learners take to the task of comprehension and to encourage them to make better form–meaning connections than they would if left to their own devices'. **Processing Instruction** is therefore a deliberate instructional intervention predicated on VanPatten's model of input processing. When learners receive or are exposed to input, they tend to rely on internal strategies (called principles in VanPatten's input processing model) to process the input. (Figure 1) As a result of their internal processing they might not be able to make correct form–meaning connections. As underscored by Wong (2004) 'the goal of Processing Instruction is to help L2 learners derive richer intake from input by having them engage in structured input activities that push them away from the strategies they normally use to make form–meaning connections'.

The three main components of Processing Instruction are as follows:

1. Learners are provided with explicit information about the target form or structure.

Figure 1. Basic principles and its sub-principles in Input Processing Approach

Principle 1. *The Primacy of Meaning Principle.* Learners process input for meaning before they process it for form.

Principle 1a. *The Primacy of Content Words Principle*: Learners process content words in the input before anything else.

Principle 1b. *The Lexical Preference Principle*: Learners will tend to rely on lexical items as opposed to grammatical form to get meaning when both encode the same semantic information.

Principle 1c. *The Preference for Non-redundancy Principle*: Learners are more likely to process non-redundant meaningful grammatical form before they process redundant meaningful forms.

Principle 1d. *The Meaning-Before-Non-meaning Principle*: Learners are more likely to process meaningful grammatical forms before non-meaningful forms irrespective of redundancy.

Principle 1e. *The Availability of Resources Principle*: For learners to process either redundant meaningful grammatical forms or non-meaningful forms, the processing of overall sentential meaning must not drain available processing resources.

Principle 1f. *The Sentence Location Principle*: Learners tend to process items in sentence initial position before those in final position and those in medial position.

Principle 2. *The First Noun Principle.* Learners tend to process the first noun or pronoun they encounter in a sentence as the subject/agent.

Principle 2a. *The Lexical Semantics Principle*: Learners may rely on lexical semantics, where possible, instead of on word order to interpret sentences.

Principle 2b. *The Event Probabilities Principle*: Learners may rely on event probabilities, where possible, instead of on word order to interpret sentences.

Principle 2c. *The Contextual Constraint Principle*: Learners may rely less on the First Noun Principle if preceding context constrains the possible interpretation of a clause or sentence.

Principle 2d. *Prior Knowledge*: Learners may rely on prior knowledge, where possible, to interpret sentences.

Principle 2e. *Grammatical Cues*: Learners will adopt other processing strategies for grammatical role assignment only after their developing system has incorporated other cues.

2. Learners are provided with information about processing strategies, both the inappropriate or inefficient one that they tend to use to process the target form or structure in the input as well as the appropriate one on which they will receive practice.

3. Learners are provided with structured input activities, practices designed to help learners abandon the inappropriate or inefficient processing strategy and make correct and appropriate form-meaning connections.

In Figure 2 we offer an example of explicit information. Here, the L2 learners are provided with more information on the processing strategy that may negatively affect the way they process the targeted form during exposure to input. Learners must be made aware of the processing strategy that they would use to process a form or a structure of the target language. For example, a common processing strategy used by L2 learners when they process input is the tendency to rely on temporal adverbs and temporal lexical markers to establish the time frame rather than processing the verbal morphology. Quite simply, if learners do not process the verbal morphology they will not acquire it.

Figure 2. Explicit information and information about the processing problem

Explicit Information

The past simple tense is one of the tenses most used to talk about events in the past. It refers to finished actions and events. Very often the Past Simple Tense ends in -ed:

> I invited John for lunch. / I played tennis with Paula.

When you talk about a finished time in the past, the English Past Simple Tense is often accompanied by a temporal adverb.

> Yesterday I smoked 20 cigarettes.

Information about the processing problem

Do not rely on the temporal adverb to understand when the action takes place as sometimes you can hear a sentence without the temporal adverb. You must pay attention to the tense ending to understand when the action takes place. In the case of describing past events pay attention to the ending of the verb: -ed.

After receiving the explicit information about the targeted linguistic feature and the information about the processing principle affecting that feature, learners are provided with different types of **structured input activities** in which the input is structured in such a way that they are pushed to process forms (in the case of the previous example, verb forms) to understand the meaning of the sentence (in the previous example, to determine the temporal reference of the sentence). In structured input activities the input is manipulated in particular ways to push learners to become dependent on form and structure to get meaning. For example, whenever we have created structured input activities for temporal verb morphology, we never include temporal lexical markers in the input. Learners only have the verb morphology to use to process the temporal framework.

In the activity seen in Figure 3, the learners' only cue to the temporal framework is the form of the verb. They must attend to the verb form to decide which part of David Beckham's life the statement refers to.

Figure 3. Structured Input Activity

David Beckham: Before and Now

<Step 1>

Listen to the following statements made by a journalist about the life of the footballer David Beckham and decide whether each statement is referring to his past life as a Manchester United Player in England or his life now as Real Madrid Player in Spain.

	MANCHESTER UNITED PLAYER (PAST)	REAL MADRID PLAYER (NOW)
1		
2		
3		
4		
5		

David Beckham ... (Sentences heard:)

1) ... receives a lot of money from advertising.
2) ... donated money to charities.
3) ... reserved more time for his family.
4) ... talked with many world leaders.
5) ... plays football with his son.

<Step 2>

Now read the sentences you have just listened to and decide if David Beckham was more famous when he was a Manchester United Player or a Real Madrid Player.

C6 Dictogloss (Grammar Dictation)

A *dictogloss* is a form of dictation, but one in which the students hear and reconstruct the whole text, rather than doing so line by line. Unlike traditional dictation, where the text is read and transcribed clause-by-clause or sentence-by-sentence, the dictogloss technique requires learners to process the whole text at once. To do this, they have to capture the meaning of the text, although they may not be able to recall the exact forms in which that meaning is conveyed. That is, they understand the teacher's account of his holidays, but they don't have a word-for-word memory of exactly what he said. So, when it comes to reconstructing the meaning of the text, they tend to draw on forms which they are already familiar with (e.g. *we drove* rather than *we'd drive*). When they compare their version of the text with the original version, they are well-positioned to notice the difference between how they expressed the meaning and how the teacher himself expressed it. The difference between *we drove* and *we'd drive* is one instance of the difference between their grammar and the teacher's (or target) grammar. It is important for the learner to notice the differences for themselves in order for them to make the necessary adjustments to their mental grammar.

It is essential, therefore, that the text should be short, and within their general level of competence — apart, that is, from the inclusion of the targeted language form. For this activity, therefore, prepared texts will probably work better than authentic ones. But the delivery should aim for authenticity. It is also important that learners are given a chance to collaborate on the reconstruction. The discussions they have at this stage about the appropriacy and accuracy of language forms are a valuable awareness-raising opportunity.

An example of a dictogloss is the following:

1. Learners discuss the sea.
2. The teacher then explains the task, and reads a short text on the sea to the class, who just listen.
3. The teacher reads the text again and the learners take notes.
4. In groups, the learners then reconstruct the text. In this activity, learners are required to reconstruct a short text by listening and noting down key words, which are then used as a base for reconstruction.

Chapter 12 MindMap

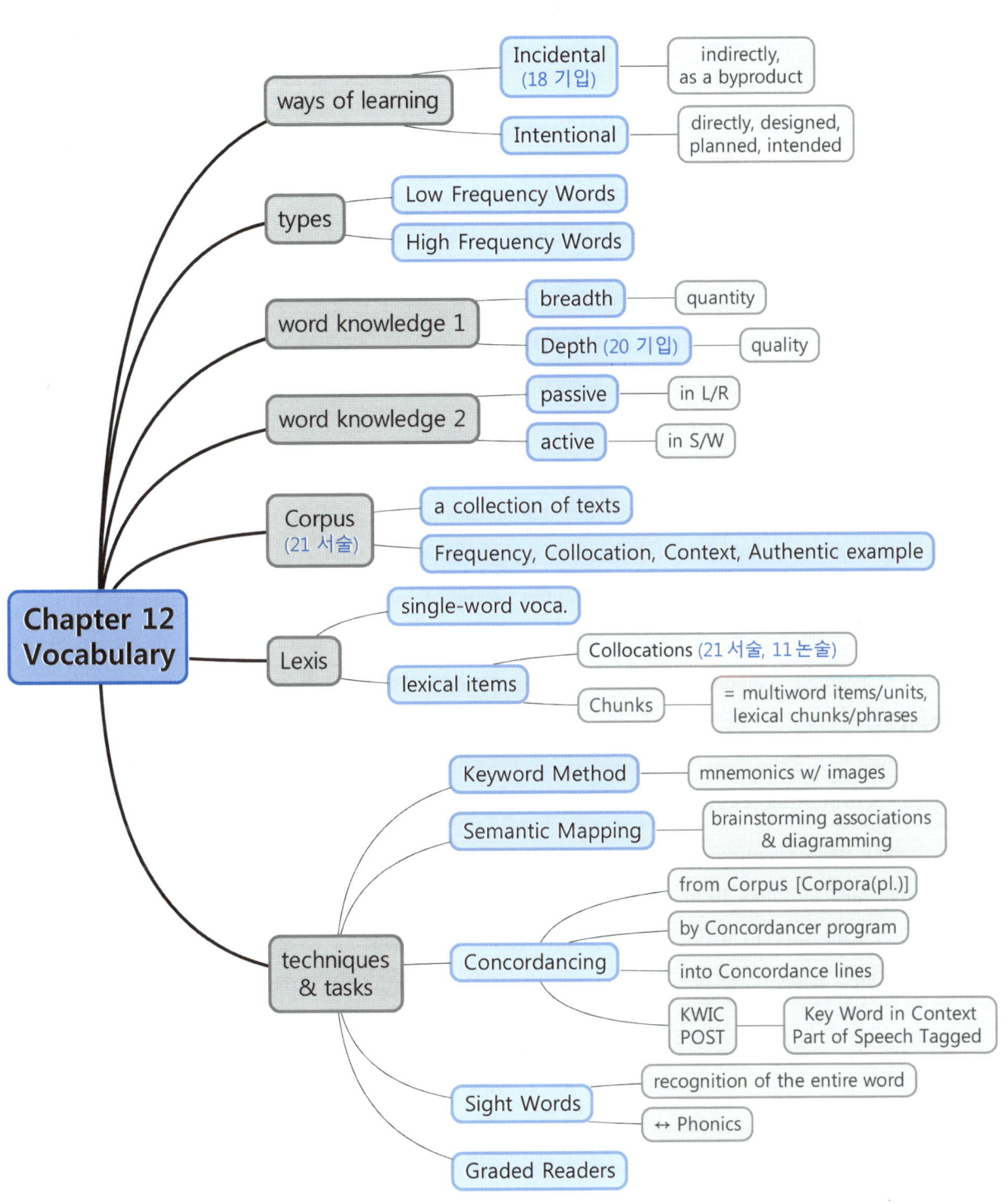

Chapter 12 Teaching Vocabulary

A Incidental vs. Intentional learning

Incidental learning	indirectly, as a byproduct
Intentional learning	(≒ explicit learning) directly, designed, planned, or intended

In L2 lexical teaching and learning, there are two types of vocabulary learning: incidental learning and intentional learning. **Incidental learning** is defined as the type of learning that is a byproduct of doing or learning something else; whereas, **intentional learning** is defined as being designed, planned for, or intended by teacher or students. In terms of vocabulary learning, incidental learning always means the approach of learning vocabulary through texts, working on tasks or doing other activities that are not directly related to vocabulary. In contrast, the intentional learning always focuses on vocabulary itself, and combines with all kinds of conscious vocabulary learning strategies and means of memorizing words. Vocabulary form, collocation, parts of speech are mainly the results of incidental learning, while the sense of a word, meaning symbolizing and innuendo between words need intentional learning (Nation 1990).

A1 Combining explicit teaching with incidental learning

In any well-structured vocabulary program, there needs to be the proper mix of explicit teaching and activities from which incidental learning can occur. With true beginners, it is probably necessary to explicitly teach all words until students have enough vocabulary to start making use of the unknown words they meet in context.

Beyond this most basic level, incidental learning should be structured into the program in a principled way. This is important for at least two reasons: meeting a word in different contexts enhances what is known about it (improving quality of knowledge), and the additional exposures help consolidate it in memory. Taking an incremental view of vocabulary acquisition, such enhancement and consolidation are both crucial. Explicit approaches to vocabulary learning, whether teacher-led in a classroom or through self-study, can only provide some elements of lexical knowledge. Even lexical information amenable to conscious study, like meaning, cannot be totally mastered by explicit study, because it is impossible to present and practice all of the creative uses of a word which a student might come across. Other types of lexical knowledge, such as collocation or connotation nuances, can only be fully grasped through numerous exposures to the word in various contexts. Therefore, explicit and incidental approaches are both necessary in the course of learning vocabulary.

A2　Vocabulary Knowledge

There are many words to know and many details to be known about each word. I. S. P. Nation (1990) sheds light on the word-learning task, suggesting that word knowledge includes the mastery of the word's:

- Meaning(s): What does the word mean? Are there multiple meanings? Are there connotations (implied additional meanings)?

- Written form: What does the word look like? How is it spelled?

- Spoken form: What does it sound like? How is it pronounced?

- Grammatical behavior: In what patterns does it occur?

- Collocations: What words are often used before or after the word. Are there certain words we must use with this word?

- Register: Is the word formal or informal? Where can I expect to hear it or use it?

- Associations: How does this word relate to other words? What words could we use in place of this one?

- Frequency: Is this word common? Is it rare? Old-fashioned?

This knowledge about the aspects of each word is referred to as **vocabulary depth**. But vocabulary depth is not language learners' only concern. In addition, they need to know an enormous number of words, referred to as **vocabulary breadth**. Word knowledge is further described by distinguishing between **receptive knowledge** (recognizing a word in reading or listening) and **productive knowledge** (using a word in writing and speaking).

B Corpus

A **corpus** (plural '**corpora**') is a collection of texts that has been assembled for the purposes of language study. Modern corpora are stored electronically and consist of many millions of words of text, both spoken and written. They range from academic texts through newspaper articles to casual conversation, and include American, British, Australian, teenager, and even learner varieties of English.

Corpus information is typically presented in the form of concordances. A **concordance** displays the results of a word search as individual lines of text, with the targeted word (or words) aligned in the center. Concordances are a convenient way of presenting learners with data for analysis, from which they can work out the regularities and patterns associated with selected words.

Another useful tool when dealing with corpus material is a **keyword program**. (Note that this is a different sense of keyword from a memory technique.) Keywords are words in the text that are not just frequent, but significantly so. For example, the fact that the most frequent word in a given text is 'the' is of little significance. 'The' is the most frequent word in almost any text. A keyword, on the other hand, is a word in a text that occurs more often in that particular text than it does across a whole range of text. A keyword program is able to plot the keywords in a text simply by comparing the text with a large corpus of text. When choosing words to pre-teach in advance of reading, a teacher need look no farther than the keywords. Also, giving learners the keywords of a text in advance of their reading the text is an excellent way of activating their knowledge. Once activated, this knowledge allows them to make better sense of the text. Also, keywords can become the focus for a concordance search, especially those words that have particular collocational or grammatical characteristics.

C Lexis

Lexis	single-word voca.	ex) dog, green, wash	
	Collocations	ex) pass the exam	lexical items
	Chunks	(= multiword items/units, lexical chunks/phrases) ex) it's up to you	

C1 Lexis

An influential book, *The Lexical Approach* by Michael Lewis published in 1993, had a significant impact on the profession in raising awareness of the importance of lexis and of the weaknesses of much classroom vocabulary work. So what is lexis? I'll give some definitions, but first it may be useful to see why there is a need for these different words.

> Which of the following items would you consider appropriate for inclusion in a lexis / vocabulary lesson (as opposed to, for example, a grammar lesson)?
>
> *computer, water, stock market, go off, pass the exam, swim against the tide, it's up to you*

In **swim against the tide**, the four words have a specific, definable meaning (perhaps in another language it could be said in a single word). It is listed in dictionaries (sometimes classed as an *idiom*). Do we need to teach this as a fixed chunk of language? It seems to be a four-word lexical item — a single unit of meaning that requires four words to be expressed. If we change any one of the words, we lose the familiar chunk — *swim along the tide* or *divide against the tide* don't seem work in the same way. Similar chunks are ***jump on the band-wagon, kick the bucket, paint the town red, put two and two together, have both feet on the ground,*** etc.

Pass the exam doesn't have quite the same kind of separate identity. The *exam* and *pass* seem more separable, ie we can think of lots of alternative words that could equally well go in front of *exam*. All the same, it's clear that *pass* very often goes together with *exam* (as do ***fail, take, enter*** and a few other words). These are all common **collocation** with *exam*, ie words that typically go together with that word. These are not fixed lexical items, but probable, common collocations.

A more difficult problem is provided by expressions such as ***It's up to you***. Is this a single lexical item, or is it a sentence that a speaker (knowing the rules of grammar) constructs afresh every time he needs it? Consider some other examples: ***it's all the same to me, what on earth ···, minding my own business, funny you should say that, sorry I'm late, wouldn't you rather ···, it'll do,*** etc. These items would probably not be found in most dictionaries, but, all the same, they do seem to have an element of being fixed items, in the same way that individual words do. It is now generally believed that native speakers do not construct expressions of this type word by word, but rather extract ready-made **chunks** of language from an internal store and then put them together with other language items in order to express complete meanings.

C2 The relationship among lexis, vocabulary, and grammar

① **Vocabulary** typically refers mainly to single words (eg ***dog, green, wash***) and sometimes to very tightly linked two- or three-word combinations (eg ***stock market, compact disc, sky blue, go off***).

② The concept of **lexis** is bigger. It refers to our 'internal database' of words and complete 'ready-made' fixed / semi-fixed / typical combinations of words that we can recall and use quite quickly without having to construct new phrases and sentences word by word from scratch using our knowledge of grammar. Lexis includes:

> a) Traditional single-word vocabulary items;
> b) Common 'going-together patterns' of words. These frequent combinations are known as collocation;
> c) Longer combinations of words that are typically used together as if they were a single item. These longer combinations (which a few years ago would probably not have been considered as anything remotely related to vocabulary) are commonly referred to as chunks or sometimes as multiword items.
> (Categories (b) and (c) are both classed as lexical items.)

③ **Grammar** refers to the generalisable patterns of the language and to our ability to construct new phrases and sentences out of word combinations and grammatical features (verb endings, etc) to express a precise (and probably unique) meaning.

We could argue that collocations and chunks occupy an intermediate zone between vocabulary and grammar.

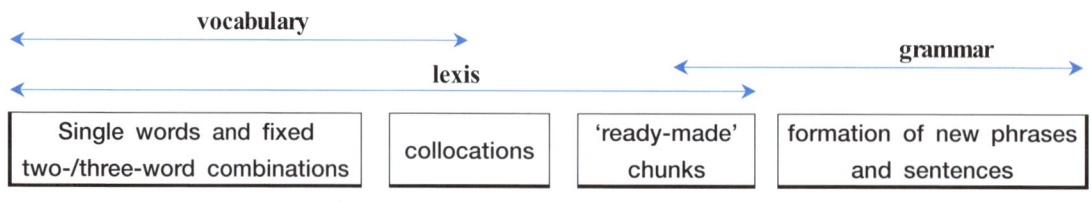

<vocabulary, lexis, and grammar>

Having said that, most teachers still use the terms vocabulary and lexis fairly interchangeably. Similarly, as the term lexical item is quite a mouthful, staff-room chat tends to avoid it, referring instead to words, collocations and chunks.

D Techniques and Tasks in teaching vocabulary

keyword method	a mnemonic technique using pronunciation and image
semantic mapping	brainstorming association & diagramming the results
concordancing	a process of looking at relationships among words
sight words	bottom-up, recognizing an entire word (↔ phonics: sounding out the word)
graded readers	with limited vocabulary, for extensive R, R for pleasure

D1 Keyword Method

Techniques for remembering things are called mnemonics. The best mnemonics have a visual element; are self-generated, i.e. not 'borrowed' from another learner or the teacher. The best-known mnemonic technique is called the **keyword technique**. This involves devising an image that typically connects the pronunciation of the second language word with the meaning of a first language word. For example, when I was learning the Maori word '*te aroha* (love)' the word sounded a little like the English word 'arrow + -er', so I pictured Cupid with a bow and arrow.

Devising keyword takes time, and a certain amount of training. Indeed, it can take more time and training than some practitioners think it is worth. However, the research evidence is compelling: there seems to be no other single technique that works as well. Therefore, when teaching new vocabulary items, it may be a good idea to allow learners a few minutes to silently and individually devise keywords. Then, if you ask them to tell their neighbors about their keywords it will not only reinforce them, but it may help train learners who are having trouble adopting this technique.

D2 Semantic Mapping

Semantic mapping generally refers to brainstorming associations which a word has and then diagramming the results. Johnson, Pittelman and Heimlich (1986) described semantic mapping as 'categorical structuring of information in graphic form'. Semantic mapping is one of the word association techniques. It is defined as a technique to make arrangement of words into a diagram, which has a key concept at the centre or at the top, and related words and concepts linked to the key concept by means of lines or arrows.

Semantic mapping has been usually used for (1) general vocabulary development, (2) pre and post-reading, (3) teaching of a study skill, (4) a link between reading and writing instruction, and (5) an assessment technique. Johnson and Pearson (1984) generalized semantic mapping as a strategy of vocabulary instruction as followed:

1. Write a key word or topic related to classroom work on a sheet of paper, the blackboard, or a transparent slide.
2. Encourage the students to think of as many words as they can that are related to the selected key word or topic.
3. Guide the students to list the words by categories.
4. Have students label the categories.
5. Discuss the relationships between these words.

D3 Concordancing

Concordancing is a process of looking at relationships among words. Even without a concordancing program, a teacher can still ask learners to look up words and strings of words on the Internet to find natural contexts. Learners can get a better understanding of how the words are used appropriately. It is a self-study technique that the learner can take away from the classroom.

Look at today's newspaper and find a phrase you don't understand. Use a search engine such as www.google.com to look for occurrences of the phrase (for example, *tongue in cheek*). Collect ten definitions or examples and review the meaning with other students.

D4 Sight Words

Sight words, which are also known as **high frequency words** and word-wall words, are simply words that students learn by sight instead of by sounding them out. They are the most commonly used words by students. Sight words instruction is an excellent supplement to phonics instruction. Phonics is a method for learning to read in general, while sight words instruction increases a child's familiarity with the high frequency words he will encounter most often. Some ESL teachers feel that the Oxford list of sight words can be more readily recognized by their ESL students. Here is a part of the list.

> I, a, the, and, he, was, to, my, it, on, in, is, went, there, you, had, am, day, she, we, for, fun, me, mum, said, be, going, got, wanted, at, but, his, home, like, of, Saturday, ...

D5 Graded readers & Vocabulary growth through reading

Graded readers are books written within a controlled vocabulary. Some graded readers are considerably reduced simplifications of well-known texts like ***Robinson Crusoe***. Others are original stories written especially for language learners within a controlled vocabulary. These are an extremely valuable resource for teaching and learning English, and teachers should be very familiar with them.

A very important means of vocabulary growth in the meaning-focused input strand is an extensive reading program. An extensive reading program involves learners reading large quantities of graded readers primarily for enjoyment. As well as being excellent for motivation and developing reading skill, this can be an important source of vocabulary growth. Learners can pick up new vocabulary and establish and enrich partly known vocabulary through such reading. Graded readers can also be used for listening, and some graded readers have accompanying tapes.

최시원 전공영어 영어교육학
English Education Conceptual

Chapter 13 MindMap

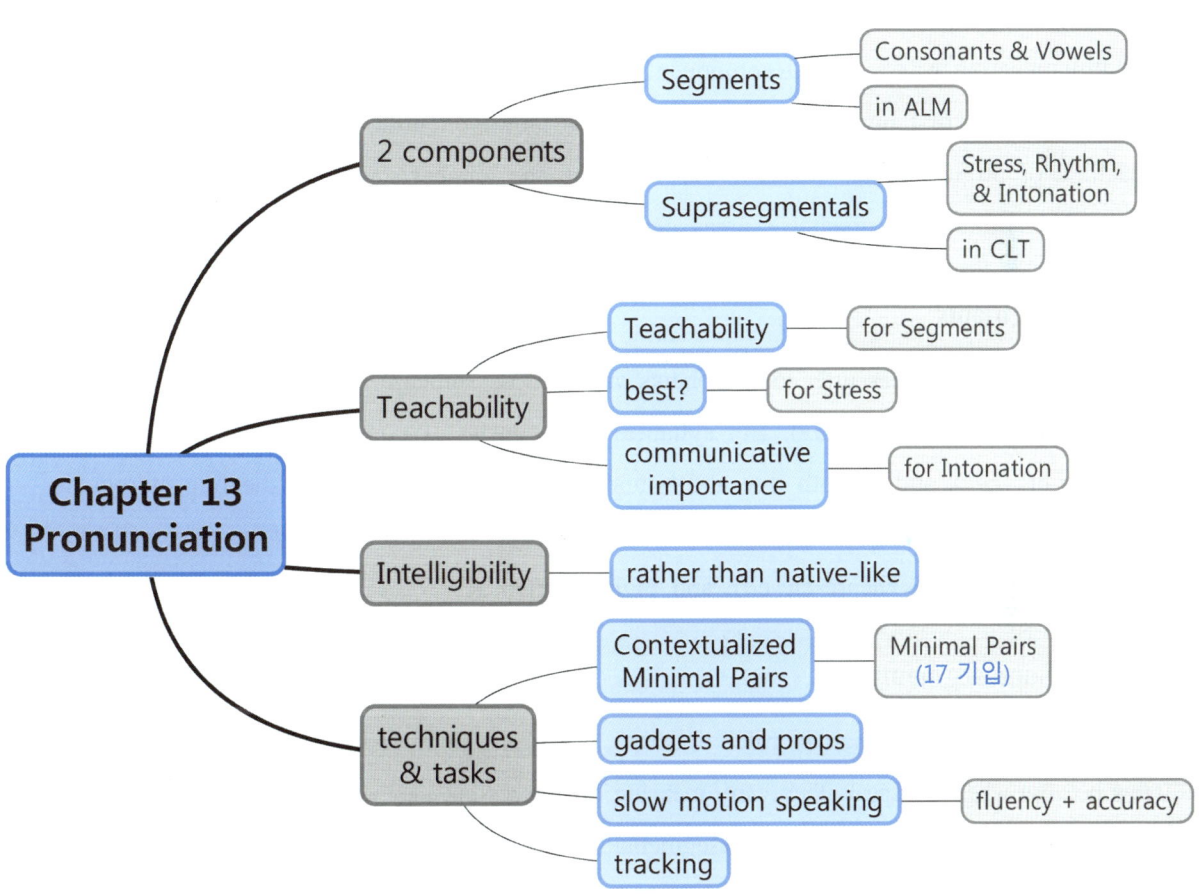

Chapter 13   Teaching Pronunciation

A   Segments vs. Suprasegmentals

segments	consonants & vowels
suprasegmentals	stress, rhythm, & intonation

Pronunciation was a central component in language teaching during the audiolingual era. When CLT was first introduced in the late 1970s, however, little attention was given to the teaching of pronunciation. When it was included, the emphasis was on rhythm, stress, and intonation (i.e. suprasegmentals), areas considered more likely to affect communication.

A1   Segments

Segmental phonemes refer to consonants and vowels. Sometimes a spoken syllable consists of one phoneme (/o/ in *okay*). But syllables also consist of combined sounds (the second syllable of *okay*), and of both free and bound morphemes. For instance, the free morpheme *hat* consists of three phonemes but only one syllable. The word *disheartened* has three syllables, four morphemes (dis+heart+en+ed), and eight phonemes.

A2   Suprasegmentals

Suprasegmental phonemes refer to stress, rhythm, and intonation. They are called like this because when we speak, they carry meaning differences but they operate 'above' the segmental phonemes. To illustrate that the suprasegmentals carry meaning, consider the sentence, 'I think I know.' It can convey four different meaning, depending on the stress:

> *I* think I know.   I think *I* know.   I *think* I know.   I think I *know*.

In these utterances, the bold italic typeface shows which word is stressed. If you say these sentences aloud, you will hear the sound and meaning differences. The differences are related to the context where the utterances occur. Consider these interpretations:

> *I* think I know. (You may not think I know the answer, but I'm pretty sure I do.)
>
> I think *I* know. (You may not know the answer, but I think I do.)
>
> I *think* I know. (I'm not entirely sure, but I think I know the answer.)
>
> I think I *know*. (I am not unsure — I am quite confident that I know the answer.)

B   Teachability issues in teaching pronunciation

Dalton and Seidlhofer (1994) try to measure pronunciation importance. They used the table below to graph out the relative **teachability** and communicative importance of segments, stress, and intonation:

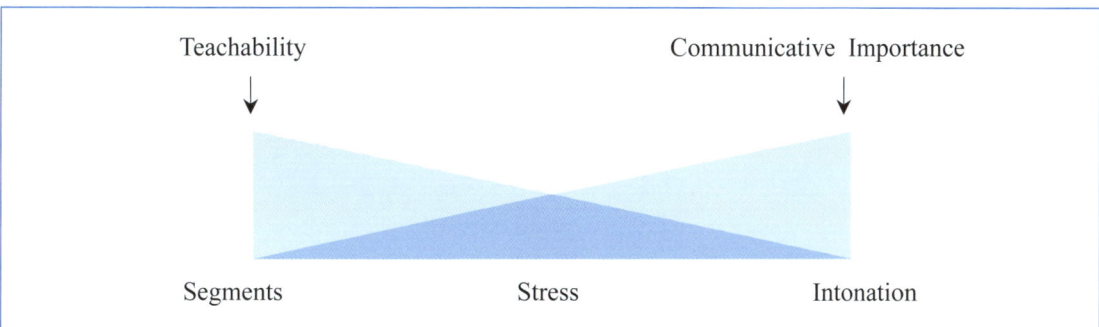

They conclude that teaching segments is easy, but teaching intonation is too hard; however, they believe that teaching stress is just right. Specifically, they believe that segments are easy to teach, but that they are not critical for clear communication. Intonation, on the other hand, is too difficult to teach even though it is critical for communication. Finally, stress is somewhat difficult to teach, and necessary for communication. Further, stress is somewhat predictable. For example, there are word stress rules for predictable stress on first syllable, last syllable, penultimate syllable, antepenultimate syllable, polysyllabic words, and compound words. Conversely, intonation is specific only to the situation. How then could one teach it? Thus, they conclude that stress should be taught because it has some predictability and is important to communication. It has the maximum overlap of communicative importance and teachability, making it a convenient focal point. It is necessarily connected to either end of the continuum: on the segmental side, word stress is decisive for the quality of individual sounds, on the intonation side, it signifies prominence.

C Intelligibility issues in teaching pronunciation

Intelligibility is the extent to which a speaker's message is understood. Harmer (2006) suggests in pronunciation teaching learners should be 'given extra information about spoken English and teachers should help them to achieve the goal of improved comprehension and intelligibility'. Harmer shows the requirement of intelligibility rather than perfection. He says 'under the pressure of such personal, political and phonological considerations, it has become customary for teachers to consider intelligibility as the prime goal of pronunciation teaching'. In some of his lesson plan Harmer shows some techniques of teaching pronunciation: focusing on individual sound, minimal pair drill, pronunciation games, sound waves practice, and learning connected speech.

Like other linguists, Thornbury (2008) also agrees that intelligibility is more important in English pronunciation. To him 'intelligibility (i.e. being understood) is more important than sounding like a native speaker'. He also suggests that while teaching, teachers should give special attention to pronunciation whether it is intelligible, receptive, in context, teachable, etc.

D Techniques and tasks in teaching pronunciation

1) Contextualized Minimal Pairs

One of the oldest techniques in pronunciation instruction is to teach students to distinguish between specifically targeted sounds, stress patterns, or intonation patterns through the use of **minimal pairs** (for example, two words which differ from each other by only one distinctive sound and which also differ in meaning). Simple pictures or drawings can be designed to provide practice in learning to distinguish such minimal pairs as: pen/pan, man/men, hand/ham, etc. In the most familiar examples the vowel sounds in words such as 'bat' and 'bet' may be contextualized as follows:

> That's a heavy bat. (Show a picture of a baseball player in a baseball stadium.)
> That's a heavy bet. (Show a picture of a gambler in a gambling casino.)

2) Gadgets and Props

Rubber bands and balls that bounce easily may be used in pronunciation classrooms to call attention to word stress, sentence stress, rhythm patterns, and features of intonation. For stress patterns at either word level or sentence level, students can be taught to stretch rubber bands dramatically to illustrate the prominence of specific syllables. Rubber balls may be used for similar purposes to illustrate words that are stressed at sentence level.

3) Slow Motion Speaking

A way to build fluency with more accurate pronunciation is through 'slow motion speaking' (SMS). To introduce SMS, the teacher models to learners how to deliberately slow down one's speech. Then, learners are given a brief excerpt of scripted language to practice aloud. Once familiar with the sample, they are asked to say it aloud along with their teacher while the teacher pronounces the excerpt in a highly unnaturally slowed-down manner. The idea is for the teacher to be slow, deliberate, and exaggerated in her or his way of slowly moving the tongue and lips while maintaining accurate sound articulation, rhythm, intonation, and pausing patterns. SMS permits learners to view close up, and to imitate, the teacher's way of producing specific sounds in context.

4) Tracking

Tracking begins with students analyzing written transcripts of English — as produced by native speakers — for which video or audio recordings are available. Either commercially produced ESL/EFL materials or transcripts from off-air recordings of television or radio shows may be used. It is important to select a recording covering a topic accessible to learners. Once learners are familiar with the transcript and know the material well, the video or audio recording is played for students and they are asked to say the material aloud while speaking along with the recorded voices. The process of working closely with such materials can continue for as long as learners find the material useful. One of tracking's distinctive features is that language learners are not being asked to repeat after the recorded voices. Rather, their challenge is to try to say the words presented in the transcript concurrent with the voices they are listening.

최시원 전공영어 영어교육학
English Education Conceptual

Chapter 14 MindMap

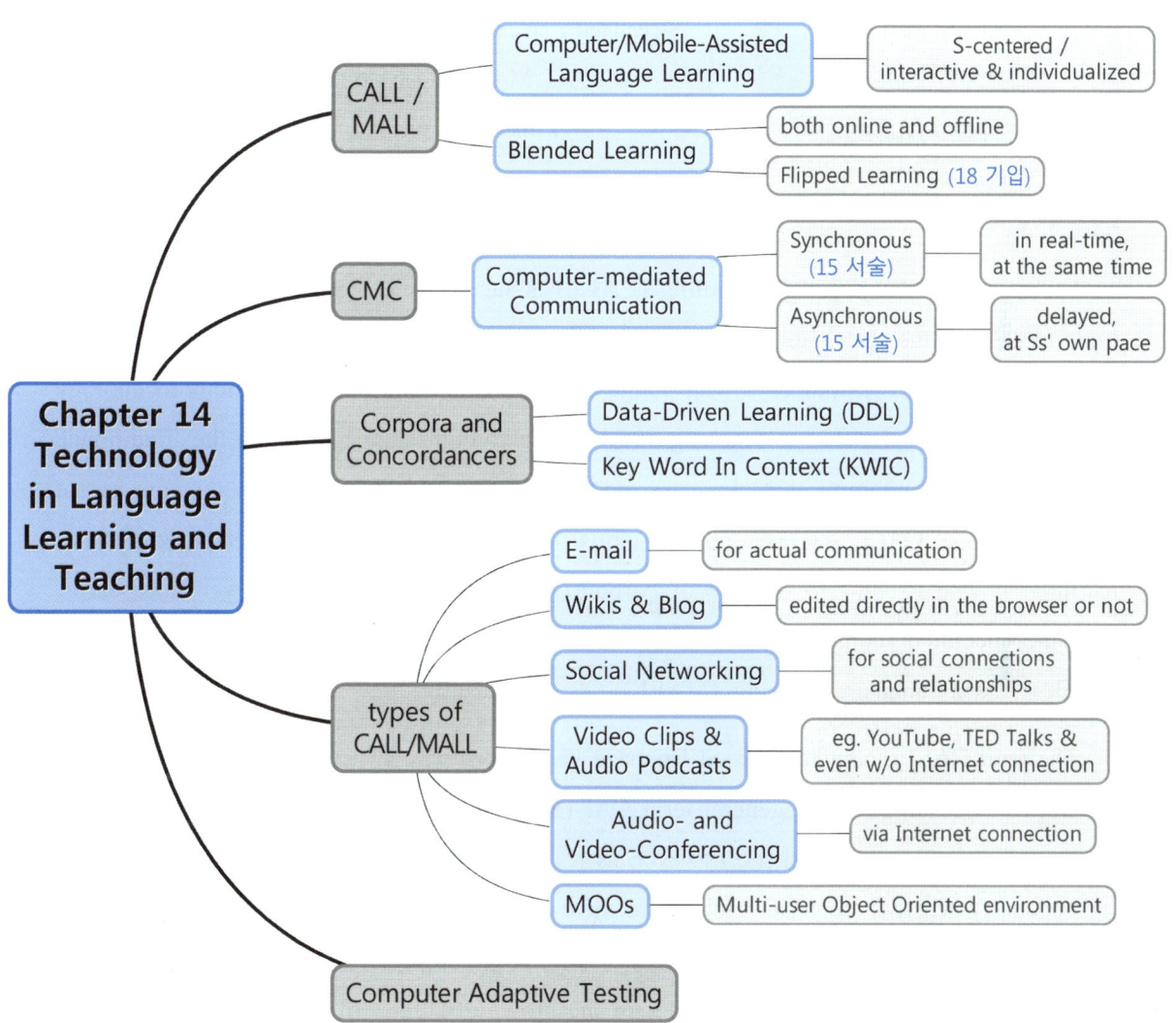

Chapter 14 Technology in Language Learning and Teaching

A   CALL & MALL

CALL / MALL	S-centered / interactive & individualized (↔ CALI)
Blended Learning	CALL/MALL + face-to-face learning
Flipped Learning	a model of blended learning

A1   CALL

Computer-assisted language learning (**CALL**) is succinctly defined in a seminal work by Levy (1997) as 'the search for and study of applications of the computer in language teaching and learning'. CALL embraces a wide range of information and communications technology applications and approaches to teaching and learning foreign languages, from the 'traditional' drill-and-practice programs that characterized CALL in the 1960s and 1970s to more recent manifestations of CALL, e.g. as used in a virtual learning environment and Web-based distance learning. It also extends to the use of corpora and concordancers, interactive whiteboards, computer-mediated communication (CMC), language learning in virtual worlds, and mobile-assisted language learning (MALL).

The term CALI (computer-assisted language instruction) was in use before CALL, reflecting its origins as a subset of the general term CAI (computer-assisted instruction). CALI fell out of favor among language teachers, however, as it appeared to imply a teacher-centred approach (instructional), whereas language teachers are more inclined to prefer a student-centred approach, focusing on learning rather than instruction. CALL began to replace CALI in the early 1980s and it is now incorporated into the names of the growing number of professional associations worldwide.

The current philosophy of CALL puts a strong emphasis on student-centred materials that allow learners to work on their own. Such materials may be structured or unstructured, but they normally embody two important features: interactive learning and individualised learning. CALL is essentially a tool that helps teachers to facilitate the language learning process. It can be used to reinforce what has already been learned in the classroom or as a remedial tool to help learners who require additional support.

A2 MALL

The ready availability of mobile devices and easy access to Wi-Fi connections multiply the possibilities for language learning 'on the move', or what we now call **Mobile-Assisted Language Learning** (**MALL**). It has provided educators greater feedom for extending learning outside traditional learning environments. Mobile devices offer immediate access to the Internet and, thus, to an abundance of 'apps' (applications) that for language learners may be more attractive alternatives compared to structured learning such as playing language games, watching movies in the L2, or listening to a radio. In particular, most mobile phones are now equipped with photo and video cameras, GPS (Global Positioning Services), Internet access, e-mail, Short Messaging Service (SMS), and Multimedia Messaging Service (MMS). Applications such as YouTube, Facebook, Skype, Twitter, and various multimedia resources are all accessible on mobile phones.

However, we should also note that the level of engagement in mobile-assisted learning may be superficial or casual rather than deep, probably due to the difficulty of working at length with a small screen and keyboard to do tasks. Ushioda (2013) states the power of mobile technologies should also motivate learners to attain deeper and more sustained levels of engagement. Some of the limitations of implementing MALL, such as reduced screen sizes, virtual keyboarding, and one-finger data-entry, remain as challenges to teachers.

A3 Blended Learning

A combination of face-to-face teaching and CALL or MALL is usually referred to as **blended learning**. Blended learning is designed to increase learning potential and is more commonly found than pure CALL (Pegrum 2009).

Since the early 2000s there has been a boom in the development of so-called Web 2.0 applications. Contrary to popular opinion, Web 2.0 is not a new version of the Web, rather it implies a shift in emphasis from Web browsing, which is essentially a one-way process (from the Web to the end-user), to making use of Web applications in the same way as one uses applications on a desktop computer. It also implies more interaction and sharing. Walker,

Davies, & Hewer (2011) list the following examples of Web 2.0 applications that language teachers are using: image storage and sharing / social bookmarking / discussion lists, blogs, wikis, social networking / chat rooms, MUDs, MOOs and MUVEs (virtual worlds) / podcasting / audio tools / video sharing applications and screen capture tools / animation tools — comic strips, movies, etc.

(A3a) Flipped Learning

The basic idea of the **flipped learning** is to make use of technology so that we do less 'teaching' in the class and focus more on group work and task based learning in the lesson. In an ELT context perhaps the teacher is explaining how a report is organized. This 'teaching stuff' can be moved out of the lesson. We can record mini lectures or screen casts where we record ourselves explaining these concepts and then put these online. The students can watch them at home and in class we can focus more on group based, task based activities that practice the knowledge that was demonstrated and explained in the videos.

The Flipped Classroom is simply a model of blended learning. It is not a methodology but rather a way of organizing learning and the learning content. In fact it really draws on several approaches to learning; namely a transmission (behaviorist approach to learning) and a social constructivist/task-based approach. At home the students are watching videos, listening to podcasts and perhaps doing quizzes to check understanding. Most of this learning is very transmission-based and does not involve collaboration or sharing of ideas. Then the students come into class where they use their knowledge in group work and tasks. This learning is more collaborative in nature and fits more with a constructivist view of learning.

B CMC

CMC (Computer-mediated Communication)	synchronous	in real-time, at the same time
	asynchronous	delayed, at students' own pace

Computer-mediated communication (**CMC**) is defined as any human communication that occurs through the use of two or more electronic devices. While the term has traditionally referred to those communications that occur via computer-mediated formats, it has also been applied to other forms of text-based interaction such as text messaging. Popular forms of

CMC include e-mail, video, audio or text chat, bulletin board systems, list-servs and MOOs. These settings are changing rapidly with the development of new technologies. Weblogs (blogs) have also become popular, and the exchange of RSS data has better enabled users to each 'become their own publisher'.

The nature of CMC means that it is easy for individuals to engage in communication with others regardless of time or location. CMC allows for individuals to collaborate on projects that would otherwise be impossible due to such factors as geography. In addition, CMC can also be useful for allowing individuals who might be intimidated due to factors like character or disabilities to participate in communication. CMC also plays a role in self-disclosure, which allows a communicative partner to open up more easily and be more expressive. When communicating through an electronic medium, individuals are less likely to engage in stereotyping and are less self-conscious about physical characteristics. The role that anonymity plays in online communication can also encourage some users to be less defensive and form relationships with others more rapidly.

B1 Synchronous vs. Asynchronous learning

Synchronous learning refers to the exchange of ideas and information with one or more participants during the same period. Examples are face-to-face discussion, online real-time live teacher instruction and feedback, Skype conversations, and chat rooms or virtual classrooms where everyone is online and working collaboratively at the same time. Since students are working collaboratively, synchronized learning helps students create an open mind because they have to listen and learn from their peers. Synchronized learning fosters online awareness and improves many students' writing skills.

Asynchronous learning may use technologies such as email, blogs, wikis, and discussion boards, as well as web-supported textbooks, hypertext documents, audio video courses, and social networking using web 2.0. Asynchronous learning is beneficial for students who have health problems or who have child care responsibilities. They have the opportunity to complete their work in a low stress environment and within a more flexible time frame. In asynchronous online courses, students proceed at their own pace. If they need to listen to a lecture a second time, or think about a question for a while, they may do so without fearing that they will hold back the rest of the class. Through online courses, students can earn their diplomas more quickly, or repeat failed courses without the embarrassment of being in a class with younger students.

Students have access to an incredible variety of enrichment courses in online learning, and can participate in college courses, internships, sports, or work and still graduate with their class.

C Types of CALL Activities

E-mail	for actual communication with individuals around the world
Wikis	websites with multiple hyperlinked pages, edited directly in the browser
Blogs	websites with multiple hyperlinked pages, constructed by an individual
Social Networking	for social connections and relationships both online and offline
Video Clips	e.g. YouTube, TED Talks
Audio Podcasts	used as authentic listening materials w/o Internet connection
Web Conferencing	(= Audio- and Video-Conferencing) via Internet connection
MOOs	(= Multi-User Object Oriented Environment) text-based Virtual Reality

C1 E-mail

E-mail may now be the most frequently and widely used means of communication for either formal or informal purposes. E-mail exchanges between students, between teachers and students, and between students and others outside the classroom involve composing, reading, and information/opinion sharing. If you want to keep class e-mails separated from your personal e-mails, it's a good idea to use other platforms such as Facebook for communicating with students.

C2 Wikis and Blogs

Wikis are websites with multiple hyperlinked pages but differ from blogs in the sense that content can be edited directly in the browser. Wikipedia is a collaboratively written encyclopedia using the wiki model. It can create a space in which students write information individually or as a group and other students add to it or amend it.

Blogs are usually constructed by an individual writer who posts regular entries of ideas, events, photos, graphics, or embedded video links. Blog sites are usually interactive, allowing visitors to leave comments. Blog assignments can be used for all levels of students using free software platforms. The writer can choose their blogs to be private or available to the public. While it is possible to receive messages from strangers, making the class blog public can encourage students to be more cautious about the quality of their writing.

C3 Social Networking

The number of users of **social networking sites** (SNSs) such as Facebook, Twitter, and LinkedIn has seen tremendous worldwide growth. SNSs allow users to develop and maintain social connections and relationships both online and offline by participating in multimodal and multisensory affordances (e.g., profiles, status updates, shared links, synchronous chats, asynchronous messages, photo sharing).

C4 Video Clips and Audio Podcasts

Videos are great materials for providing language input in a meaningful context. Popular websites such as YouTube, Vimeo, and TED Talks offer countless video clips in a variety of genres: music videos, documentaries, sports highlights, TV talk shows, commercials, soap operas, sitcoms, and so on. However, the video links are useless if there is no Internet connection in the classroom. In that circumstance, **podcasts** would be good alternatives for authentic listening materials in various topical areas such as academic lectures, talk-radio broadcasts, interviews, and audiobooks.

C5 Audio- and Video-Conferencing

Another promising popular technology is the carrying out of conferences over a digital microphone or a video camera installed in computers, smart phones, or portable tablet PCs. The current top **video conferencing** software may include Skype, Google Hangouts, FaceTime, and Adobe Connect. With this technology teachers can provide students with one-on-one tutoring sessions as well as additional consultations from any location. It can also be used to invite guest speakers or native speakers of a target language who can speak with students in the classroom.

C6 MOOs

Educational multi-user virtual environments are not new. The earliest form was called a **MOO** (**Multi-User Object Oriented environment**). A MOO is a text-based virtual reality environment that allows users to go online to the same place at the same time to communicate with one another and manipulate and interact with cyber-objects. Educational MOOs emerged in the early 90s to provide a virtual environment to support learning. They ranged from MOOs to support the learning of a second language to those focused on building online communities of practice. Tapped In, for example, is an example of a MOO for teacher professional development:

[Tapped In: An online teacher community: http://tappedin.org/]

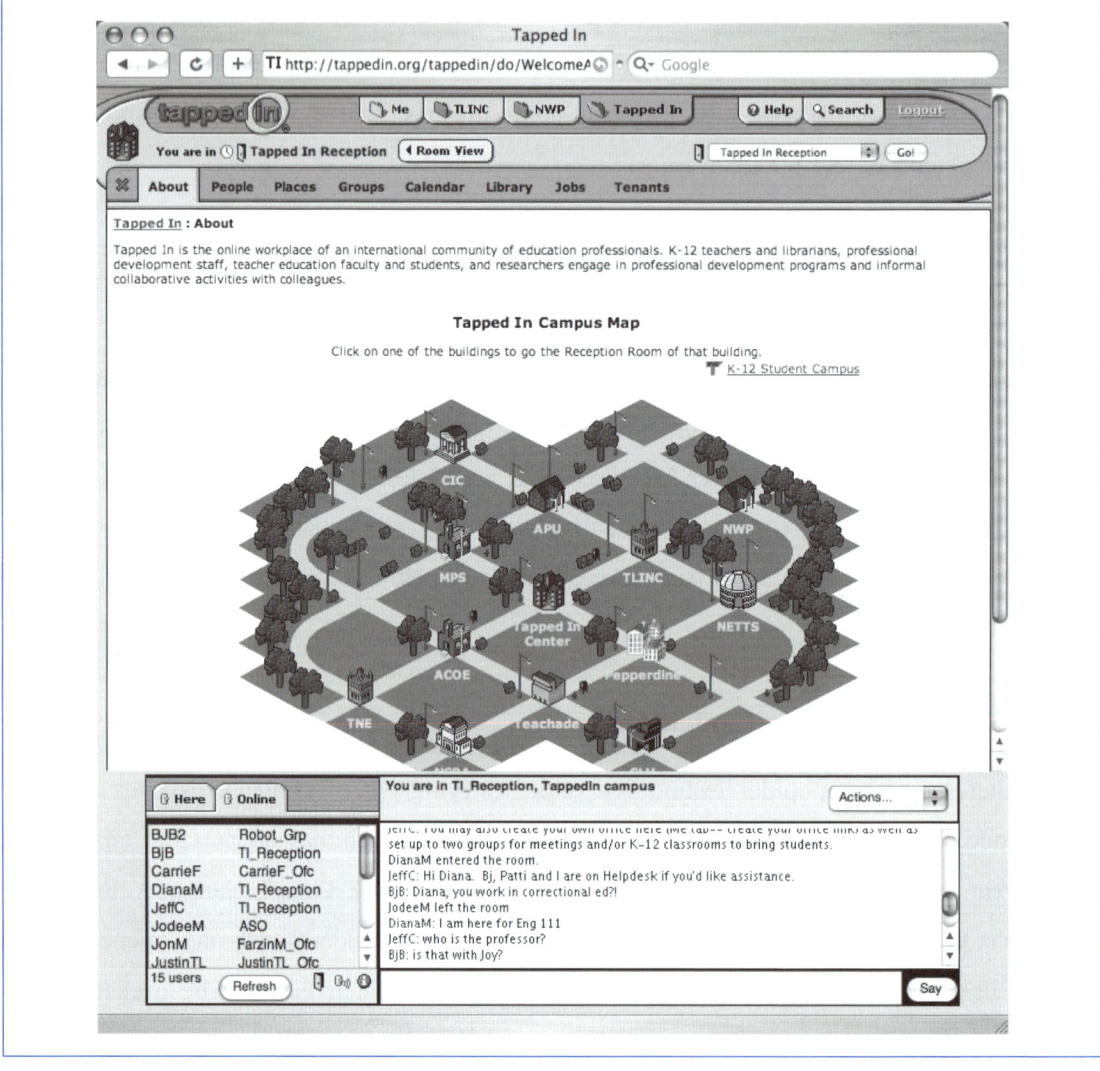

More immersive three-dimensional virtual environments called MUVEs (Multi-User Virtual Environments) or virtual worlds have emerged in recent years and are of increasing interest to education. Virtual worlds, such as Second Life, do not have fixed rules and goals, and hence are distinguishable from games. That is, virtual worlds provide flexible and unstructured environment that may stimulate user creativity, and there is no limit on how to use the space. For educational use, this means that one can create virtually any learning activity in any discipline depending on his/her instructional design capability and skill level with the virtual world tools.

C7 Online Grammar Exercises

Grammar Clinic is an online application that asks users to identify sentence-level errors (sentence fragments, run-on sentences, article use, verb use, noun use, preposition use, relative pronoun use, punctuation use, etc.) and to correct them. Users receive immediate feedback on their performance, and a short grammar handbook comes with the application.

D Corpora and Concordancers

Corpus (pl. Corpora)	authentic discourse data
Concordancing	searching for words in context and collocations
Concordancer	a computer program that automatically constructs a concordance
Concordance (line)	a comprehensive index of the words used in a corpus
KWIC (= key word in context)	the keyword is shown highlighted in the middle of the display, with the text forming its context on either side
POST (= part of speech tagged)	a special label assigned to each word in a corpus to indicate the part of speech and often also other grammatical categories such as tense, number, case, etc.

Corpora have been used for many years as the basis of linguistic research and also for the compilation of dictionaries and reference works such as the Collins Cobuild series. It was Tim Johns (1991) who raised the profile of the use of concordancers in the language classroom with his concept of **Data-driven learning** (**DDL**). DDL encourages learners to work out their own rules about the meaning of words and their usage by using a concordancer to locate examples in a corpus of authentic texts. It is also possible for the teacher to use a **concordancer** to find examples of authentic usage to demonstrate a point of grammar or typical collocations, and to generate exercises based on the examples found.

```
2720 hits    Standardized to 2,720 per million (hits/corpus size x 1,000,000)
             Click any KEYWORD for more context
001.  []     discouragement, or the temptation to abandon our efforts, " WOULD show that one placed excessive trust in purely human m
002.  []     the kind to go violent. Were you in love with that girl"? " WOULD it make any difference to you if I were, Mary Jane"? S
003.  []     ered Steinha^ger to herself, several times, memorizing it. " WOULD you first read the poem aloud to me and then let me re
004.  []     exteriors indicated. We showed them to each other and said " WOULD you have guessed ..."? Squatting on our haunches besid
005.  []     gly. One girl expressed what was obviously in their minds. " WOULD you advise us to act the same way? You might have fail
006.  []     ind. ## Next morning, he found a note in the refrigerator. " WOULD you mind wrapping your onion"? said this note. "The sm
007.  []     s information"? he asked. "Haven't the faintest, Captain". " WOULD you mind sending him up here? I'd like to talk to him"
008.  []     uipped for the job". The resulting setup, it was declared, " WOULD be similar to that which is in successful operation in
009.  []     wed. After he had gone, Kate asked Uncle Randolph proudly, " WOULD you take their oath"? And the old man had given a sly
010.  []     rs, which is interested in developing part of the project. # WOULD BAR VEHICLES# The plan for eliminating traffic hazards
011.  []     that date to pay for other social security costs. #OUTLAYS WOULD INCREASE# Officials estimated the annual tax boost for
012.  []     has been submitted for Congressional approval, $26,000,000 WOULD be spent through universities and private voluntary ag
```

(from www.lextutor.ca)

Robb (2003) shows how it is possible to use Google as a concordancer, but he also points out a number of drawbacks, for instance there is no control over the educational level, nationality, or other characteristics of the creators of the texts that are found, and the presentation of the examples is not as easy to read as the output of a dedicated concordancer that places the **key words** (i.e. the search terms) **in context**.

E Computer Adaptive Testing

Computer adaptive testing (**CAT**) is a form of computer-based test that adapts to the examinee's ability level. For this reason, it has also been called tailored testing. CAT successively selects questions for the purpose of maximizing the precision of the exam based on what is known about the examinee from previous questions. From the examinee's perspective, the difficulty of the exam seems to tailor itself to their level of ability. For example, if an examinee performs well on an item of intermediate difficulty, they will then be presented with a more difficult question. Or, if they performed poorly, they would be presented with a simpler question. Compared to static multiple choice tests that nearly everyone has experienced, with a fixed set of items administered to all examinees, computer-adaptive tests require fewer test items to arrive at equally accurate scores.

Chapter 15 MindMap

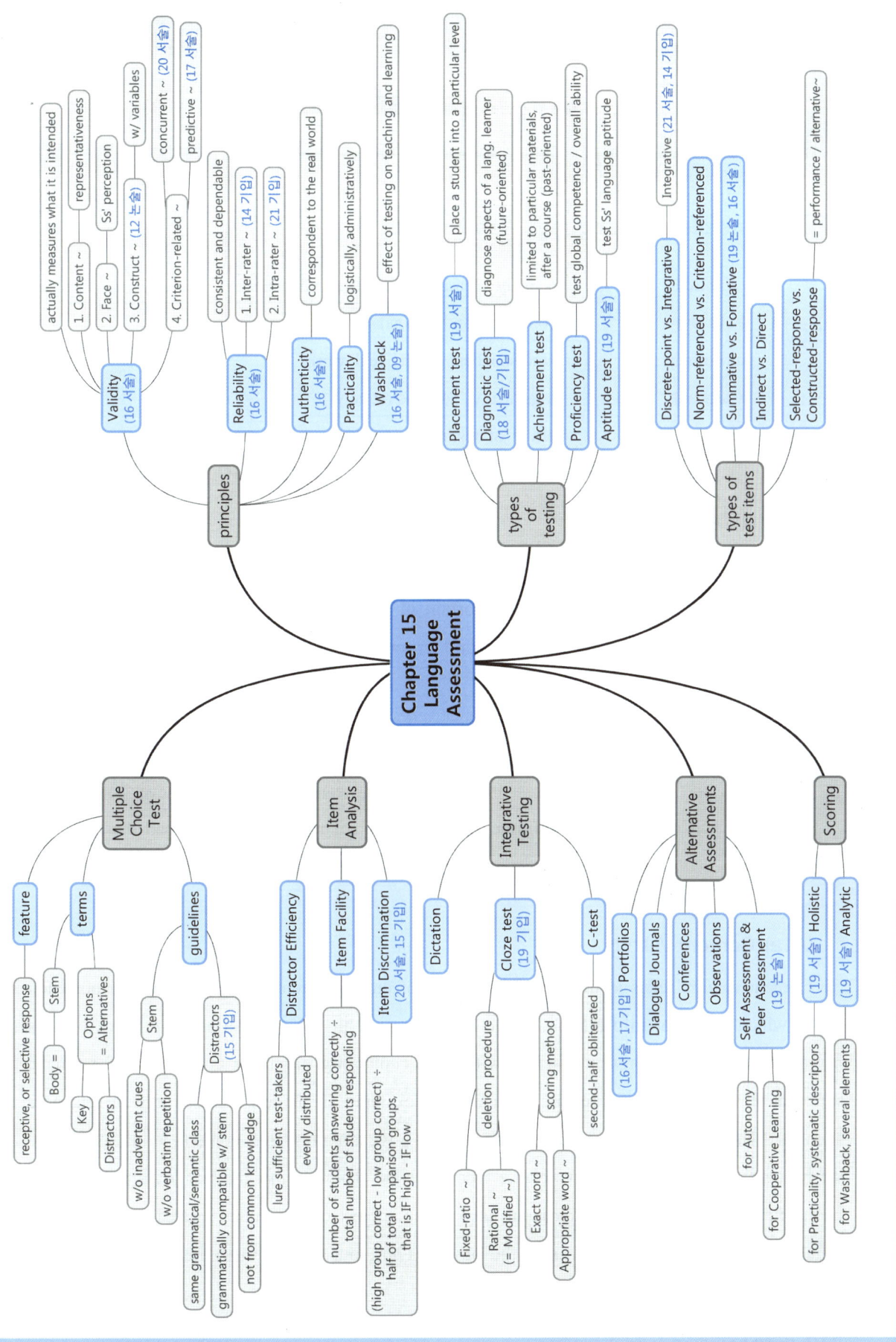

Chapter 15 Language Assessment

A Principles of Language Assessment

Validity	actually measures what it is intended
Reliability	consistent and dependable
Authenticity	correspondent to the real world
Practicality	logistically, administratively
Washback	effect of testing on teaching and learning

A1 Validity

Validity refers to the degree to which the test actually measures what it is intended to measure. Four types of validation are important in your role as a classroom teacher: content validity, face validity, construct validity, and criterion-related validity.

	Content ~	the representativeness of the test
	Face ~	the participants' perceptions of the test
	Construct ~	measuring the underlying construct, the higher level concepts
Criterion-related ~	Concurrent ~	supported by other concurrent performance beyond the test
	Predictive ~	assessing a test-taker's likelihood of future success

(A1a) Content Validity

Content validity refers to the representativeness of our measurement regarding the phenomenon about which we want information. If we are interested in the acquisition of relative clauses in general and plan to present learners with an acceptability judgment task, we need to make sure that all relative clause types are included. For example, if our test consists only of sentences such as "The boy who is running is my friend," we do not have content validity because we have not included other relative clause types such as "The dog that the boy loves is beautiful." In the first sentence the relative pronoun *who* is the subject of its clause, whereas in the second sentence the relative pronoun *that* is the object. Thus, our testing instrument is not sensitive to the full range of relative clause types, and we can say that it lacks content validity.

(A1b) Face Validity

Face validity is closely related to the notion of content validity and refers to the familiarity of our instrument and how easy it is to convince others that there is content validity to it. If, for example, learners are presented with reasoning tasks to carry out in an experiment and are already familiar with these sorts of tasks because they have carried them out in their classrooms, we can say that the task has face validity for the learners. Face validity thus hinges on the participants' perceptions of the research treatments and tests. If the participants do not perceive a connection between the research activities and other educational or second language activities, they may be less likely to take the experiment seriously.

(A1c) Construct Validity

Construct validity refers to the degree to which the research adequately captures the construct of interest. Constructs are higher level concepts which are not directly observable or measurable while variables (sometimes used interchangeably with indicators or measures) seek to measure the underlying construct. Thus, construct validity can be enhanced when multiple variables of a construct are used. Construct validity is an essential topic in second language acquisition research precisely because many of the concepts investigated are not easily or directly defined. In second language research, concepts such as language proficiency, aptitude, exposure to input, and linguistic representations are of interest. However, these concepts are not directly measurable in the way that height, weight, or age are. That is why we use construct validity to measure those concepts. Imagine, for example, that you have been given a procedure for conducting an oral interview. The scoring analysis for the interview weighs several factors into a final score: pronunciation, fluency, grammatical accuracy, vocabulary use, and sociolinguistic appropriateness. The justification for these five factors lies in a theoretical construct that claims those factors as major components of oral proficiency. So, on the other hand, if you were asked to conduct an oral proficiency interview that accounted only for pronunciation and grammar, you could be justifiably suspicious about the construct validity of such a test.

(A1d) Criterion-related Validity

Criterion validity refers to the extent to which tests used in a research study are comparable to other well-established tests of the construct in question. For example, many language programs attempt to measure global proficiency either for placement into their own program or to determine the extent to which a student might meet a particular language requirement. For the sake of convenience, these programs often develop their own internal tests, but there may be little external evidence that these tests are measuring what the programs assume they are measuring. One could measure the performance of a group of students on the local test and a well-established test (e.g., TOEFL in the case of English, or in the case of other languages, another recognized standard test). Should there be a good correlation, one can then say that the local test has been demonstrated to have criterion-related validity. Criterion-related evidence usually falls into one of two categories: concurrent and predictive validity.

① **Concurrent validity**: A test has **concurrent validity** if its results are supported by other concurrent performance beyond the assessment itself. For example, the validity of a high score on the final exam of a foreign language course will be substantiated by actual proficiency in the language.

② **Predictive validity**: The **predictive validity** of an assessment becomes important in the case of placement tests, admissions assessment batteries, language aptitude tests, and the like. The assessment criterion in such cases is not to measure concurrent ability but to assess (and predict) a test-taker's likelihood of future success.

A2 Reliability

Test **reliability** refers to the consistency of scores on a test. A number of sources of *un*reliability may be identified:

- the test itself (its construction), known as test reliability

- the administration of a test

- the test-taker, known as student-related reliability

- the scoring of the test, known as rater (or scorer) reliability

Among these, rater reliability is usually categorized into the following: inter-rater reliability and intra-rater reliability.

Inter-rater ~	Two or more scorers yield consistent scores of the same test.
Intra-rater ~	One scorer yields consistent scores in different situations.

(A2a) Inter-rater Reliability:

Inter-rater reliability occurs when two or more scorers yield consistent scores of the same test. Failure to achieve inter-rater reliability could stem from lack of adherence to scoring criteria, inexperience, inattention, or even preconceived biases.

(A2b) Intra-rater Reliability:

Intra-rater reliability is an internal factor, a common occurrence for classroom teachers. Violation of such reliability can occur in cases of unclear scoring criteria, fatigue, bias toward particular 'good' and 'bad' students, or simple carelessness.

A3 Authenticity

Bachman & Palmer define **authenticity** as 'the degree of correspondence of the characteristics of a given language test task to the features of a target language task'. In a test, authenticity may be present in the following ways:

① The language in the test is as natural as possible.

② Items are contextualized rather than isolated.

③ Topics and situations are interesting, enjoyable, and humorous.

④ Some thematic organization to items is provided, such as through a story line.

⑤ Tasks represent, or closely approximate, real-world tasks.

The authenticity of test tasks in recent years has increased noticeably. Two or three decades ago, unconnected, boring, contrived items were accepted as a necessary component of testing. Things have changed. It was once assumed that large-scale testing could not include performance of the productive skills and stay within budgetary constraints, but now many such tests offer speaking and writing components. Reading passages are selected from real-world sources that test-takers are likely to have encountered or will encounter. Listening comprehension sections feature natural language with hesitations, white noise, and interruptions. More and more tests offer items that are 'episodic', in that they are sequenced to form meaning units, paragraphs, or stories.

A4   Practicality

Practicality refers to the logistical, down-to-earth, administrative issues involved in making, giving, and scoring an assessment instrument. These include 'cost, the amount of time it takes to construct and to administer, ease of scoring, and ease of interpreting/reporting the results'.

A5   Washback

The effect of testing on teaching and learning is known as **washback**. When students take a test, ideally they will receive information (feedback) about their competence, based on their performance. That feedback should 'wash back' to them in the form of useful diagnoses of strengths and weaknesses. Washback also includes the effects of an assessment on teaching and learning prior to the assessment itself, that is, on preparation for the assessment. Washback enhances a number of basic principles of language acquisition: intrinsic motivation, autonomy, self-confidence, language ego, interlanguage, and strategic investment, among others.

One way to enhance washback is to comment generously and specifically on test performance. In reality, letter grades and a score showing the number of right or wrong give absolutely no information of intrinsic interest to the student. At best, they give a relative indication of a formulaic judgment of performance as compared to others in the class — which fosters competitive, not cooperative, learning. With this in mind, when you return a written test or a data sheet from an oral production test, consider giving more than a number, grade, or phrase as your feedback.

A little bit of washback may also accrue to students through a specification to the student of the numerical scores on the various subsections of the test. A subsection on verb tenses, for example, that yields relative low score may serve the diagnostic purpose of showing the student an area of challenge.

Finally, washback also implies that students have ready access to you to discuss the feedback and evaluation you have given. An interactive, cooperative, collaborative classroom can promote an atmosphere of dialogue between students and teachers regarding evaluative judgment.

B Types of Testing: in terms of Purposes

Placement test	placing a student into a particular level
Diagnostic test	diagnosing aspects of a language learner (future-oriented)
Achievement test	limited to particular materials, after a course (past-oriented)
Proficiency test	testing global competence / overall ability
Aptitude test	predicting a person's future success in advance

B1 Placement tests

The purpose of **placement tests** is to place a student into a particular level or section of a language curriculum or school. Although the ultimate objective of a placement test is to correctly place a student into a course or level, a very useful secondary benefit is diagnostic information on a student's performance, which in turn gives teachers a head start on assessing their students' abilities.

B2 Diagnostic tests

The purpose of **diagnostic tests** is to diagnose aspects of a language that a student needs to develop or that a course should include. Usually, such tests offer a checklist of features for the administrator (often the teacher) to use in pinpointing difficulties.

B3 Achievement tests

Achievement tests are (or should be) limited to particular materials addressed in a curriculum within a particular time frame and are offered after a course has focused on the objectives in questions.

It's tempting to blur the line of distinction between a diagnostic test and a general achievement test. Achievement tests analyze the extent to which students have acquired language features that have already been taught; diagnostic tests should elicit information on what students need to work on in the future. Therefore, a diagnostic test will typically offer more detailed, subcategorized information on the learner.

B4 Proficiency tests

The purpose of **proficiency tests** is to test global competence in a language. A proficiency test is not limited to any one course, curriculum, or single skill in the language; rather, it tests overall ability.

B5 Aptitude tests

Aptitude tests are given to a person ***prior*** to any exposure to the second language to predict a person's future success. Language aptitude tests are designed to measure a person's capacity or general ability to learn a foreign language and to be successful in that undertaking. Aptitude tests are considered to be independent of a particular language.

C Types of Test Items

only one skill, analytic	Discrete-point	Integrative	more than two skills, global
mean, median, standard deviation, percentile rank	Norm-referenced	Criterion-referenced	feedback on specific course or lesson objectives
at the end of a course	Summative	Formative	in the process of a course
performing a task related	Indirect	Direct	actually performing the task
select one of the alternatives	Selected-response	Constructed-response	develop S's own answer (= performance / alternative ~)

C1 Discrete-point vs. Integrative test

Discrete-point tests are constructed on the assumption that language can be broken down into its component parts and that those parts can be tested successfully. Those components are basically the skills of listening, speaking, reading, writing, the various hierarchical units of language (phonology, morphology, lexicon, syntax, discourse) within each skill, and subcategories within those units.

The discrete-point approach met with some criticism as we emerged into an era of emphasizing communication, authenticity, and context. The criticism was, in short, that communicative competence is so global and requires such integration (hence the term **integrative testing**) that it cannot be captured in additive tests of grammar and reading and vocabulary and other discrete points of language.

Two types of the test have been held up as examples of integrative tests: cloze tests and dictations. A **cloze** test is a reading passage that has been 'mutilated' by the deletion of roughly every sixth or seventh word; the test-taker is required to supply words that fit into those blanks. John Oller (1979) claimed that cloze test results are good measures of overall proficiency. According to theoretical constructs underlying this claim, the ability to supply appropriate words in blanks requires a number of abilities that lie at the very heart of competence in a language: knowledge of vocabulary, grammatical structure, discourse structure, reading skills and strategies, and an internalized 'expectancy' grammar (that enables one to predict an item that will come next in a sequence).

The argument for claiming **dictation** as an integrative test is that it taps into grammatical and discourse competencies required for other modes of performance in a language. Further, dictation test results tend to correlate strongly with other tests of proficiency. Success on a dictation requires careful listening, reproduction in writing of what is heard, efficient short-term memory, and, to an extent, some expectancy rules to aid the short-term memory.

C2 Norm-referenced vs. Criterion-referenced test

The extent to which a test is practical sometimes hinges on whether a test is designed to be norm-referenced or criterion-referenced.

In **norm-referenced tests**, each test-taker's score is interpreted in relation to a mean, median, standard deviation, and/or percentile rank. The purpose in such tests is to place test-takers along a mathematical continuum in rank order. Typical of norm-referenced tests are standardized tests intended to be administered to large audiences, with results quickly disseminated to test-takers.

Criterion-referenced tests, on the other hand, is designed to give test-takers feedback on specific course or lesson objectives, that is, the 'criteria'. Classroom tests involving smaller numbers, and connected to a curriculum, are typical of criterion-referenced testing. Here, more time and effort on the part of the teacher (test administrator) are usually required in order to deliver the feedback.

C3 Summative vs. Formative test

Summative assessments aim to measure, or summarize, what a student has grasped and typically occurs at the end of a course or unit of instruction. A summation of what a student has learned implies looking back and taking stock of how well that student has accomplished objectives, but it does not necessarily point the way to future progress.

The purpose of **formative assessments** is to evaluate students in the process of 'forming' their competencies and skills with the goal of helping them to continue that growth process. The key to such formation is the delivery (by the teacher) and internalization (by the student) of appropriate feedback on performance, with an eye toward the future continuation (or formation) of learning.

C4 Direct vs. Indirect test

Direct testing involves the test-taker in actually performing the target task. In an **indirect test**, learners are not performing the task itself but rather a task that is related in some way. For example, if you intend to test learners' oral production of syllable stress and your test task is to have learners mark (with written accent marks) stressed syllables in a list of written words, you could, with a stretch of logic, argue that you are indirectly testing their oral production. A direct test of syllable production would require that students actually produce target words orally.

The most feasible rule of thumb for achieving content validity in classroom assessment is to test performance directly. Consider, for example, a listening/speaking class that is doing a unit on greetings and exchanges that includes discourse for asking for personal information (name, address, hobbies, etc.) with some form-focus on the verb be, personal pronouns, and question formation. The test on that unit should include all of the above discourse and grammatical elements and involve students in the actual performance of listening and speaking.

C5 Selected-Response vs. Constructed-Response test

The most familiar form of assessment is one in which the test-taker is asked to select each response from a set of specified alternatives. Because the test-taker chooses an option rather than creating an answer from scratch, such an assessment is called a **selected-response assessment**. Such assessments include multiple-choice, matching, and true-false tests.

Alternatively, an assessment can require a student to develop his or her own answer in response to a stimulus, or prompt. An assessment of this form, such as one that requires an essay or a solution to a mathematical problem, is called a **constructed-response assessment**. Neither the prompts nor the responses need be written, however. Responses commonly include any form whose quality can be judged accurately, from live performances to accumulated work products. For this reason, constructed-response assessments are also called **performance assessments**. In our study, we also used the less technical term **alternative assessment** as a synonym for both of these terms.

[Features of Selected- and Constructed-Response Measures]

Feature	Selected-Response			Constructed-Response		
	Rarely	Some-times	Usually	Rarely	Some-times	Usually
Easy to develop			✔	✔		
Easy to administer			✔		✔	
Easy to score			✔	✔		
Similar to real world in performance demands ('authentic')	✔					✔
Efficient (requires limited time)			✔	✔		
Credible to stakeholders			✔		✔	
Embodies desired learning activities	✔					✔
Sound basis for determining quality of scores			✔		✔	
Effective for factual knowledge			✔			✔
Effective		✔				✔

D Multiple-choice Tests

D1 Principles and Terms for MCQ

principles	Practicality		easy to administer
	Reliability		consistent and dependable
terms	Stem (= Prompt)		the body of the item
	Options (= Alternatives)	Key	the correct response
		Distractors	the rest

The two principles that stand out in support of multiple-choice formats are, of course, practicality and reliability. With their predetermined correct responses and time-saving scoring procedures, multiple-choice items offer overworked teachers the tempting possibility of an easy and consistent process of scoring and grading. But you might spend even more time designing such items than you save in grading the test. Of course, if your objective is to design a large-scale standardized test for repeated administrations, then a multiple-choice format does indeed become viable.

As you face the task of designing the test, let's first consider some important terminology.

① Multiple-choice items are all receptive, or selective response, items in that the test-taker chooses from a set of responses (commonly called a supply type of response) rather than creating a response. Other receptive item types include true/false questions and matching lists.

② Every multiple-choice item has a **stem** (the 'body' of the item that presents a stimulus) and several (usually between three and five) **options** or **alternatives** to choose from.

③ One of those options, the **key**, is the correct response, whereas the others serve as **distractors**.

D2 Guidelines for making closed-ended test tasks

Closed-ended response tasks are suitable for testing skills involved in reading and listening because they involve comprehension skills. They do not require the test taker to produce or generate a response. Closed-ended response tasks can be particularly suitable for beginning level learners precisely because they do not require language production and because they are highly structured.

Most closed-ended test tasks are some form of what is commonly known as multiple-choice questions, although there are some variations that are not. Matching tasks in which the test taker must match one set of items, such as specific words, to another set, such as different 'parts of speech' or grammatical terms, are an example. However, even this format can be conceived of as multiple-choice in that the grammatical items constitute a set of multiple-choice answers, only one of which is correct as a descriptor of each. Multiple-choice question formats include a stem, or prompt, and alternative responses. The **stem** is, in effect, the question. The alternatives that are not correct are called **distractors**.

What follows are general guidelines for constructing multiple-choice types of closed-ended test tasks. These guidelines are summarized in the following table. We present guidelines for preparing stems and response alternatives.

[Checklist for devising closed-ended tests]

[The stem]
1. Is the stem simple and concise?
2. Are there unnecessary double negatives or other complex wordings in the stem?
3. Does the stem assess what it is supposed to?
4. Are there inadvertent cues to the right answer?
5. Is the stem a verbatim repetition of material taught in class? If so, is this desirable?

[The response alternatives]
1. Are the distractors of the same grammatical and semantic class as the correct response?
2. Are the response alternatives grammatically compatible with the stem?
3. Are all the alternatives equally attractive?
4. Are the distractors informative?
5. Are the alternatives equally difficult, complex, and long?
6. Is there more than one correct alternative?
7. Does the wording of the alternatives match the stem?
8. Can the correct response be derived from common knowledge?
9. Are the alternatives suitably simple?
10. Can the answer to any items be derived from other items?
11. Do any of the alternatives refer to other items?

1) The stem

The stem, or prompt, in a multiple-choice task can be linguistic or nonlinguistic in nature. Nonlinguistic stems consist of pictures or **realia** (i.e., real objects). Linguistic stems can consist of single words, phrases, sentences, written text, oral passages, or discourse.

① The stem should be presented in a simple, concise form so that the task or problem posed by the item is clear and unambiguous. In other words, it should be clear to the test taker what is called for after reading or hearing the stem. For example, the following item is ambiguous because it leads to more than one possible correct answer:

> • She watched her carefully _____ her coat on.
>   a. put*
>   b. puts
>   c. to put
>   d. while putting*

② In most cases, it is advisable to avoid using negatively worded stems since they make extra and often unnecessary demands on the test taker. For example:

> • Which of the following is not true?

③ Make sure the stem is testing what it is supposed to be testing. In particular, make sure that the point that is being tested is the only source of difficulty in the stem. Otherwise, the task will demand more than you want to test. For example, if the item is testing vocabulary, make sure that any language used to provide context for the target item is familiar and comprehensible to the student; otherwise you might be testing knowledge of more than one vocabulary item. For example:

> • Jane *donated* a candelabrum to the charity bazaar.
>   a. gave*
>   b. sold
>   c. sent
>   d. wore

In this stem, the target word is ***donated***, but the use of the words ***candelabrum*** and *bazaar* may confuse and mislead students because they are not familiar with them. Or if it is a sentence comprehension item, for example, make sure that obscure vocabulary that could impede comprehension is avoided, that is, unless you want to see whether the students can infer the meaning of unknown words from context. Obscure vocabulary in a sentence comprehension item turns the task from sentence comprehension to vocabulary knowledge.

④ Avoid stems that inadvertently give clues to the right answer for unimportant or uninteresting reasons. For example:

> • Charlie is always late for school, so his mother is going to buy an _____ clock for him.
> a. ring
> b. alarm*
> c. morning
> d. bell

The correct answer in this case (alarm) is cued by the article *an* in addition to the meaning; *an* is always followed by a word that begins with a vowel, and *alarm* is the only alternative that begins with a vowel.

⑤ It is often advisable to avoid making the stem identical to material that has been taught or used in class in order to avoid correct responding on the basis of memory alone. There may be exceptions to this, such as testing for comprehension of idiomatic expressions.

2) The response alternatives

Like the stem, the alternative responses in a multiple-choice item can be linguistic or nonlinguistic in nature. The latter can consist of pictures or realia. For example, the examiner says a word, and the students must select from among four alternative pictures the one that corresponds to the word. More commonly, alternative responses are expressed in linguistic form. For example, the examiner says a word, and the students select from among four spoken alternative words the one that is a synonym of the target.

① Distractors should belong to the same general grammatical or semantic category as the correct response. In other words, avoid distractors that are different from the correct alternative in structural or semantic terms. If the test taker has a general idea of the type of response called for, such differences might give inadvertent clues that certain responses are wrong.

For example, if the stem consists of a sentence with a word missing (i.e., cloze format), then all alternative responses should belong to the grammatical category needed to fill in the blank. For example:

> T: Another place to put our adverb?
> - She walked _____ up the steps to the library.
>   a. weak
>   b. slowly*
>   c. try
>   d. wisdom

In this case, the test taker might recognize that an adverb is called for. Since *slowly* is the only adverb among the alternatives, it would be selected regardless of its meaning. This would be an appropriate set of distractors if you want to test the test takers' understanding that an adverb, and not some other part of speech, is called for in this gap.

In reading comprehension tasks, the distractors should refer to the text in some way. Alternatives that are totally unrelated to the stem can be eliminated by the test taker simply on the basis of general understanding. For example:

> Japan has few natural resources. To prosper and survive, the country must import raw materials, maintain high standards of manufacturing, and sell finished goods in foreign markets.
>
> - Japanese prosperity depends *most* on:
>   a. discovering new raw materials
>   b. importing manufactured goods
>   c. her people's religion
>   d. high levels of international trade*

In this item, distractor c. could be eliminated easily because it has no relationship to the text.

② When the stems are incomplete statements that call for completion, use distractors that are grammatically compatible with the stem. For example, in the item on Japanese prosperity, if alternative (d) had read *to sell finished goods internationally*, the item would have been much more difficult and confusing to the test taker because the grammatical form of the alternative does not fit with the stem.

③ In principle, all distractors should be equally attractive and plausible to the test taker; that is to say, each distractor will be chosen equally often by test takers who do not choose the right answer. Distractors that are never or seldom chosen instead of the right answer are not serving any useful function. In practice, it is difficult to create distractors that are equally attractive, but some effort should be put into achieving this.

When devising distractors, it might be helpful to (a) define the grammatical or semantic category to which the distractors should belong, and (b) think of alternatives that have some association with the stem or correct choice. In order to determine the attractiveness of distractors, it is necessary to keep a record of how often each distractor for a given question is chosen.

One method of identifying distractors is to choose them from the errors that students make in their spoken or written use of the language. Choosing distractors in this way means that you are likely to include plausible distractors that are attractive to the students who do not know the right answer.

④ Choose distractors that can tell you something about where the students are going wrong if they select them. A related point, avoid trick alternatives that distract the test taker for trivial or unimportant reasons. For example:

> - Definition item: to cook by exposing to direct heat
>   a. roost
>   b. burn
>   c. broil*
>   d. fry

Roost is a trivial and tricky distractor because it confuses word meaning and pronunciation in a way that is not useful. It was chosen because of its resemblance to ***roast***.

⑤ Choose distractors that have comparable difficulty, complexity, and length. Distractors that are obviously different from the alternatives might be especially salient to the test taker with the result that they are more likely to be eliminated or accepted. For example:

> Choose the best definition of the underlined word:
> - Mary is a very bright student; she got As in all of her courses.
>   a. difficult
>   b. erudite*
>   c. shiny
>   d. friendly

Erudite is a poor alternative since it is a much more sophisticated word than the others and might be chosen for that reason alone.

⑥ Avoid including more than one correct alternative. In this regard, avoid distractors that might be correct in another dialect, regional variation, or modality of the language. For example, if you are testing spoken language, avoid using language in the distractors that might be considered appropriate in the written form of the language. An exception to this is if you want to test sociolinguistic skills. The best way to avoid more than one correct alternative is to have someone else review your test items.

There should be no 'missing link' between the stem and the alternative responses that would make more than one of them correct. This can happen when students assume some additional plausible context. For example:

> - He left the office early _____ he could do some shopping.
>   a. so*
>   b. if*
>   c. unless
>   d. that

In this item, both *so* and *if* could be correct depending on the context you have in mind.

⑦ Avoid using alternative answers that contain words or phrases that match the stem if the other alternatives do not contain similar matching elements. An alternative that matches the stem while others do not might be chosen on the basis of the matching elements alone. In some cases this might lead to a correct choice, whereas in other cases it can lead to an incorrect choice. This is particularly important in comprehension tests.

⑧ It should not be possible to choose the correct response on the basis of general knowledge. In other words, choosing the correct response should depend on the content of the test. One way of examining this possibility is to have someone answer the questions without reading or hearing the text. For example:

> • When tourists from Canada go to Florida on vacation, they travel _____.
>   a. north
>   b. west
>   c. east
>   d. south*

⑨ The alternative responses should be as simple as possible in keeping with the complexity of the test purposes. Avoid repetitious wording, redundancy, and unnecessary detail in the responses. For example:

> • Robert went to the hospital _____.
>   a. because he wanted to visit his sick brother
>   b. because he wanted to have his leg examined
>   c. because he was a volunteer worker in the gift shop
>   d. because his brother has asked him to

In this case, it would be better to include all of the repetitious elements in the stem: ***Robert went to the hospital because*** ⋯

⑩ In reading comprehension tasks, when several items are based on a single text, the answer to one question should not be given by the wording of another. For example:

> (1) What did Mary serve Sam?
>   a. leftover casserole
>   b. scrambled eggs
>   c. hamburger and fries
>   d. fresh salmon*
>
> (2) Where did Sam go for dinner?
>   a. to Mary's*
>   b. home
>   c. to the school cafeteria
>   d. to Joe's Restaurant

⑪ Avoid answers that refer to several other answer choices. For example:

> • She didn't go to the party because she _____.
>   a. was sick
>   b. had nothing to wear
>   c. was expecting an important call
>   d. b and c but not a

3) Assembling multiple-choice questions

The following are a number of points to take into consideration when putting multiple-choice items together for a test or examination.

① Make sure the stem is distinct from the alternative answers. In written tests this can be achieved by inserting extra spaces between the stem and the alternative responses and by listing and indenting the alternatives on separate lines. In oral tests, the stem can be distinguished from the alternative responses by presenting the stem in one voice, say a female voice, and alternatives in another voice, a male voice.

> *Poor presentation*
> - The population of Denmark is: (a) 2 million, (b) 4 million, (c) 7 million, (d) 15 million
>
> *Good presentation*
> - The population of Denmark is:
>   a. 2 million
>   b. 4 million
>   c. 7 million
>   d. 15 million

② Identify the stems and alternatives using different symbols: for example, numbers for the stems and letters for the alternatives. When using separate answer sheets, make sure that your method of identifying stems and alternatives on the test corresponds to that presented on the students' answer sheet.

③ The correct alternative should occur equally frequently in each option position. Avoid presenting the correct choice in a particular position.

④ Use as many alternatives as are both possible and reasonable. The chances of selecting the correct alternative by guessing alone diminishes with more alternatives. With three alternatives, students have a 33% chance of getting the correct answer by guessing; with five alternatives, the chances of a correct response due to guessing are reduced to 20 percent. However, increasing the number of alternatives makes it increasingly difficult to construct plausible, attractive, and appropriate distractors.

⑤ Allow plenty of space between questions so that the test does not appear to be compressed and jammed together.

Good closed-ended test tasks require considerable time and thought to prepare. Whether it is worth investing the time and thought needed to devise these kinds of tests depends on how the test results will be used and the importance of the decisions based on those results. Clearly, the investment of a great deal of time and thought is warranted when there are a large number of students to be tested. Another consideration when deciding whether to use a closed-ended test format is authenticity: arguably, many closed-ended test formats often do not reflect the way authentic language is used. They may nevertheless be useful for evaluating specific aspects of language learning. In some cases, closed-ended test tasks do call on the kinds of language performance your students will be expected to demonstrate. As in other aspects of classroom-based evaluation, one form of testing is not necessarily desirable under all circumstances and for all purposes. Rather, judicious use of each form may be called for.

D3 Item Analysis

Distractor Efficiency	luring a sufficient number of test-takers & evenly distributed
Item Facility	(= Item Difficulty) easy or difficult for the group of test-takers
Item Discrimination	differentiating between high- and low-ability test-takers

(D3a) Distractor Efficiency

Distractor efficiency is one more important measure of a multiple-choice item's value in a test and one that is related to item discrimination. The efficiency of distractors is the extent to which (a) the distractors 'lure' a sufficient number of test-takers, especially lower-ability ones, and (b) those responses are somewhat evenly distributed across all distractors. Those of you who have a fear of mathematical formulas will be happy to hear that there is no formula for calculating distractor efficiency and that an inspection of a distribution of responses will usually yield the information you need.

Consider the following. This is a multiple-choice item with five choices, and responses across upper- and lower-ability students are distributed as follows:

Choices	A	B	C*	D	E
High-ability students (10)	0	1	7	0	2
Low-ability students (10)	3	5	2	0	0

* Note: **C** is the correct response.

No mathematical formula is needed to tell you that this item successfully attracts seven of the ten high-ability students toward the correct response, whereas only two of the low-ability students get this one right. The item might be improved in two ways: (a) Distractor D doesn't fool anyone. No one picked it, and therefore it probably has no utility. A revision might provide a distractor that actually attracts a response or two; (b) distractor E attracts more responses (two) from the high-ability group than the low-ability group (zero). Why are good students choosing this one? Perhaps it includes a subtle reference that entices the high group but is 'over the head' of the low group, and therefore the latter students don't even consider it.

The other two distractors (A and B) seem to be fulfilling their function of attracting some attention from lower-ability students.

(D3b) Item Facility

Item facility (IF) is the extent to which an item is easy or difficult for the proposed group of test-takers. You may wonder why that is important if in your estimation the item achieves validity. The answer is that an item that is too easy or too difficult really does nothing to separate high-ability and low-ability test-takers. It is not really performing much 'work' for you on a test.

IF simply reflects the percentage of students answering the item correctly. The formula looks like this:

$$IF = \frac{\text{\# of students answering the item correctly}}{\text{Total \# of students responding to that item}}$$

For example, if you have an item on which 13 out of 20 students respond correctly, your IF index is 13 divided by 20 or .65(65%). There is no absolute IF value that must be met to determine if an item should be included in the test as is, modified, or thrown out, but appropriate test items will generally have IFs that range between .15 and .85. Two good reasons for occasionally including a very easy item (.85 or higher) are to build in some affective feelings of 'success' among lower ability students and to serve as warm-up items. Very difficult items can provide a challenge to the highest-ability students.

(D3c) Item Discrimination

Item discrimination (ID) is the extent to which an item differentiates between high- and low-ability test-takers. An item on which high-ability students (who did well on the test) and low-ability students (who did not) score equally well would have poor ID because it did not discriminate between the two groups. Conversely, an item that garners correct responses from most of the high-ability group and incorrect responses from most of the low-ability group has good discrimination power.

Suppose your class of 30 students has taken a test. Once you have calculated final scores for all 30 students, divide them roughly into thirds — that is, create three rank-ordered ability groups including the top 10 scores, the middle 10, and the lowest 10. To find out which of your 50 or so test items were most 'powerful' in discriminating between high and low ability, eliminate the middle group, leaving two groups with results that might look something like this on a particular item:

Item 23	No. Correct	No. Incorrect
High-ability students (top 10)	7	3
Low-ability students (bottom 10)	2	8

Using the ID formula (7-2=5÷10=0.50), you would find that this item has an ID of 0.50, or a moderate level.

The formula for calculating ID is

$$ID = \frac{\text{High group no. correct} - \text{low group no. correct}}{\frac{1}{2} \times \text{total of your two comparison groups}} = \frac{7-2}{\frac{1}{2} \times 20} = \frac{5}{10} = 0.50$$

The result of this example item tells you that the item has a moderate level of ID. High discriminating power would approach a perfect 1.0, and no discriminating power at all would be zero. In most cases, you would want to discard an item that scored near zero. As with IF, no absolute rule governs the establishment of acceptable and unacceptable ID indices.

One clear, practical use for ID indices is to select items from a test bank that includes more items than you need. You might decide to discard or improve some items with lower ID because you know they won't be as powerful an indicator of success on your test.

E   Integrative Testing

E1   Dictation

Dictation is a widely researched genre of assessing listening comprehension. In a dictation, test-takers hear a passage, typically of 50 to 100 words, recited three times: first at normal speed; then with long pauses between phrases or natural word groups, during which time test-takers write down what they have just heard; and finally at normal speed once more so they can check their work and proofread.

E2 Cloze test

Fixed-ratio	deletion procedure	every seventh word (± two)
Rational		all words according to grammatical or discourse functions
Exact	word scoring method	only the exact word in the origin
Appropriate		any word grammatically correct and makes good sense

The word cloze was coined by educational psychologists to capture the Gestalt concept of 'closure', that is, the ability to fill in gaps in an incomplete image (visual, auditory, or cognitive) and supply (from background schemata) omitted details.

In written language, a sentence with a word left out should have enough context that a reader can close that gap with a calculated guess, using linguistic expectancies (formal schemata), background experience (content schemata), and some strategic competence. Based on this assumption, **cloze** tests were developed for native-language readers and defended as an appropriate gauge of reading ability. Some research on SLA vigorously defends cloze testing as an integrative measure not only of reading ability but also of other language abilities. It was argued that the ability to make coherent guesses in cloze gaps also taps into the ability to listen, speak, and write. With the decline in enthusiasm for the search for the ideal integrative test in recent years, cloze testing has returned to a more appropriate status as one of a number of assessment procedures available for testing reading ability.

Cloze tests are usually a minimum of two paragraphs in length to account for discourse expectancies. They can be constructed relatively easily as long as the specifications for choosing deletions and for scoring are clearly defined. Typically every seventh word (± two) is deleted (**fixed-ratio deletion procedure**), but many cloze-test designers instead use a **rational deletion procedure** of choosing deletions according to the grammatical or discourse functions of the words. Rational deletion also allows the designer to avoid deleting words that would be difficult to predict from the context. For example, in the sentence "Everyone in the crowd enjoyed the gorgeous sunset.", the seventh word is 'gorgeous', but learners could easily substitute other appropriate adjectives.

Two approaches to the scoring of cloze tests are commonly used. The **exact word scoring method** gives credits to test-takers only if they insert the exact word that was originally deleted. The second method, **appropriate word scoring method**, credits the test-takers for supplying any word that is grammatically correct and makes good sense in the context.

The choice between the two methods of scoring is one of practicality/reliability versus face validity. In the exact word approach, scoring can be done quickly (especially if the procedure uses a multiple-choice technique) and reliably. The second approach takes more time because the teacher must determine whether each response is indeed appropriate, but students will perceive the test as being fairer because they won't get 'marked off' for appropriate, grammatically correct responses.

The following excerpts from a longer essay illustrate the difference between rational and fixed-ratio deletion and between exact word and appropriate word scoring.

Fixed-ratio deletion (every seventh word)

The recognition that one's feelings of (1) _____ and unhappiness can coexist much like (2) _____ and hate in a close relationship (3) _____ offer valuable clues on how to (4) _____ a happier life. It suggests, for (5) _____, that changing or avoiding things that (6) _____ you miserable may well make you (7) _____ miserable but probably no happier.

Rational deletion (prepositions and conjunctions)

The recognition that one's feelings (1) _____ happiness (2) _____ unhappiness can coexist much like love and hate (3) _____ a close relationship may offer valuable clues (4) _____ how to lead a happier life. It suggests, (5) _____ example, that changing (6) _____ avoiding things that make you miserable may well make you less miserable (7) _____ probably no happier.

In both versions there are seven deletions, but the second version allows the test designer to tap into prediction of prepositions and conjunctions in particular. The second version also provides more washback as students focus on targeted grammatical features.

Both of these scoring methods could present problems, with the first version presenting a little more ambiguity. Possible responses might include the following:

Fixed-ratio deletion version, blank	Rational deletion version, blank
3: *may, might, could, can*	4: *on, about*
4: *lead, live, have, seek*	6: *or, and*
5: *example, instance*	7: *but, and*

E3 C-test

Some variations on standard cloze testing have appeared over the years; one of the better known is the C-test. In the **C-test**, the second half (according to the number of letters) of every other word is obliterated and the test-taker must restore each word. Many consider this technique to be 'even more irritating to complete than cloze tests'.

> ### C-test
> The recognition th__ one's feel___ of happ_____ and unhap_____ can coe___ much li__ love a__ hate i_ a cl___ relati_____ may of___ valuable cl___ on h__ to le__ a hap____ life. I_ suggests, f__ example, th__ changing o_ avoiding thi__ that ma__ y__ miserable may we__ make y__ less mise_____ but prob___ no hap____.

F Alternative Assessments

Portfolios	a purposeful collection of students' work
Dialogue Journals	an interaction between T and S thru dialogues or responses
Conferences	a conversation between T and S about a draft
Observations	assessing students without their awareness for authenticity
Self- and Peer-Assessment	for autonomy and for cooperative learning

F1 Portfolios

One of the most popular forms of alternative assessment within a communicative framework is the construction of portfolios. A **portfolio** is 'a purposeful collection of students' work that demonstrates to students and others their efforts, progress, and achievements in given areas'. Portfolios include essays, compositions, poetry, book reports, art work, video or audio recordings of a student's oral production, journals, and virtually anything else one wishes to specify. In earlier decades of our history, portfolios were thought to be applicable only to younger children who assembled a portfolio of art and written work for presentation to a teacher and/or a parent. But now, learners of all ages and in all fields of study are benefiting from the tangible, hands-on nature of portfolio development.

In order to use portfolios as a form of classroom-based assessment, teachers need to give clear directions to students on how to get started (many students will never have compiled a portfolio before and may be mystified about what to do). Showing a sample portfolio from a previous student might help to stimulate thoughts on what to include. And if feasible, teachers need to utilize web-based or online opportunities for portfolio compilation and sharing. Many teachers now have class websites that give teacher and students easy access to announcements, supplementary materials, discussions, and posting of student-generated material.

F2 Dialogue Journals

A journal is a log or 'account' of one's thoughts, feelings, reactions, assessments, ideas, or correctness. Most classroom-oriented journals are what have now come to be known as **dialogue journals**. Recently, the assessment qualities of journal writing have assumed an important role in the teaching-learning process. Because most journals are — or should be — a dialogue between student and teacher, they afford a unique opportunity for a teacher to offer various kinds of feedback to learners.

F3 Conferences

For a number of years, conferences have been a routine part of language classrooms, especially of courses in writing. **Conferencing** has become a standard part of a process approach to teaching writing, as the teacher, in a conversation about a draft, facilitates the improvement of the written work. Such interaction has the advantage of allowing one-on-one communication between teacher and student such that the specific needs of a student can receive direct feedback. Conferences can be in-person (for maximum exchange of ideas) or computer-based through blogs and other online media.

Through conferences, a teacher can assume the role of a facilitator and guide, rather than a master controller and deliverer of final grades. In this embracing atmosphere, students can feel that the teacher is an ally who is encouraging self-reflection. It's important to consider a conference as a dialogue that is ***not*** to be graded. Conferences are by nature formative, not summative; formative assessment points students toward further development, rather than offering a final summation of performance.

F4 Observations

One of the characteristics of an effective teacher is the ability to ***observe*** students as they perform. Teachers are constantly engaged in a process of taking students' performance and intuitively assessing it and using those evaluations to offer feedback.

On the other hand, observations can become systematic, planned procedures for real-time, almost surreptitious recording of student verbal and nonverbal behavior. One of the objectives of such observation is to assess students as much as possible without their awareness (and possible consequent anxiety) of the observation, so that the naturalness of their linguistic performance will be maximized. Checklists, charts, rating scales, systematic note-taking, and teachers' journals can all help to support our intuitive observations and to provide a source of identifiable feedback to students.

You will probably find moderate practicality and reliability in observations, especially if the objectives are kept simple. Face validity and content validity are likely to get high marks because observations are likely to be integrated into the ongoing process of a course. Authenticity is high because, if an observation goes relatively unnoticed by the student, then there is little likelihood of contrived situation. Washback can be high if you take the time and effort to help a student to become aware of your data on their performance.

F5 Self- and Peer-Assessment

A conventional view of language pedagogy might consider **self- and peer-assessment** to be an absurd reversal of the teaching-learning process. But a closer look at the acquisition of any skill reveals the importance, if not the necessity, of self-assessment and the benefit of peer-assessment. Successful learners extend the learning process well beyond the classroom and the presence of a teacher or tutor, autonomously mastering the art of self-assessment. And where peers are avaliable to render assessment, why not take advantage of such additional input?

Research has shown a number of advantages of self- and peer-assessment: speed, direct involvement of students, the encouragement of autonomy, and increased motivation because of self-involvement in the process of learning. Of course, the disadvantage of *subjectivity* (which leads to unreliability) looms large, and must be considered whenever you propose to involve students in self- and peer-assessment.

G Holistic vs. Analytic Scoring

Holistic scoring	a systematic set of descriptors, for Practicality
Analytic scoring	descriptors on several elements, for Washback

G1 Holistic Scoring

The following scoring scale is a prime example of **holistic scoring**. Each point on a holistic scale is given a systematic set of descriptors, and the reader-evaluator matches an overall impression with the descriptors to arrive at a score.

Test of Written English scoring guide

Scores

6   **Demonstrates clear competence in writing on both the rhetorical and syntactic levels, though it may have occasional errors.**

   A paper in this category
   - effectively addresses the writing task
   - is well organized and well developed
   - uses clearly appropriate details to support a thesis or illustrate ideas
   - displays consistent facility in the use of language
   - demonstrates syntactic variety and appropriate word choice

5   **Demonstrates competence in writing on both the rhetorical and syntactic levels, though it will probably have occasional errors.**

   A paper in this category

- may address some parts of the task more effectively than others
- is generally well organized and developed
- uses details to support a thesis or illustrate an idea
- displays facility in the use of language
- demonstrates some syntactic variety and range of vocabulary

4   **Demonstrates minimal competence in writing on both the rhetorical and syntactic levels.**
    A paper in this category
    - addresses the writing topic adequately but may slight parts of the task
    - is adequately organized and developed
    - uses some details to support a thesis or illustrate an idea
    - demonstrates adequate but possibly inconsistent facility with syntax and usage
    - may contain some errors that occasionally obscure meaning

3   **Demonstrates some developing competence in writing, but it remains flawed on either the rhetorical or syntactic level, or both.**
    A paper in this category may reveal one or more of the following weaknesses:
    - inadequate organization or development
    - inappropriate or insufficient details to support or illustrate generalizations
    - a noticeably inappropriate choice of words or word forms
    - an accumulation of errors in sentence structure and/or usage

2   **Suggests incompetence in writing.**
    A paper in this category is seriously flawed by one or more of the following weaknesses:
    - serious disorganization or underdevelopment
    - little or no detail, or irrelevant specifics
    - serious and frequent errors in sentence structure or usage
    - serious problems with focus

1   **Demonstrates incompetence in writing.**
    A paper in this category
    - may be incoherent
    - may be undeveloped
    - may contain severe and persistent writing errors

G2 Analytic Scoring

For classroom instruction, holistic scoring provides little washback into the writer's further stages of learning. Classroom evaluation of learning is best served through **analytic scoring**, in which as many as six major elements of writing are scored, thus enabling learners to hone in on weaknesses and capitalize on strengths. Scores in five or six major elements help call the writers' attention to areas of needed improvement. Practicality is lowered in that more time is required for teachers to attend to details within each of the categories to render a final score or grade, but ultimately students receive more information about their writing.

[Rubric in English for Level 3 Task 3 in NEAT]

	Scoring Dimensions			
	Task Completion	Content	Organization	Language Use
score	- An email made up of 40~50 words - Suggests the type of clothes to bring to the writer's Australian friend - Makes sympathizing remarks toward the Australian friend's concern	- Presents appropriate response to the Australian friend concerning the cold weather in Korea - Provides adequate suggestion for his/her friend - Provides appropriate details in suggestion	- Introductory remarks for a reply to a friend's email - Has a sentence of presenting appropriate response to the Australian friend's concern - Appropriate placement of suggesting remarks - Appropriate ending - Coherent	- Uses only English and appropriate vocabulary - Variety in sentence structures - Few grammar errors - Few errors in spelling
5	The writer completely addresses the assigned writing task.	The writer provides relevant content that is complete, concrete, and thoroughly developed.	The writer develops an adequate organizational structure, including an effective introduction, body, and conclusion. Main ideas are complete and logically sequenced.	Few grammar or spelling errors are evident. Vocabulary usage is generally controlled and ideas are expressed clearly.

4	The writer makes a reasonable, mostly complete, attempt to address the writing task.	The writer provides relevant content that is mostly complete.	The writer develops a mostly complete organizational structure, including an introduction, body, and conclusion. The sequencing of main ideas is mostly complete and logical.	Some grammar or spelling errors are evident, but they do not distract from the writer's message. Vocabulary usage is mostly correct, although some words may be misused.
3	The writer makes a reasonable, but incomplete, attempt to address the writing task.	The writer provides some relevant content, but it may be incomplete or undeveloped.	The writer develops an incomplete organizational structure that may include a weak introduction, body, and conclusion. The sequencing of main ideas may be incomplete and illogical.	Some grammar or spelling errors may affect the communication of the writer's message. Some control of vocabulary usage is evident, although errors may affect communication of the writer's message.
2	The writer makes a poor, incomplete attempt to address the writing task.	The writer attempts to provide relevant content, but it may be irrelevant, undeveloped, and incomplete.	The writer attempts to develop an organizational structure, but it is incomplete. Main ideas may not be evident or logical.	Numerous errors in grammar, spelling, and vocabulary usage negatively affect the communication of the writer's message.
1	The writer fails to address the writing task.	The writer fails to provide any content that is relevant or complete.	The writer fails to develop a meaningful organizational structure or logical progression of main ideas.	Pervasive errors in grammar, spelling, and vocabulary usage significantly impair communication of the writer's message.
0	Answer not suitable for the given task (scribbling, use of obscene words, etc.); no answer provided; over 70% is written in any language other than English; evidence of writing anything that is not consistent with the given topic.			

최시원 전공영어 영어교육학
English Education Conceptual

APPENDIX

★ Glossary on English Education

A

- **Accessibility Hierarchy** A continuum of relative clause types such that the presence of one type implies the presence of other types higher on the hierarchy.

- **acculturation** The process of adapting to a new culture. This involves understanding different systems of thought, beliefs, emotions, and communication systems.

- **accuracy** The use of correct forms of grammar, vocabulary, spelling and pronunciation. See also fluency.

- **achievement test** See **test**.

- **acquisition** Learning a language without studying it, just by hearing and / or reading and then using it. This term is used to describe language being absorbed without conscious effort, i.e. the way children pick up their mother tongue. Language acquisition is often contrasted with language learning. For some researchers, such as Stephen Krashen, 'acquisition' is unconscious and spontaneous, and 'learning' is conscious, developing through formal study.

- **active vocabulary** The words and phrases which a learner is able to use in speech and writing. It is contrasted with **passive vocabulary**.

- **adaptation** The process through which a teacher makes changes in textbook materials to have them better fit a particular group of students.

- **additive bilingualism**   See **bilingualism**.

- **adjunct instruction** An approach to content-based language teaching in which L2 students concurrently enroll in a language and a content course; the tasks and assignments are generally coordinated between the language and content instructors. See content and language integrated learning, content-based instruction, sheltered instruction, and theme-based instruction.

- **advance organizer** An organizational framework that is presented in advance of a lesson to emphasize its central idea, e.g., having students skim a reading text or using a graphic organizer to present key ideas and vocabulary.

- **affective filter** An invisible psychological filter that can either facilitate or hinder second language acquisition.

- **alternative assessments** Ways other than standardized tests to get information about what students know and where they need help, such as oral reports, projects, performances, experiments, and class participation.

- **analytical approach** According to David Wilkins, one of two broad approaches to syllabus design; this approach uses topics, text, tasks and experiential content rather than linguistic content as its point of departure and is favored by communicative approaches to language teaching (e.g., task-based language teaching, content-based language teaching). See synthetic approach.

- **analytic rubric** An assessment tool that rates the various components of student performance and provides scores for each one. See holistic rubric.

- **anxiety** One of the affective factors that have been found to affect L2 acquisition. Different types of anxiety have been identified: trait ~ (a characteristic of a learner's personality) and state ~ (apprehension that is experienced at a particular moment in response to a definite situation). ~ may be both facilitating (i.e. it has a positive effect on L2), or debilitating (i.e. it has a negative effect).

- **approach** A theory about the nature of language and how languages are learned.

- **asking for clarification** Asking for an explanation of what a speaker means, e.g. *What do you mean*?

- **assessment** A general term to refer to various types of testing or evaluation.

- **asynchronous computer-mediated communication** Communication via computer that is not simultaneous, but delayed, as with email.

- **authentic** A term that describes language or tasks that approximate those used in the real world for non-pedagogical purposes, i.e., for genuine communication. See **authenticity**.

- **authenticity** The degree to which texts and tasks are 'real' rather than artificially created. See **authentic**.

- **authentic task (or real world task)** A task which involves learners in using language in a way that replicates its use in the 'real world' outside the language classroom. See **pedagogic task**.

- **authentic text** A text which is not written or spoken for language teaching purposes. A newspaper article, a rock song, a novel, a radio interview and a traditional fairy tale are examples of authentic texts. A story written to exemplify the use of reported speech, a dialogue scripted to exemplify ways of inviting and a linguistically simplified version of a novel would not be authentic texts. See **simplified texts**.

- **automaticity** The degree of routinized control that one has over linguistic knowledge.

- **autonomy** See **learner autonomy**.

B

- **back-channeling** When a listener signals understanding, surprise, agreement, etc. to a speaker as the speaker is speaking, e.g. *I see, uhhu, mm,* etc.

- **backwash effect** (in testing) The effect of a test on teaching.

- **basic interpersonal communication skills (BICS)** According to Jim Cummins, a learner's language proficiency that is characterized by a command of every-day, conversational or social language. See **cognitive academic language proficiency (CALP)**.

- **bilingualism** Being able to communicate effectively in two or more languages, with more or less the same degree of proficiency. There are various types of ~. In the case of additive ~, a speaker adds a second language without any loss of competence to the first language. This can lead to balanced ~. In the case of subtractive ~, the addition of a second language leads to gradual erosion of competence in the first language.

- **blended learning** Learning which involves a combination of e-learning and face-to-face learning.

- **bottom-up processing** The process whereby a learner applies existing knowledge of sound segments, words, phrases etc. to make sense of or to produce a spoken or written text. See top-down processing.

C

- **CA** See **contrastive analysis**.

- **CALL (Computer Assisted Language Learning)** The use of computer technology to assist processes of language learning.

- **care-taker speech** Speech produced by care-takers when they talk to young children. Care-takers typically use simplified syntactic structures, exaggerated pronunciation and a slow rate of speech. See also **child-directed speech; motherese**.

- **child-directed speech** The language addressed to a child. See also **care-taker speech**.

- **chunks** Sequences of words that are repeatedly used together, for example *you know what I mean, by the way, I don't know*; easily identified using corpus research.

- **clarification request** A device used in conversation to ask for more information when something has not been understood.

- **closed question** A question which leads to a yes / no answer or another very short response, e.g. *Did you come to school by bus? Yes. What did you have for breakfast? Toast.* See **open question**.

- **closed task** A task for which there is a single correct answer, solution, or outcome.

- **cloze** A type of assessment in which randomly-selected or deliberately-selected words in a written passage have been deleted and the test taker fills in the blanks.

- **CMC** See **computer-mediated communication**.

- **code-switching** One kind of intra-speaker variation. It occurs when a speaker changes from one variety or language to another variety or language in accordance with situational or purely personal factors.

- **cognitive academic language proficiency (CALP)** According to Jim Cummins, a learner's language proficiency that is characterized by not only a command of basic interpersonal communication skills (BICS) but also those language and literacy skills required for academic study. See **basic interpersonal communication skills (BICS)**.

- **cognitive strategies** Learning strategies that 'operate directly on incoming information, manipulating it in ways that enhance learning'. They involve such operations as rehearsal, organizing information, and inferencing.

- **cognitive style** Some psychologists consider that individuals have characteristic ways of perceiving phenomena, conceptualizing and recalling information. Various dimensions of ~ have been identified, including **field dependence** and **field independence**.

- **coherence** When ideas in a spoken or written text fit together clearly and smoothly, and so are logical and make sense to the listener or reader.

- **cohesion** The way spoken or written texts are joined together with logical grammar or lexis, e.g. conjunctions (Firstly, secondly), lexical sets, referring words (it, them).

- **cohesive device** A feature in a text which provides cohesion, e.g. use of topic-related vocabulary throughout a text, of sequencing words (then, next, after that, etc.), of referencing words (pronouns – he, him, etc.), of conjunctions (however, although, etc.).

- **collocation** Words that belong together, such as *to make a case*.

- **communication strategies** Strategies used when learners do not have the correct language for the concept they wish to express. e.g. paraphrase and mime.

- **communicative activity** A classroom activity in which learners need to talk or write to one another to complete the activity.

- **communicative competence** The ability to use the language effectively for communication. Gaining such competence involves acquiring both sociolinguistic and linguistic knowledge (or, in other words, developing the ability to use the language accurately, appropriately, and effectively).

- **Communicative Language Teaching (CLT)** An approach to language teaching dating from the 1970s that emphasizes the learning of language for (and by) meaningful interactions with others either through speech or writing, but usually with everyday speech as an initial priority.

- **Community Language Learning** A language teaching method developed by Charles Curran based on a counseling model; students decide what they want to say, the teacher translates these utterances into the target language, and once many expressions have been elicited, the teacher writes the expressions on board and explains their structure.

- **compensation strategies** Strategies used when learners do not know, or cannot immediately recall a word or words needed when speaking or writing.

- **Competition Model** One model of language processing based on how people interpret sentences.

- **comprehensibility** The perceived ease with which a speaker can be understood. See **intelligibility**.

- **comprehensible input** The understandable input that learners need for learning. Input that is slightly more advanced than the learner's current level of grammatical knowledge.

- **comprehensible output** The language produced by the learner (the 'output').

- **comprehension** Understanding a spoken or written text.

- **comprehension check** A device used in conversation to ensure that one's interlocutor has understood.

- **computer-mediated communication (CMC)** Communication that takes place over computer networks.

- **concordancer** Computer software that searches for words or phrases in text files and displays targets in a list with surrounding context.

- **concordancing** The study through the use of a computer-based corpus of the context in which a lexical item occurs.

- **confirmation check** A device used in conversation to determine whether one has been understood correctly.

- **connectionism** An approach that assumes that learning takes place based on the extraction of regularities from the input.

- **consciousness-raising** Often synonymous with language awareness, but emphasizing the cognitive processes of noticing input or making explicit learners' intuitive knowledge about language, in the belief that an awareness of form will contribute to more efficient acquisition.

- **constructed response type** Assessment tools that require students to provide a response using language that they have learned.

- **content and language integrated learning (CLIL)** The term for any subject that is taught through the medium of a language other than the mother tongue, e.g. History through English, etc.

- **content-based language teaching (CBLT)** An approach to the teaching of language in which content is the driving force behind the course or curriculum; it is often drawn from regular school subjects such as science, geography and mathematics or topics of themes of interest to students; also referred to as **content-based language instruction**.

- **context** 1. The situation in which language is used or presented, e.g. a story about a holiday experience could be used as the context to present and practise past tenses. 2. The words or phrases before or after a word in discourse which help someone understand that word.

- **contrastive analysis (CA)** The analysis of differences between languages which can be used to explain a language learner's developmental errors and interlanguage competence.

- **Contrastive Analysis Hypothesis** The prediction that similarities between two languages do not require learning and that the differences are what need to be learned.

- **controlled practice** See **practice**.

- **conversation analysis** The study of 'talk-in-interaction', which attempts to describe the organization of conversation in terms of its sequential systems, rules, and structures.

- **corpus data** Samples of language use normally recorded from real situations.

- **correction code** A series of symbols a teacher may use to mark learners' writing so that they can correct mistakes by themselves, e.g. P = punctuation mistake, T = tense mistake.

- **corrective feedback** An intervention that provides information to a learner that a prior utterance is incorrect. See also **feedback**.

- **creative thinking** Generating new ways of looking at a situation.

- **criterion-referenced assessment** The interpretation of a learner's performance in relation to explicitly stated goals or standards critical language awareness.

- **critical period** A time during early childhood (approximately the first decade of life) when language can be acquired natively. Language learned after this period invariably exhibits non-native features.

- **Critical Period Hypothesis** This states that there is a period (i.e. up to a certain age) during which the learners can acquire an L2 easily and can achieve native-speaker competence, but that after this period L2 acquisition becomes more difficult and is rarely entirely successful.

- **critical reading** A reading practice which attends to the ideological underpinning of text, as signalled not so much by what a writer chooses as a topic but how people, places and events are talked about.

- **critical thinking** The ability to analyze information.

- **cue card / prompt card** A card on which there is / are (a) word(s) or picture(s) to prompt or encourage learners to produce particular language, often during a controlled practice activity or drill, e.g. a teacher presenting *I like +ing / I don't like +ing* could have a number of picture cue cards with different activities (*swimming, reading,* etc). Learners have to respond to the cue card using *I like +ing* or *I don't like +ing*.

- **curriculum** (pl. curricula) A specification of the goals, objectives, content, procedures, and evaluation instruments underpinning a course of study, typically for a program entailing more than one course. See syllabus.

D

- **declarative knowledge** Knowledge that learners have about something. This information is relatively accessible to conscious awareness. See also **procedural knowledge**.

- **deductive approach** An approach to the presentation of new material which begins by the teacher presenting the rules for a given teaching point, then providing examples that illustrate the rule; also referred to as **rule-driven learning**. See **inductive approach**.

- **deductive thinking** Going from the general to the specific. See also **inductive thinking**.

- **designer methods** A term coined by David Nunan to describe methods developed and promoted by one individual and spread by disciples, e.g., Silent Way, Community Language Learning.

- **detail, read for detail, listen for detail** To listen to or read a text in order to understand most of what it says or particular details. See **gist, global understanding**.

- **diagnostic test** See **test**.

- **dialogue journals** Written (electronically or by hand) or orally-recorded discussions between students and teachers about school-related or other topics of interest to students.

- **discourse** The organization of language beyond the level of the sentence and the individual speaking turn, whereby meaning is negotiated in the process of interaction. The study of discourse is called **discourse analysis**.

- **dictation** An activity which typically involves the learners in writing down what the teacher reads aloud.

- **dicto-comp** A technique for practising composition in language classes. A passage is read to a class, and then the students must write out what they understand and remember from the passage, keeping as closely to the original as possible but using their own words where necessary.

- **dictogloss** A classroom activity in which students listen to a text read aloud to them and then reconstruct it in writing from their notes; can be done individually or in pairs or groups.

- **differentiated instruction** This is also referred to as 'individualized' or 'customized' instruction. The curriculum offers several different learning experiences within one lesson to meet students' varied needs or learning styles; for example, providing instruction according to the different ability levels in a classroom.

- **discourse** An instance of spoken or written language that has describable, internal form and meaning (e.g., words, structures, cohesive devices) relating coherently to an external function or purpose and a given audience or interlocutor.

- **discourse analysis** The study of language in use (both spoken and written) that extends beyond sentence boundaries.

- **discourse competence** The ability of a learner to construct coherent and cohesive oral and written discourse in the target language and to interact with others (e.g., in conversations, email, business letters) in a coherent and acceptable manner. See **communicative competence, linguistic competence, socio-cultural competence,** and **strategic competence**.

- **discrete-point test** A language **test** which measures knowledge of individual language items, such as a grammar test which has different sections on tenses or adverbs. Tests consisting of **multiple-choice** items are usually discrete-point tests. ~s can be contrasted with integrative tests. An **integrative test** is one which requires a learner to use several language skills at the same time, such as a dictation test, because it requires the learner to use the knowledge of grammar, vocabulary and listening comprehension.

- **display question** A question (usually posed by the teacher) asking the learner to provide specific information related to the lesson content (e.g., from a written text or as part of a grammar drill or homework correction task); typically display questions require lower order thinking skills or rote memory. See **referential question**.

- **drill** A **technique** teachers use for encouraging learners to practise language, mainly sounds or sentence patterns. It involves guided repetition or practice. In a **choral drill** the teacher says a word or sentence and the learners repeat it together as a class. In an **individual drill** the teacher says a word or sentence and one learner repeats it. Choral and individual drills are called **repetition drills**. In a **substitution drill** the teacher provides a sentence and a different word or phrase which the learner must use (or substitute) in exactly the same structure, e.g. *Teacher: I bought a book. Pen. Learner: I bought a pen.*

E

- **eclectic** (adj.) An approach to language teaching in which the teacher uses techniques and activities taken from different methods.

- **editing** The practices, in L2 composition classes, that students engage in to correct discrete language errors in their writing, i.e. errors in grammar, vocabulary, sentence structure, spelling, etc. See also **revision**.

- **elicitation** Any technique designed to get the learner to produce language in speech or writing.

- **ellipsis** The omission of words or phrases which can be understood from the co-text (textual ellipsis) or the situation (situational ellipsis); common informal speech and writing.

- **English as a Foreign Language (EFL)** English language programs in countries where English is not the common or official language.

- **English as a lingua franca (ELF)**   The varieties of English that are emerging in Europe and Asia as a result of non-native speakers of English using English to communicate with other non-native speakers. See English as a foreign language, English as a second language, English as an international language.

- **English as an international language (EIL)**   A term that recognizes that English has spread well beyond its original borders and now exhibits numerous varieties, with more non-native than native users; used across national boundaries for purposes of diplomacy, business, science, entertainment, etc., often quite apart from its historical and cultural origins. See English as a foreign language, English as a lingua franca, English as a second language.

- **English as a Second Language (ESL)**   English language programs in countries where English is the dominant or official language. Programs designed for non-English-speaking immigrants in the USA are ESL programs.

- **English for Academic Purposes (EAP)**   The study or teaching of English with specific reference to an academic (usually a university- or college-based) course.

- **English for Specific Purposes (ESP)**   A term that refers to teaching or studying English for a particular career (like law or medicine) or for business in general.

- **e-Portfolio**   A digital collection of an individual student's work and achievements.

- **error analysis**   A procedure for analyzing second language data that begins with the errors learners make and then attempts to explain them.

- **errors**   The incorrect forms (vis-à-vis the language being learned) that learners produce.

- **expanding circle**   Based on B. B. Kachru, countries where English is learned as a foreign language (such as China, Japan, and Brazil) and where the target English variety is an Inner Circle model such as American or British English. See **inner circle** and **outer circle**.

- **explicit knowledge**   Knowledge about language that involves awareness. See also **declarative knowledge, explicit learning, implicit knowledge, implicit learning, procedural knowledge**.

- **explicit learning**   Acquisition of language that involves deliberate hypothesis testing as learners search for structure. See also **declarative knowledge; explicit knowledge; implicit knowledge; implicit learning; procedural knowledge**.

- **explicit teaching**   An approach in which information about a language is given to the learners directly by the teacher or the textbook.

- **explicit vocabulary learning**   The learning of vocabulary by means of overt and intentional strategies, such as techniques of memorization. (= **intentional** ~)

- **extensive listening / reading**   Listening to or reading long pieces of text, such as stories or newspapers, i.e. it is listening or reading for general or global understanding, often of longer texts. See **intensive listening / reading**.

- **extrinsic motivation**   When an individual is motivated by outside factors or other people (as opposed to being motivated from within).

- **extroversion**   Refers to where an individual's attention is focused; namely, the world and people outside of the individual. See also **introversion**.

F

- **feedback**   An intervention in which information is provided to a learner that a prior utterance is correct or incorrect. See also **corrective feedback**.

- **field-dependence**   A personality style in which an individual uses the context for interpretation. See also **field-independence**.

- **field-independence**   A personality style in which an individual does not use the context for interpretation. See also **field-dependence**.

- **first language**   See **mother tongue, L1 / L2**.

- **flipped learning**   A model of blended learning focusing on group work and task-based learning in the classroom.

- **fluency**   The ability to read, speak, or write easily, smoothly, and expressively. See accuracy. See also **accuracy**.

- **focused task**   A communicative task that is designed to get learners to practice a predetermined linguistic form. See **task, unfocused task**.

- **focus-on-form**   Instruction that overtly draws students' attention to linguistic elements as they arise in lessons which focus mainly on meaning or communication. See **focus-on-forms**.

- **focus-on-forms**   An approach that is evident in the traditional approach to grammar teaching based on a structural syllabus, with the underlying assumption that language learning is a process of accumulating distinct linguistic elements or constituents. See **focus-on-form**.

- **foreigner talk**   The modified language used when addressing a nonnative speaker.

- **foreign language learning**   The learning of a second language in a formal classroom situation that takes place in a country where the NL is spoken (e.g., learning French in the United States; learning Hebrew in Japan).

- **formal instruction**   This occurs in classrooms when teachers try to aid learning by raising the learners' consciousness about the target language rules. Formal instruction can be deductive (the learners are told the rules) or inductive (learners develop a knowledge of the rules through carrying out language tasks).

- **formal syllabus**   Aims and content of teaching that focus upon systems and rules of phonology, morphology, vocabulary, grammar and upon discourse and genres as text. Also referred to as structural, grammatical, lexical, genre-based syllabuses.

- **formative assessment**   Assessments used while instruction is in progress to promote student learning. See **summative assessment**.

- **fossilization**   The cessation of learning. Permanent plateaus that learners reach resulting from no change in some or all of their interlanguage forms. See also **interlanguage; stabilization**.

- **functional syllabus**   Aims and contents of teaching that focus upon the purposes of language use, from specific speech acts within conversation to larger texts such as particular genres serving specific social functions.

- **functions**   The things people do through language, for example, instructing, apologizing, and complaining.

G

- **gist, global understanding, listening / reading for gist, listening / reading for global understanding** To read or listen to a text and understand the general meaning of it, without paying attention to specific details. See **detail, read for detail, and listen for detail**.

- **global errors** According to Marina Burt and Carol Kiparsky, errors that lead to misunderstanding or miscommunication of a sentence. See **local errors**.

- **graded reader / simplified reader** A book where the language has been made easier for learners. These are often books with stories or novels where the language has been simplified.

- **graphic organizer** A diagram or chart (such as a spider map or a T-graph) used to organize or represent knowledge graphically with the intent of enhancing comprehension, learning, and critical thinking ability; also referred to as visual organizer or concept map. See **KWL chart**.

- **guided writing** A piece of writing that learners produce after the teacher has helped them prepare for it by, for example, giving the learners a plan to follow, or ideas for the type of language to use. See **process writing** and **product writing**.

H

- **hesitation** A pause before or while doing or saying something.

- **heterogeneous groups** Groups of students of mixed abilities.

- **holistic rubric** An assessment tool that rates student performance as a whole and generates a single score. See analytic rubric and rubric.

I

- **immersion education** A type of foreign language program which typically serves language majority students in North American contexts.

- **implicit knowledge**   Knowledge about language that does not involve awareness of that knowledge. See also **declarative knowledge; explicit learning; explicit knowledge; implicit learning; procedural knowledge**.

- **implicit learning**   Acquisition of knowledge about the underlying structure of a complex stimulus environment without doing so consciously. See also **explicit knowledge; explicit learning; implicit knowledge**.

- **implicit vocabulary learning**   The learning of vocabulary primarily by incidental means, such as unconscious exposure to and experience of using words. (= **incidental** ~)

- **inductive approach**   Presentation of new material which begins by the teacher presenting examples, then guiding the students to arrive at the rule based on the examples presented; also referred to as discovery learning. See **deductive approach**.

- **inductive thinking**   Going from the specific to the general. See also **deductive thinking**.

- **inferencing**   The means by which the learner forms hypotheses, through attending to input, or using the situational context to interpret the input.

- **information gap activity**   An activity in which selected information is known by one participant but not the other and the participants must discover and share the information to complete the task.

- **information transfer**   An activity in which learners move information from one source to another, e.g. reading an explanation then completing a diagram with key words from the explanation.

- **initiation-response-evaluation (IRE)**   A classroom interactional sequence in which the teacher asks a student a display question and then signals whether the students' response is correct or not followed by a brief evaluation. See **initiation-response-feedback (IRF)**.

- **initiation-response-feedback (IRF)**   A classroom interactional sequence in which the teacher asks the student a referential question; after the student responds, the teacher provides feedback and uses the student's response to continue the conversational exchange (often over multiple turns). See **initiation-response-evaluation (IRE)**.

- **inner circle**   Based on B. B. Kachru, countries where English is a native language (such as the United Kingdom, the United States, and Canada). See **expanding circle** and **outer circle**.

- **input** The language that is available to learners; that is, exposure.

- **input enhancement** A technique that attempts to make parts of the input salient.

- **input modification** The ways in which teachers alter their classroom language based on their perceptions of learners' proficiency level.

- **instrumental motivation** Motivation that comes from the rewards gained from knowing another language. See also **integrative motivation**.

- **intake** The part of the language input that is internalized by the learner.

- **integrative motivation** Motivation that comes from the desire to acculturate and become part of a target language community. See also **instrumental motivation**.

- **integrated skills** An integrated skills lesson combines work on more than one language skill. For example reading and then writing or listening and speaking.

- **integrative test** See **discrete-point test**.

- **intelligibility** The extent to which a message can actually be understood. See **comprehensibility**.

- **intensive course** A course which takes place over a short period of time, but which consists of a large number of hours.

- **intensive listening / reading** Reading or listening to focus on how language is used in a text. See **extensive listening / reading**.

- **interaction** 'Two-way communication' between listener and speaker, or reader and text.

- **interactionist approaches** Approaches that consider conversational interaction as a locus of learning.

- **interference** ~ happens when the learner's mother tongue affects performance in the target language, especially in pronunciation, lexis or grammar.

- **interlanguage** The language produced by an individual learner in the process of learning a foreign language. Interlanguage is constantly changing and developing as learners learn more of the second language.

- **interlanguage transfer**   The influence of one L2 over another in instances where there are multiple languages acquired after the L1.

- **interlocutor**   The person with whom one is speaking.

- **intertextuality**   The use of others' texts (or one's own previous texts) in shaping a newly-created text, for example by citing other authors or alluding to commonly known works.

- **intrinsic motivation**   Motivation that comes from within the individual.

- **introversion**   Refers to where an individual's attention is focused, namely, towards the individual's own inner world. See also **extroversion**.

- **IRF (initiation, response, follow-up)**   A common pattern of classroom discourse based on a teacher's initiation move, a student's response, and a teacher's follow-up. Also called **IRE (initiation, response, evaluation)**.

J

- **jigsaw activity**   An activity in which individuals receive different but related parts of something, and then work together to complete the whole; in jigsaw reading and listening tasks, individuals receive parts of a text that is shared and reconstructed in groups.

K

- **key-pal**   The electronic equivalent of a pen pal. Key-pals are friends who communicate using electronic media — they exchange e-mails instead of traditional paper-based letters.

- **kinesthetic learner**   See **learning style**.

- **KWL chart**   A graphic organizer commonly used for promoting strategic reading or listening; the chart motivates students to engage in the text by having them discover what they already know (the K stage), what they want to know (the W stage), and what they have learned (the L stage); also referred to as a KWHL chart (with H representing the How stage). See **graphic organizer**.

L

- **L1** First language / the mother tongue.

- **L2** Second language.

- **language chunks** Short phrases learned as a unit (e.g. *thank you very much*); patterned language acquired through redundant use, such as refrains and repetitive phrases in stories.

- **language awareness** A learner's understanding of the rules of how language works and his / her ability to notice language.

- **language competences** See **communicative language competences**.

- **Language Experience Approach (LEA)** A method of teaching first and second language literacy in which a group of students first experiences some activity or event together; then, drawing upon that common experience, the students dictate statements describing the experience to the teacher (or another student) who writes them down; this story is then used for various reading and language practice activities; particularly effective for beginning and intermediate English as a second or foreign language students, and for showing the relationship between oral and written language.

- **language performance** The use of specific linguistic means to carry out a task. Language performance can refer to either the process or the product.

- **language proficiency** What a learner can do and / or how well he / she can perform using language, given an identified and defined purpose.

- **language transfer** The use of the first language (or other languages known) in a second language context. See also **interference; negative transfer; positive transfer**.

- **learner autonomy** The capacity learners have to take charge of their own learning. This implies choice of aims, content, approaches and / or forms of evaluation based on reflection related to individual needs and interests.

- **learner's style** A learner's strategic, motivational, or affective predilection for, or orientation to, language learning or use; also referred to as **learning style**.

- **learning** A cumulative process whereby individuals gradually assimilate increasingly complex and abstract entities (concepts, categories, and patterns of behaviour or models) and / or acquire skills and competences. It is the internalization of rules and formulas which can be used to communicate in the **L2**. Krashen uses this term for formal learning in the classroom.

- **learning log** The use of a notebook or a book in which students write about experiences in and out of school or record responses and reactions to learning and learning activities. They are sometimes referred to as **dialogue journals** or diaries.

- **learning strategy** A strategic plan undertaken by a learner in learning. Strategies can be employed by learners to assist with the storage of information, to help with the construction of language rules, and to help with an appropriate attitude towards the learning situation.

- **learning style** The preferred way of taking in and processing new information and / or skills.

- **lexical approach** A way of teaching language that focuses on lexical items or chunks such as words, multi-word units, collocations and fixed expressions rather than grammatical structures.

- **lexical item** An item of vocabulary which has a single element of meaning. It may be a compound or phrase: *bookcase, post office, put up with*. Some single words may initiate several lexical items; e.g. *letter: a letter of the alphabet / posting a letter*.

- **lexical phrases** Recurrent phrases and patterns of language which have become institutionalized through frequent use. Phrases such as '*Can I help you?*' or '*Have you heard the one about ... ?*' are lexical phrases.

- **lexical syllabus** A syllabus which makes the learning of frequent vocabulary central to the content of a language course.

- **lexis** Individual words or sets of words, e.g. *homework, study, whiteboard, get dressed, be on time*.

- **lingua franca** A language used to communicate with others when there is no common first language.

- **linguistic competence** The accuracy and extent of a learners' phonological, lexical, and grammatical proficiency in a second or foreign language.

- **linguistic relativity** The popular belief that differences in the structures of languages also reflect or create differences in the way people perceive or think about the world around them. Also called **Sapir-Whorf hypothesis**.

- **listen and do / make / draw** A classroom activity where learners listen to the teacher or to another learners and while they are listening they perform an action (listen and do), make something (listen and make) or draw something (listen and draw). These activities are usually used as comprehension tasks.

- **listen for detail** See **detail**.

- **listen for gist, global understanding** See **gist**.

- **local errors** According to Marina Burt and Carol Kiparsky, errors that involve only a small portion of a sentence (for example, missing articles) but do not lead to misunderstanding of a proposition. See **global errors**.

- **look-and-say methods** Reading methods which ask learner readers to learn a large sight vocabulary, often through words presented on flash cards. See also **phonics**.

M

- **materials** Anything which is used to help teach language learners.

- **materials adaptation** Making changes to materials in order to improve them or to make them more suitable for a particular type of learner. Adaptation can include reducing, adding, omitting, modifying and supplementing.

- **metacognition** The ability to reflect on one's thinking and exercise control over cognitive processes through planning, monitoring, and evaluation.

- **metacognitive strategy** Many L2 learners are able to think consciously about how they learn and how successfully they are learning. ~s involve planning learning, monitoring the process of learning, and evaluating how successful a particular strategy is.

- **metalanguage** The language we use when talking about language itself. This may consist of terminology – sentence, noun, past tense, intonation, discourse - or the type of grammar rules that can be found in reference grammars and some school books.

- **metalinguistic knowledge** Explicit, formal knowledge about language that can be verbalized, usually including metalinguistic terminology, such as 'present tense', 'indefinite article', etc.

- **methodology** (1) A set of step-by-step procedures for teaching a language. (2) Procedures and principles for selecting, sequencing, and justifying learning experiences.

- **mind map** See **word map**.

- **minimal pairs** Pairs of words distinguished by one phoneme only, e.g., pin - bin; frequently used for practising sound contrasts in a foreign language.

- **miscue analysis** The manner of evaluating how a reader draws on syntactic, graphophonemic and semantic knowledge in his or her sampling of text with a view to establishing reader strengths and weaknesses.

- **mistake** A deviation in learner language that occurs when learners fail to perform their competence. It contrasts with an **error**.

- **mixed ability, mixed level** The different levels of language or ability of learners studying in the same class.

- **modification** An attempt by a speaker to simplify or elaborate a normal discourse pattern in order to make a message more accessible to a listener.

- **Monitor Model** A model of second language acquisition based on the concept that learners have two systems (acquisition and learning) and that the learned system monitors the acquired system.

- **MOO (multi-user object-oriented) environment** Software that allows multiple users to interact in real time on the internet. Users may exchange virtual 'objects', hyperlink to maps or games, create password-secured private spaces, etc.

- **motherese** The language addressed to a young child. See also **care-taker speech; child-directed speech**.

- **mother tongue** The very first language that you learn as a baby, which is usually the language spoken to you by your parents. Also called **L1** or **first language**. See also **L1 / L2**.

- **motivation** The characteristic that provides the incentive for learning.

- **multiple intelligences** (**MI**) A theory of intelligence that characterizes human intelligence as having multiple dimensions that must be acknowledged and developed in education. The theory of MI is based on the work of the psychologist Gardner who posits 8 intelligences.

- **multiple-choice questions / items** A task-type in which learners are given a question and three or four possible answers or options. They choose the correct answer from the options they are given.

N

- **native language** Primary or first language spoken by an individual. See also **L1**.

- **natural order** Some people believe there is an order in which learners naturally learn some items in their first or other languages. Some language items are learned before others and it can be difficult for teachers to influence this order.

- **needs analysis** Analysis to determine what students need to be able to do in English in their educational or professional situation.

- **negative evidence** Information provided to a learner concerning the incorrectness of a form. See also **positive evidence**.

- **negative transfer** The use of the first language (or other languages known) in a second language context resulting in a nontarget-like second language form. See also **interference; language transfer; positive transfer**.

- **negotiated syllabus** An approach to course design that involves learners in decision-making about what they are going to learn.

- **negotiation of meaning** The attempt made in conversation to clarify a lack of understanding.

- **norm-referenced assessment** An assessment in which an individual or group's performance is compared with a larger group. See also **criterion-referenced assessment**.

- **notion** In the notional-functional syllabus, one of the two organizational principles determining the selection of items to be taught; this principle takes into consideration the ideas or meanings (e.g., time, quantity, duration, location) that learners need to express. See function.

- **notional-functional syllabus** A language syllabus organized around the communicative purposes (or functions) for which people use language and the ideas (notions) that are being communicated; also referred to as **functional-notional syllabus**. See **notion, function**.

O

- **objective** The breaking down of goals into achievable and measurable parts.

- **open(-ended) comprehension questions** A task or question that does not have a right or wrong answer, but which allows learners to offer their own opinions and ideas or to respond creatively, e.g. *Why do you think the writer likes living in Paris?*

- **open task** A task with more than one possible answer, solution, or outcome.

- **outcome** Result. This is what the teacher hopes will be the result in terms of learning at the end of the lesson.

- **outer circle** Based on B. B. Kachru, countries (such as India and Nigeria) where the English varieties spoken are localized and the role of English is that of an institutionalized variety that is influenced by local languages and different from Inner Circle varieties. See **inner circle** and **expanding circle**.

P

- **paradigmatic** A relation of substitution that typically occurs across clauses or sentences with the paradigmatic forms occurring in the same grammatical slot, e.g. Is that a new watch? No, it's my old one. See **syntagmatic**.

- **paralinguistics** The study of elements that accompany language use but are not part of language per se (e.g., body language, gestures, facial expressions).

- **passive vocabulary** The vocabulary that students are able to understand compared to that which they are able to use. Contrasted with **active vocabulary**.

- **pedagogic task** A task which does not replicate a real world task but which is designed to facilitate the learning of language or skills which would be useful in a real world task. Completing one half of a dialogue, filling in the blanks in a story and working out the meaning of ten nonsense words from clues in a text would be examples of pedagogic tasks, i.e. in pedagogic tasks, learners are required to do things which it is extremely unlikely they would be called upon to do outside of the classroom. See also **real-world tasks**.

- **peer assessment** judgements about learner performance, normally according to set and explicit criteria, made by same or similar age learners.

- **performance assessment** Typically, this involves observation of classroom performance to assess how well learners express themselves during specific tasks by checking performance against criteria.

- **personality** A set of traits that characterize an individual.

- **phonics** Reading methods which emphasize sound-symbol relationships in written language by, e.g., asking learner readers to match up letters in words to a sound equivalent. See also **look-and-say methods, whole-word methods**.

- **placement test** See **test**.

- **portfolio** A collection of various samples of a student's work during a particular course such as writing samples. See also **portfolio assessment**.

- **portfolio assessment** A test on a collection of materials designed to demonstrate progress over time.

- **positive evidence** Evidence based on forms that actually occur. See also **negative evidence**.

- **positive transfer** The use of the first language (or other languages known) in a second language context when the resulting second language form is correct. See also **interference; language transfer; negative transfer**.

- **PPP** An approach to teaching language items which follows a sequence of presentation of the item, practice of the item, and then production (i.e. use) of the item.

- **practice**

  - **controlled practice, restricted practice** When learners use the target language repeatedly and productively in situations in which they have little or no choice of what language they use. The teacher and learners focus on accurate use of the target language.

  - **less controlled, freer practice, free practice** When learners use the target language but have more choice of what they say and what language they use.

- **prefabricated patterns** Parts of language that are learned as a whole without knowledge of the component parts.

- **presentation** 1. When the teacher introduces new language usually by focusing on it, often by using the board and speaking to the whole class. 2. When a learner or learners gives a talk to their class or group.

- **pre-teach (vocabulary)** Before introducing a text to learners, the teacher can teach key vocabulary from the text which s/he thinks the learners do not already know and which is necessary for them to understand the main points of a text.

- **prior knowledge** The knowledge a learner already has about a topic or subject. It is the past knowledge a learner brings to a new learning situation.

- **problem solving** Learners work in pairs or groups to find the solution to a problem. Problem-solving activities usually help develop oral **fluency**.

- **procedure** The details of exactly what is going to happen in each stage of a lesson, e.g. learners practise the language of complaints in a role-play in pairs.

- **procedural knowledge** Knowledge that relates to cognitive skills that involve sequencing information. This information is relatively inaccessible. See also **declarative knowledge**.

- **procedural syllabus** A syllabus consisting of a series of tasks sequenced in order of difficulty with learners acquiring language by negotiating these tasks under teacher guidance and with no focus on language form. The syllabus was developed in Bangalore, South India by a team led by N.S. Prabhu.

- **Processability Theory** A theory that proposes that production and comprehension of second language forms only takes place to the extent that they can be handled by the linguistic processor. Understanding how the processor functions allows one to understand developmental paths.

- **process approach** An approach to the teaching of writing that focuses on understanding and teaching the process that experienced writers use in composing; generally involves consideration of audience and purpose, strategies for idea generation, and revision and feedback on multiple drafts of a paper. See **product approach**.

- **process-oriented instruction** Pedagogy that develops learners' ability to enhance the cognitive and social processes of their learning through explicit teaching and implicit scaffolding.

- **process syllabus** A framework for classroom decision-making based upon negotiation among teacher and students applied to any chosen aspect of the curriculum.

- **process writing** An approach to writing, which thinks of writing as a process which includes different stages of writing such as planning, drafting, re-drafting, editing, and proofreading. See also **guided writing** and **product writing**.

- **product writing** An approach to writing which involves analysing and then reproducing models of particular text types. See also **guided writing** and **process writing**.

- **productive skills** When learners produce language, speaking and writing are productive skills. See **receptive skills**.

- **proficiency** One's (functional) ability in a given second or foreign language.

- **proficiency test** See **test**.

- **project work** An activity which focuses on completing an extended task or tasks on a specific topic.

- **prompt** (v., n.) To help learners think of ideas or to remember a word or phrase by giving them a part of it or by giving another kind of clue. When a teacher suggests a word that the learner hasn't remembered, e.g. *Learner: I want to ⋯⋯ in an office. Teacher: Work? Learner: Yes, I want to work in an office*. A teacher can also use a word prompt to correct a learner, e.g. *Learner: He don't like that. Teacher: Grammar. Learner: Sorry – he doesn't like that*.

- **prompting** Assisting students in thinking beyond their response to a question.

- **proofreading** Reading a text in order to check whether there are any mistakes in spelling, grammar, punctuation, etc. See also **process writing**.

- **prop** An object used by the actors performing in a play or film. Teachers may give learners props to use when they are doing a role play in class.

R

- **raise awareness** To help learners start to understand something that they may not already know by drawing attention to it. For example, if you teach **learning strategies**, it can raise learners' awareness of how to learn.

- **rapport** The relationship between the teacher and learners.

- **rationale** The reason for doing something, e.g. the rationale for pre-teaching vocabulary before learners read a text is to help learners read the text more easily. When teachers plan a lesson, they think about a rationale for activities and procedures.

- **read for detail** See **detail**.

- **read for gist, global understanding** See **gist**.

- **realia** (pl.) Three-dimensional objects used for instruction. Real objects such as clothes, menus, timetables and leaflets that can be brought into the classroom for a range of purposes.

- **recasts** Reformulations of an incorrect utterance that maintain the original's meaning.

- **receptive skills** When learners do not have to produce language; listening and reading are receptive skills. See **productive skills**.

- **re-draft** When a piece of writing is changed with the intention of improving it. A writer's first draft may be re-drafted. See **process writing**.

- **referential question** A question (usually posed by the teacher) that has no single correct answer and typically requires the learner to provide an original, creative answer (e.g., the learner's opinion on an issue); typically such questions require a higher level of thinking on the part of the learner. See **display question**.

- **reformulation** A teacher's correction of learner errors by repeating the sentence correctly, but without drawing the learners' attention to the error. Compare with **recast**.

- **register** The formality or informality of the language used in a particular situation. Formal register or language is that used in serious or important situations, e.g. in a job application. Informal register or language is that used in relaxed or friendly situations, e.g. with family or friends. Register may also refer to language which is specific to a particular group, e.g. technical register, scientific register.

- **reliability** The extent to which a test or assessment procedure measures consistently.

- **repair strategy** An utterance which corrects or modifies what has just been said.

- **repetition** To say something again, often for practice. This is often done in **drills**.

- **resources** The variety of sources teachers can draw on in the process of locating, selecting and / or producing ideas, texts, activities, tasks and reference materials useful for their learners.

- **response** A reply or reaction to communication such as a laugh, a smile, saying something. Teachers and learners may respond to each other in writing, speech or in the form of a facial expression.

- **restructuring** Changes or reorganization of one's grammatical knowledge.

- **review** When a learner, often guided by the teacher, looks again at language that has already been taught in order to remember this language better. Teachers may choose to review vocabulary or grammatical structures in the classroom, for example, in order to help learners consolidate the language or to prepare for a **test**.

- **revision** The practices in L2 composition classes in which students 'look again' at their writing holistically in order to improve areas such as organization, adequate use of evidence, focus, etc. See also **editing**.

- **rhyme**   1. Words that sound similar because they have the same ending, e.g. *hat, cat*. 2. A song or poem with words that sound the same at the end of each line, e.g. *I believe I can fly. I believe I can touch the sky.*

- **risk taking**   The extent to which people are willing to do something without being certain of the outcome.

- **rubric**   An assessment tool that includes criteria for evaluating levels of student performance. See **holistic rubric** and **analytic rubric**.

S

- **Sapir-Whorf hypothesis**   See **linguistic relativity**.

- **scaffolding**   The support given to language learners to enable them to perform tasks and construct communications which are at the time beyond their capability.

- **scan**   To read a text quickly to pick out specific information, e.g. finding a phone number in a phone book. See **detail, gist, global understanding, skim**.

- **schema**   A pre-existing knowledge structure in the memory of human beings, essential to discourse processing; plural: schemata.

- **schema theory**   A theory of language processing based on the notion that past experiences lead to the creation of mental frameworks that help us make sense of new experiences.

- **second language / L2**   The term is used to refer to a language which is not a mother tongue but which is used for certain communicative functions in a society. See **foreign language**.

- **second language acquisition (SLA)**   The learning of another language after the first language has been learned. The use of this term does not differentiate among learning situations. See also **L2**.

- **segmental sounds**   Individual sounds (consonants and vowels). Compare with **suprasegmentals**.

- **selected response item type**   an assessment tool that requires students to select an answer or response to demonstrate learning, e.g., multiple choice items.

- **selective listening** Attending to specific information that had been signalled prior to listening.

- **self-assessment** A judgement made by the learner on his or her own performance, knowledge, strategies, etc.

- **self-regulation** A learner's executive control processes related to use of cognitive, affective, and sociocultural strategies.

- **sheltered instruction** An approach to content-based language teaching in which L2 students study subjects in the regular curriculum; usually taught by a subject matter instructor who has special training in strategies for making the content accessible to L2 students and assisting them with language development. See **adjunct instruction, content and language integrated learning, content-based instruction,** and **theme-based instruction**.

- **silent period** The time when learners who are beginning to learn a first (or second) language prefer to listen (or read) before producing the language, e.g. babies have a silent period when they listen to their parents before starting to try to speak themselves.

- **Silent Way** A language teaching method developed by Caleb Gattegno; using an array of visuals (colored rods of different sizes, sound charts, and word charts), the teacher gets students to practice a new language point while saying very little in the process; only the target language is used with no explanation allowed.

- **simplified texts** These are texts which have been made simpler so as to make it easier for learners to read them. The usual principles of simplification involve reduction in length of the text, shortening of sentences, omission or replacement of difficult words or structures, omission of qualifying clauses and omission of non-essential detail.

- **simplification** Making something easier. Simplifying language or tasks is a common **scaffolding** strategy, for example.

- **simultaneous bilingualism** The acquisition of two languages at the same time both as L1s, i.e. by the time a child is, say, three years old.

- **skill** The knowledge and experience needed to perform a specific task or job. The four language skills are listening, speaking, reading, and writing. See **receptive skills, productive skills**.

- **skill-building theory** A view claiming that: (1) knowledge originates in an explicit form and is gradually proceduralized into an implicit form through practice; and (2) explicit knowledge develops into implicit knowledge through communicative practice; also referred to as skill-acquisition theory.

- **skim** To read a text quickly to get a general idea of what it is about. See **detail, gist, global understanding**.

- **SLA** See **Second Language Acquisition**.

- **socio-cultural competence** Knowledge, skills, and functional abilities that are associated with values, beliefs, norms, and behavior of a particular society and in the context of daily communication and social interaction, i.e., knowing how to speak and behave appropriately. See **communicative competence, discourse competence, linguistic competence,** and **strategic competence**.

- **Sociocultural Theory** A theory based on work by the Russian psychologist Vygotsky that considers knowledge / learning arises from a social context. Learning, being socially mediated, comes from face-to-face interaction. Knowledge is internalized from learners jointly constructing knowledge in dyadic interactions.

- **speech act** A type of verbal action (i.e. the functions for which language is used), such as promising, apologizing, inviting.

- **stabilization** The plateaus that learners reach when there is little change in some or all of their interlanguage forms. See also **fossilization; interlanguage**.

- **standardized test** A test that is in the same format for all who take it. It often relies on multiple-choice questions and the testing conditions — including instructions, time limits, and scoring rubrics — are the same for all students, though sometimes accommodations on time limits and instructions are made for disabled students.

- **strategy** A conscious or nonconscious thought or behavior used by an individual to achieve a language learning or use goal.

- **structural approach** A way of teaching which uses a syllabus based on grammatical structures. The order in which the language is presented is usually based on how difficult it is thought to be.

- **substitution drill** See **drill**.

- **subtractive bilingualism** See **bilingualism**.

- **summative assessment** Assessments used to summarize student learning upon completion of course or program of instruction. See **formative assessment**.

- **suprasegmental features** Pronunciation features which extend over multiple sounds (e.g., stress, rhythm, and intonation); also referred to as prosody. See **segmental sounds**.

- **syllabus** The selected and organized content (areas of knowledge and particular skills and abilities) appropriate to the particular aims of a course.

- **syllabus design** Procedures and principles for selecting, sequencing, and justifying the learning content of a course.

- **synchronous computer-mediated communication** Communication via computer networks which takes place in real time, such as on-line chat.

- **syntagmatic** Linear relations that are expressed within the same clause or sentence such as a lexical collocation (e.g., an auspicious occasion) or the position in which an indirect object occurs (I gave John the book / I gave the book to John). See **paradigmatic**.

- **synthetic approach** According to David Wilkins, one of two broad approaches to syllabus design; this approach is based on the analysis and specification of discrete linguistic items and is favored by traditional approaches to language teaching (e.g., grammar translation). See **analytic approach**.

T

- **target language (TL)** The language being learned.

- **task** An activity in the classroom which involves language use to achieve a communicative purpose.

- **task-based syllabus** Aims and contents of teaching focusing upon the creation and interpretation of meaning and organized on the basis of appropriate sequences and permutations of communicative tasks and metacommunicative (form-focused or learning-focused) tasks.

- **teacher talk** Teachers' adjustments to both language form and language function in order to facilitate communication.

- **technique** A specific classroom device or activity, [such as a role-play] that is consistent with a method and therefore in harmony with an approach. Some techniques are used in more than one method, e.g. modelling & repetition.

- **test** A formal **assessment** of a learner's language. An **achievement test** is used to see how well learners have learned the language and skills taught in class. Achievement tests are often at the end of term or end of the year and test the main points of what has been taught in that time. A **diagnostic test** is used to identify problems and strengths that learners have with language or skills. It helps the teacher plan what to teach, or what not to teach, in future. A **placement test** is often used at the beginning of a course in a language school in order to identify a learner's level of language and find the best class for them. A **proficiency test** is used to see how good learners are at using the target language. The contents of a proficiency test are not chosen according to what has been taught, but according to what is needed for a particular purpose, e.g. English for studying at university, English for general communication.

- **think-aloud procedure** A procedure which involves having research subjects (including teachers and learners) verbalize their thoughts as they are undergoing some process, such as lesson planning or revising a composition. See **think-aloud protocol**.

- **think-aloud protocol** The resulting record (whether it be an audio-recording, a videotape, or a transcript) of research involving a think-aloud procedure. See **think-aloud procedure**.

- **top-down processing** Using background knowledge and expectations about what is being said or written to understand a message.

- **Total Physical Response (TPR)** A method for teaching a foreign language developed by James Asher in the 1970s that is based on connecting language to movement through a series of commands, such as *Stand up* or *Sit down*; still used widely as a technique in teaching ESL or EFL for learners with beginning levels of proficiency.

- **transfer** Knowledge of the L1 is used to help in learning the L2. Transfer can be positive, when the two languages have similar structures, or it can be negative, when the two languages are different, and L1-induced errors occur.

- **turn** The smallest unit of interaction between at least two speakers.

- **turn taking** (1) the part of conversation analysis that deals with how two or more speakers manage their turns in a conversation; (2) as part of the interactive dynamic of classrooms, the roles of speakers and listeners shift frequently, with turns initiated, delegated, relinquished, borrowed, stolen, interrupted, offered, overlapping, etc.

U

- **unfocused task** A fluency-oriented communicative task for which learners are not made aware of the specific linguistic feature being practiced; generally these types of tasks elicit general samples of language use. See **focused task, task**.

- **usage** Widdowson uses the term ~ to refer to 'that aspect of performance which makes evident the extent to which the language user demonstrates his knowledge of linguistic rules'. The term contrasts with **use**.

- **use** Widdowson uses the term ~ to refer to that aspect of performance which 'makes evident the extent to which the language user demonstrates his ability to use his knowledge of linguistic rules for effective communication'.

- **U-shaped learning** Learning whereby early forms appear to be correct, followed by a period of incorrect forms, with a final stage of correct forms.

- **utterance** A complete unit of speech in spoken language. An utterance can be shorter than a sentence, e.g. *A: When's he coming? B: Tomorrow*. 'Tomorrow' is an utterance here.

V

- **validity** The extent to which a test or assessment procedure measures what it claims to measure.

W

- **wait time** The amount of time which elapses after a teacher poses a question to an individual student or to the class as a whole.

- **washback** The influence or effect of assessment on instruction.

- **Web 2.0** The second generation of the Worldwide Web, seen as a platform to enable interactivity and shared dynamic content, rather than static webpages.

- **Webinar** A web-based seminar or professional development opportunity, featuring both visual and audio material available online in real time and typically allowing for interaction with participants from around the world; often recorded and made available asynchronously after the initial broadcast.

- **webquest** A project which requires learners to use Internet resources and websites to find information.

- **Whole Language** A teaching method that focuses on reading for meaning in context.

- **whole-word-method** A method for teaching children to read in the mother tongue, in which children are taught to recognize whole words rather than letter-names (as in the alphabetic method) or sounds (as in phonics). See also **phonics**.

- **word map, mind map** A diagram which is used to make a visual record of vocabulary on the same topic, e.g. car bus.

- **working memory** Memory that involves storage capacity and processing capacity.

Z

- **zone of proximal development (ZPD)** According to Lev Vygotsky, the difference between what a child can achieve alone and what s/he can achieve with the help of the adult (parent or teacher) or more skilled peer.

MEMO

MEMO

MEMO

최시원 전공영어 영어교육학

ISBN 979-11-90700-84-9

- 발행일 · 2020年 12月 14日 초판 1쇄
- 발행인 · 이용중
- 저 자 · 최시원
- 발행처 · 도서출판 배움
- 주 소 · 서울시 영등포구 영등포로 400 신성빌딩 2층 (신길동)
- 주문 및 배본처 · Tel : 02) 813-5334 Fax : 02) 814-5334

저자와의
협의하에
인지생략

본서의 **無斷轉載·複製**를 禁함. 본서의 무단 전재·복제행위는 저작권법 제136조에 의거 5년 이하의 징역 또는 5,000만 원 이하의 벌금에 처하거나 이를 병과할 수 있습니다. 파본은 구입처에서 교환하시기 바랍니다.

정가 20,000 원